ELON

RELATIONS OF DEVELOPMENT AND AGING

This is a volume in the
Arno Press collection

GROWING OLD

Advisory Editor
Leon Stein

See last pages of this volume
for a complete list of titles

RELATIONS OF DEVELOPMENT AND AGING

Compiled and Edited by
JAMES E. BIRREN

ARNO PRESS

A New York Times Company
New York • 1980

830979

Editorial Supervision: BRIAN QUINN

Reprint Edition 1980 by Arno Press Inc.

Reprinted by permission of James E. Birren
Reprinted from a copy in the Library of the University of Missouri

GROWING OLD
ISBN for complete set: 0-405-12813-4
See last pages of this volume for titles.

Manufactured in the United States of America

Library of Congress Cataloging in Publication Data

Birren, James E   ed.
   Relations of development and aging.

   (Growing old)
   A symposium presented before the Gerontological
Society at the 15th annual meeting, Miami Beach, Fla.
   Reprint of the 1964 ed. published by Thomas,
Springfield, Ill., which was issued as publication
no. 582 of American lecture series.
   Includes bibliographies.
   1. Growth--Congresses. 2. Aging--Congresses.
I. Title. II. Gerontological Society. III. Series.
QP84.B5 1980   612'.67   79-8659
ISBN 0-405-12775-8

RELATIONS OF
DEVELOPMENT AND AGING

Publication Number 582
AMERICAN LECTURE SERIES ®

A Monograph in
The BANNERSTONE DIVISION *of*
AMERICAN LECTURES IN GERIATRICS AND GERONTOLOGY

Series Editor
JAMES E. BIRREN, Ph.D.

U.S. Department of Health, Education and Welfare
Public Health Service
National Institutes of Health
Bethesda, Maryland

RELATIONS OF DEVELOPMENT AND AGING

*A symposium presented
before the
Gerontological Society
at the 15th Annual Meeting,
Miami Beach, Florida,
with financial support of
The Ford Foundation*

Compiled and Edited by
JAMES E. BIRREN, Ph.D.

CHARLES C THOMAS · **PUBLISHER**
Springfield • Illinois • U.S.A.

Published and Distributed Throughout the World by
CHARLES C THOMAS · PUBLISHER

BANNERSTONE HOUSE
301-327 East Lawrence Avenue, Springfield, Illinois, U.S.A.

NATCHEZ PLANTATION HOUSE
735 North Atlantic Boulevard, Fort Lauderdale, Florida, U.S.A.

With THOMAS BOOKS careful attention is given to all details of manufacturing and design. It is the Publisher's desire to present books that are satisfactory as to their physical qualities and artistic possibilities and appropriate for their particular use. THOMAS BOOKS will be true to those laws of quality that assure a good name and good will.

Printed in the United States of America

0-5

CONTRIBUTORS

John E. Anderson, Ph.D., Professor Emeritus, formerly Director, Institute of Child Development, University of Minnesota, Minneapolis, Minnesota.

James E. Birren, Ph.D., Chief, Section on Aging, National Institute of Mental Health, Bethesda, Maryland

Margaret Blenkner, D.S.W., Director of Research, Benjamin Rose Institute, Cleveland, Ohio

B. S. Bloom, Ph.D., Professor of Education, University of Chicago, Chicago, Illinois

John A. Clausen, Ph.D., Director, Institute of Human Development, University of California, Berkeley, California

D. B. Dill, Ph.D., Department of Anatomy and Physiology, Indiana University, Bloomington, Indiana

W. H. Forbes, Ph.D., M.D., Harvard School of Public Health, Boston Massachusetts

Stanley M. Garn, Ph.D., Chairman, Department of Growth and Genetics, The Fels Research Institute, Yellow Springs, Ohio

Robert J. Havighurst, Ph.D., Professor, Committee on Human Development, University of Chicago, Chicago, Illinois

Jerome Kagan, Ph.D., Chairman, Department of Psychology, The Fels Research Institute, Yellow Springs, Ohio

Mary O. Kibler, A.B., The Fels Research Institute, Yellow Springs, Ohio

Raymond G. Kuhlen, Ph.D., Professor of Psychology, Syracuse University, Syracuse, New York

Philip S. Lawrence, Sc.D., Chief, Health Interview Survey Branch, National Center for Health Statistics, Public Health Service, U.S. Department of Health, Education, and Welfare, Washington, D.C.

Robert Morris, D.S.W., Professor, The Florence Heller Graduate School for Advanced Studies in Social Welfare, Brandeis University, Waltham, Massachusetts

Bernice L. Neugarten, Ph.D., Associate Professor, Committee on Human Development, University of Chicago, Chicago, Illinois

Jerry L. Newton, M.A., Department of Anatomy and Physiology, Indiana University, Bloomington, Indiana

Philip Nolan, Jr., Department of Growth and Genetics, The Fels Research Institute, Yellow Springs, Ohio

Christabel G. Rohmann, B.A., Department of Growth and Genetics, The Fels Research Institute, Yellow Springs, Ohio

Lester W. Sontag, M.D., Director, The Fels Research Institute, Yellow Springs, Ohio

James W. Terman, M.A., School of Medicine. Indiana University, Bloomington, Indiana

Alfred H. Washburn, M.D., Emeritus Director, Child Research Council, Denver, Colorado

v

PREFACE

Man develops and ages under continually changing influences of the societies which he creates. More children grow up advantageously and more adults live into a productive later life than ever before, but many do not. What is the optimum pattern of the environment for man's development throughout the life span? Some partial answers can be given and are already incorporated in the features of the social, psychological, and biological conditions of life in modern communities. Somewhat more is known about growth and development than about senescence, yet much of development has been studied without regard to the context of the whole life span. This gives rise to intriguing and important questions about the late life consequences of the biological, phychological, and social conditions of early life. The forces affecting the individual over the life span are complex yet it is not useful to merely say they are complex and let matters rest. The task of the scholar and researcher is to specify how they are complex based upon studies of man and lower organisms. This book represents an effort to specify some of the complexities of development and aging and to specify the limits of our knowledge.

What follows are the papers presented at the 1962 meeting of the Gerontological Society together with subsequent revisions and additions of papers which had special relevance to the topic. The content of the papers varies: there are contributions to concepts and theories, as well as reports of specific research. Some papers have the character of reviews and others limit discussion to work from particular laboratories. This diversity would appear to be appropriate to encourage further explorations of the subject. Though of high interest and promise, the subject matter is not a highly articulate field of knowledge. This partly results from the difficulties in carrying out research over long intervals of the life span and also from the absence of concepts about the transformations of organisms over the life span, particularly from the adult to the "old." The subject matter tends to divide along the lines of separate scientific disciplines with interesting and important gaps appearing when one views it through the perspective of the unity of science encouraged by the study of the life span.

The specific background for this book lies in the interest expressed in 1960, by the Research Committee of the Gerontological Society, to organize a symposium on the relations of growth and aging as part of the annual program of the Society. In November 1961, the Research and Program Committees met jointly and approved plans which resulted in this book. Arrangements for the Symposium were made possible by a grant from the Ford Foundation to the Gerontological Society. The Chairman of the Research Committee was Robert J. Havighurst and the Chairman of the Program Committee, Ewald W. Busse. Membership of the joint Research and Program Committee was: Walter M. Beattie, Jr., Austin B. Chinn, Robert W. Kleemeier, Thomas McGavack, Mary C. Mulvey, Bernice L. Neugarten, Gordon C. Ring, Ethel Shanas, Bernard L. Strehler, and Morris Zelditch. The Gerontological Society gratefully acknowledges the assistance of the Ford Foundation in making possible the symposium which led to this volume.

JAMES E. BIRREN

CONTENTS

RELATIONS OF
DEVELOPMENT AND AGING

SECTION A

Background; Concepts and Issues

Chapter 1

INTRODUCTION TO THE STUDY OF DEVELOPMENT AND AGING IN THE LIFE CYCLE

ROBERT J. HAVIGHURST AND JAMES E. BIRREN

This book consists of papers by biologists and social scientists on the subject *Relations of Development and Aging.*

In order to study relations of events in early life to events in later life, the ideal method would seem to be that of observing a group of people as they move through the life cycle. But this method has been used very little, and its use has mainly been limited to the United States of America. The cost in time and money is great, and a continuity of research effort and research personnel must be guaranteed or at least assumed as a matter of faith in the oncoming generations of one's colleagues.

THE CONCEPT OF EARLY AND LATE LIFE RELATIONSHIPS

There is a good deal of evidence that early life experience, biological and social, has consequences in later life. For example, the heart lesions of rheumatic fever in childhood may lead to rheumatic heart disease in adulthood. Again, there is a good deal of psychological theory which holds that early childhood experience results in adult personality traits.

A particularly attractive but erroneous theory regards the life cycle as reversing itself during the later years, with the adult personality regressing through an antique form of adolescence and finally falling into second childhood. This view had some support for a time from people who applied Freudian personality theory

5

naively. Since the secretion of sex hormones decreases after about age fifty, it was supposed that this decrease might lead to a kind of "reverse puberty," with concomitant personality changes.

Although such speculations have not proved valuable, a broader scientific basis for the study of early and late life relationships has been laid in longitudinal studies of human development in individuals and groups of people.

BIOGRAPHICAL STUDIES OF THE LIFE-SPAN

The study of a single life span is the subject-matter of biography and autobiography. The 19th Century saw a few well-documented studies of individual children made by careful and reasonably objective observers. Interesting as these studies are, they often have little value for understanding human development, and because of their susceptibility to bias many essential data may be omitted or misinterpreted. Biographical materials seem to have a use as sources of suggestions for variables to be included in studies with appropriate statistical, sampling, or experimental controls.

LONGITUDINAL STUDIES OF GROUPS OF PEOPLE

Longitudinal studies of groups of children commenced in the United States about 1915. Walter F. Dearborn of Harvard commenced the *Harvard Growth Study*, which measured children in the Boston area from early in the primary school grades to late in high school. About the same time, Professor Louis Terman of Stanford University, commenced his *Study of Genius*, with intelligence and other measurements on children in the upper 2 or 3 per cent of the population on intelligence tests. In the 1930's, several important longtudinal studies of children and adolescents were begun. T. Wingate Todd and W. W. Greulich at Western Reserve, Harold Stuart at Harvard, Harold Jones at the University of California at Berkeley, Jean Walker Macfarlane and Nancy Bayley working separately also at Berkeley, Alfred Washburn at Denver, and Lester Sontag at the Fels Research Institute, all started studies of groups of children at birth or as early as the age of ten.

Several of these studies terminated after ten years or so, but others were continued, sometimes after a lapse of several years. Terman's study has been continued by later colleagues at Stanford; his subjects are now mostly in their fifties. The University of California Adolescent Study which started with ten year olds in 1932 has been continued by Mary Cover Jones and others, with the subjects now in their forties. The Fels Institute study has been going long enough to include people who were studied as infants and whose own children are now being studied in the same series.

A number of relatively short longtudinal studies of adults have been made, including the Kansas City Study of Adult Life which followed a group originally aged fifty to eighty-nine for five years. Also, some groups of people who were studied at one time were sought out and restudied years later. Owens' study of veterans of World War I helped to modify our belief about the course of adult intelligence when he reported the testing of groups of veterans years after they had first been tested. The National Institute of Mental Health has made a five year follow-up of a group of healthy elderly men of average initial age of seventy-two years. The Gerontology Branch of the National Heart Institute is also undertaking longitudinal studies of aging in adult men. Kallmann and his associates have made a systematic attempt to follow a group of senescent identical and fraternal twins. The Skodak and Skeels study of adopted children of below-average mothers has recently been revived and the children are being studied as adults.

In the studies which extended from the childhood to the adulthood of groups of people it has been possible to establish the existence of some continuity of behavior, as well as to show some striking changes of behavior in certain areas.

PROBLEMS OF LONGITUDINAL RESEARCH

One of the severe limitations of a longitudinal study is the fact that the study tends to be limited by the concepts and methods with which it started. While new ideas and new methods of measurement may be introduced during the course of the study, the data so obtained do not reach back to the beginning. For example, the Terman study and the California Adolescent Study did not employ projective tests, and this important source of data is missing from them today.

There are also the practical problems of the cost of a longitudinal study which includes a comprehensive description of the biological and psychological characteristics of the subjects as well as an assessment of their social environment. The maintenance of continuity in the research staff is a considerable disadvantage compared with the faster cross sectional research.

Conceptual Problems

In the absence of much data from longitudinal studies over the life span there is a tendency to use different methods and different concepts for the different age levels, and to regard children, adolescents, adults, and old people as members of different species.

There is also a problem faced by the specialist of a particular discipline—the tendency to see the variables in his own discipline as causal, and to ignore such possibilities in other discipline as well as overlook significant interaction effects. Thus the biologist may have difficulty to accept social forces and conditions as causes of human development and variations in health. On the other hand, the social scientist may easily ignore certain "emergent" biological factors, such as changes in the nervous system with resultant behavior changes in later life, or the consequences of disease.

It is not easy to see the continuing process of socialization in adults, even though such a process is clearly seen in children. Continuity of childhood, adolescence, adulthood and old age may be postulated, but the methods of studying this continuity and the concepts for describing it are still inadequate.

VALUES IN LIFE-SPAN DEVELOPMENTAL STUDY

The principal value of studies over the life span is the contribution it makes to the "problem-oriented professions"—the professions that seek to alleviate problems and to make human life more satisfactory. Developmental studies provide normative data for practioners in psychiatry, public health, social service, and adult education. Information from studies about the developmental sequences that lead to competence and to happiness, or their opposites, guide the work of these professions.

CURRENT RESEARCH PROBLEMS AND POSSIBILITIES

There is now such a great commitment of resources to research —government and private foundation money—that the cost barrier to long-term developmental studies is less of a major problem. Still, there have been no recent commitments to such studies. Meanwhile, attention is being given to the "natural experiments" in which different societies subject people to different cultural forces through the life span. The cultural differences in socialization allow comparison of the adult members of different societies and thus give information concerning the major forces on development. Anthropologists are hastening to study the few remaining primitive societies in New Guinea and elsewhere, with special attention to the entire life span.

More attention will probably be given to comparative studies of adult life and of aging in modern societies, where the cultural differences are relatively small, but nevertheless clear and specific enough to allow the discovery of cause-effect sequences. For instance, there may be cross-national differences in attitudes toward work which are related to the retirement practices and attitudes toward retirement in various societies.

Life-Span Studies and the Disciplines

Longitudinal studies and life-span research tend to encourage cross-discipline research. There is something about a longitudinal study that causes the scientist to think outside of the limits of his particular discipline, and to seek the cooperation of other disciplines. While the longitudinal studies of the past were generally commenced by medical men, they soon involved social scientists, as well. Where such studies are started by social scientists, there is generally a concern with health and with body functioning soon involving biologists.

Life-span studies thus tend to work against the trend toward greater specialization and greater diversity among the sciences and toward a unification of science.

Several factors have changed the context of human developmental studies such as the proportion of adults surviving to sixty years and beyond, changing employment and production patterns as a result of automation and the rising costs of medical and social services of dependent persons, as well as the proportion of free compared with employed time. Not all such issues are or should be compressed into the rubric of research and science. Some touch deeply personal and social values. While the subject matter may be clouded with emotion, man need not be conceived, mature and die without being knowledgeable about the forces which shape his life, nor need he avoid manipulating these forces to his advantage.

Chapter 2

PSYCHOLOGICAL RESEARCH ON CHANGES AND TRANSFORMATIONS DURING DEVELOPMENT AND AGING

JOHN E. ANDERSON

The psychologist who studies development from birth to maturity and the psychologist who studies aging in later life have common interests. They deal with a living person who changes *with* and *in* time because of internal forces which motivate him and because of external stimulation which impinges upon him from many sources. For both, the living person is a manifold of traits, abilities, skills and attitudes functioning within a very complex field of forces known as the environment. But the living person, whether young or old, does not change all at once or in every aspect of his being; there are stable as well as changing characteristics. Development and aging alike are not a series of random, unprogrammed events but are a series of orderly changes of many types.

The scientific task is to disentangle the complex, in order to obtain an orderly picture of the parts and of the whole that will enable us to predict the course of events within limits by separating stability from change, and by determining the rate and amount of change. But this is not enough. The scientist also seeks systematic knowledge of the manner in which the living person can be modified by appropriate stimulation and motivation, not only in order to understand the principles and factors that make for change and stability but also to improve the status and functioning of the ongoing young or old person.

The life cycle begins with conception and ends with death. There is rapid upward change in infancy and childhood, slower upward change in youth, a long stable period of adult life, and downward changes in later adult life. While the variation in the length of life and in the proportions of the life cycle that are devoted to growth and to decline among various species is very great, there are also basic similarities in the life cycles of living organisms.

Although the terms development and aging may be used for all age changes, in this paper *development* is used for the upward and *aging* for the downward changes. For the moment, we do not ask whether the changes in living persons are internally or externally determined but simply say that in addition to an order of genetic maturing, the cultural background creates a pattern of orderly, age-linked stimulation that becomes part of the observed process. For example, children enter school at six and thereafter undergo fairly uniform learning experiences and old people retire at definite ages in accordance with law and custom.

Development and aging alike involve *irreversible* changes in time, which cannot be detected over very short periods but which become obvious or are easily measured over a longer period. These changes are *continuous* and *cumulative*. The adaptability of the person depends upon an interplay between structures and functions which themselves change with age and on an interplay between his traits and the demands of the environment. What the eighteen year old may do with much energy, the fifty-five year old may do with less but better directed energy. Hence, account must be taken of the *task* set by the environment and of the capacity of a living organism to make internal adjustments to meet such tasks.

MAPPING CHANGES AS FUNCTIONS OF TIME OR OF CHRONOLOGICAL AGE

The simplest way in which to secure information about age changes is to measure groups of persons at various ages, selected from the population in a similar way, and plot their scores with age as the abscissa and some average of their scores as the ordinate. The resulting curves—or the statistics upon which they are based—reveal stability or change within cross sections of the population.

For example, we may compare five year olds with seven year olds, or sixty-five year olds with seventy year olds. If measures are taken on the same individuals in the same manner at successive intervals of times a longitudinal study is made. Or there may be follow-up studies at a later age level of the same persons who had been studied earlier. In studying young children, an interval of a year or even of a half year will reveal change; with older children longer intervals are necessary. In older adults intervals of one year may reveal little or no change; five years or even more may be necessary to bring out trends. Thus, the length of the interval between measures bears some relation to the rate at which increase or decrease occurs.

But because chronological age covers such a wide range of variance within the individuals who make up the samples, its use as a time clock has some limitations. To reduce this variance and obtain clearer results, norms which have previously been obtained by standardizing measures against chronological age, such as physical age, skeletal age, dental age, mental age, social age and so on, may be employed. Each of these makes for greater homogeneity. But because after very early childhood many aspects of growth and development are either uncorrelated or have low correlations, one measure cannot be substituted for another; hence reference back to the base in terms of chronological age may be needed or implied.

Because of variance in individual development, investigators have sought anchoring points, either in terms of maximal or minimal rates of change. When growth curves are superimposed by means of such points, amazing basic similarities in the form of the growth curves are revealed. Shuttleworth's (14) earlier longitudinal study of this phenomena is brilliant. So far as I know, no such technique has been used in studying change in older persons.

In infancy and early childhood every part and function grows so rapidly that almost anything that is measured shows marked trends with age; in late adolescence the rate has slowed down to such an extent that some searching has to be done to reveal processes that are changing. At the beginning of decline, the changes are slight and confined to a few characteristics; at very old ages changes are so great and occur in such a wide variety of parts and functions that they can hardly be missed and are patent to even the most casual observer.

Since there are three cycles of growth: 1) a fetal cycle, 2) a childhood cycle, and 3) an adolescent cycle, some measures of physical growth slow down as the end of a cycle is approached and speed up with the onset of the new cycle. Measures of behavior are unlikely to reveal these shifts. There are then a wide variety of growth patterns represented by various families of curves. Some functions grow rapidly in childhood and slowly in adolescence, others slowly in childhood and rapidly in adolescence, and still others at a more uniform but gradually decreasing rate throughout. Moreover the age at which terminal points (full maturity without further growth) appear varies with the function studied. Thus, the eye reaches adult size at two years, while arms and legs do so in late adolescence.

For most functions in adults and older persons, there is a long stable period with little change from twenty-five years to roughly forty-five years, followed by a period from forty-five to sixty-five years in which there is some evidence of downward change. From sixty-five years onward the decrements become greater. But, as with measures of development, the form of the curves, the point of onset, and the period of maximum decline vary with the structure or function measured. For example, measures of speed begin to fall off slightly between thirty and thirty-five (enough to move highly selected athletes out of top flight competition); strength begins to decline at forty-five years or thereabouts while coordination remains stable until sixty-five years or thereabouts. Note, however, that in particular individuals because of disease, accident, and possibly because of genetic factors change may begin earlier and that in other persons it begins much later.

Because each structure and function has its own characteristic pattern of growth and decline we must study it for itself and plot its course. We must also determine the correlations between the growth and decline of the various structures and functions empirically. In order to describe the aging person and to design complex experiments, much mapping must be done through age-oriented and normative studies. There is no simple, straightforward easily comprehended course of development and aging. In general the task of measuring, plotting, and analyzing the age relations and their interrelations has been fairly well done for growth and development—even though more could well be done—while for aging, in spite of a rapidly growing scientific literature, much more mapping, plotting, and analyzing remains to be done.

DEVELOPMENTAL STAGES, CHOICE POINTS, OR MORE ABRUPT CHANGES

Developmental psychologists are not only concerned with the gradual changes involved in growth and in aging but also with the various transformations that result from maturaticn, from learning, from insults and traumatic experiences and from the accidents of fortune or imposed choices. Although these changes generally occur over a shorter period of time, the primary distinction is not made in terms of abruptness but in terms of the quality of the changes or the manner in which they give new direction to parts of, or to the whole of the life pattern. They can be thought of as phases which noticeably transform the orientation of the person and his relations to his environment, and may be defined as emergents. In some instances, particularly where maturation is involved, they form stages or steps in a heirarchy of more and more complex behavior with new properties or aspects of functioning emerging with each step.

Perhaps they are better viewed from another angle as choice points, (see Anderson 1), a term used to designate a phenomenon in time which changes the direction or shape of the living organism and creates a "tree" in the topological sense, (see Ore 11), which differs from the "tree" that would have appeared had another choice been made. If we view the living person, whether young or old, as an open-end system of irreversible relations both within the living system itself and in its personal and social relations with the surrounding field of forces, we can think of a choice point, whether the decision be made by the person or forced upon him by outside circumstances, as a new orientation of the person. However, it should be clear that the choice point cannot be defined in terms of the immediate moment but in terms of the consequences which follow subsequently over a period of time. It may also be preceded by antecedents which also occur over a period of time.

What may follow are changes in the manner in which the person spends his time and energy, the types of interests and activities he manifests, and the interpersonal and social relations in which he engages. There may be modifications in his perception of himself and of other persons. The same consequences would not have followed, had choice fallen on other alternatives.

MATURATION: TRANSITIONS AND TRANSFORMATIONS

Between conception and death, some events which are common to all members of a species occur in an orderly sequence. While some individuals go through the sequences more rapidly than others, the variation of individuals about nodal points in time or chronological age is small compared to that between species. The course of events defined in various ways as unfolding, differentiation, maturation, growth, development, and even aging, seems strongly linked with constitutional elements. For the whole and for individual components, the unfolding occurs within growth potentials which have upper and lower limits. Presumably similar potentials and limits also exist for downward changes.

For example, the transition from infancy to childhood is marked by the appearance of walking and of symbolic responses; that from childhood to adolescence by puberty which involves marked changes in glandular secretions.

In their classic studies of infant development, both Shirley and Gesell describe the gradual changes that occur in the sensori-motor systems underlying the appearance of locomotion as well as the stages in which the infant quite suddenly goes from sitting to crawling, crawling to creeping, and creeping to walking. Once through a stage, the infant does not return to the earlier one but continues with the more effective method of locomotion. When he finally walks he elaborates the motor responses by climbing, running, and jumping, and moves into a much enlarged world in which many objects and experiences previously inaccessible become accessible and manipulable. Walking appears on the average between thirteen and fourteen months, plus or minus some weeks—a very narrow age span in relation to the whole life cycle—in a wide range of human beings observed in various climates under various environmental conditions. Encouragement, training and favorable conditions may advance its appearance in individual children by several weeks and limited opportunities may delay it slightly.

Similarly, although babbling and other vocal habits have been forming for some months, the use of the first word symbolically appears on the average at about fifteen months, and the use of the first sentence some six months later. The range of differences among individuals and among various cultures is relatively small. The use of symbols in the form of language transforms the child into a social being who can communicate with others and who can learn more quickly and efficiently through language as a mediating process.

Puberty or the awakening of sex appears on the average at about the age of twelve years in girls and about two years later in boys. In both sexes it is preceded by a prepuberal period of two years in which many small and gradual changes occur throughout. the body and is succeeded by a similar period of progressive post-puberal changes. Puberty changes the outlook upon life, modifies all personal and social relations and transforms the child into an adult.

Note that the phenomena just described are primarily maturational in character and that they appear in virtually all human beings (except for cases of extreme pathology), that they are independent of the wishes of the individual or his parents, and that, while they may be affected in some degree by environmental conditions, the possibilities of marked advancement or delay in their appearance are distinctly limited. Further the time of their appearance is compressed into a short period in comparison with the length of the life cycle. Also within a few months or years at most, marked changes in the individual and in his relations with his environment follow. Moreover, both the associated physical and psychological changes have been described in considerable detail by scientists.

There is some question whether or not stages comparable to these childhood maturational stages appear in older persons. The nearest analog to puberty is the menopause in the female which has some resemblance to puberty in terms of its base in glandular secretion, its universality, and its abruptness, and in the time over which it extends. But in 85 out of 100 females there seems to be no noticeable lasting effect on physique or behavior. The menopause, however, has not been as extensively studied on substantial and representative samples of the population as has puberty.

Welford (17) in studying substantial samples of workers, obtained age curves for withdrawal from work that involves timestress which are striking in terms of the sharpness of the drop with age and the generality of the phenomenon. These suggest an age-bound phenomenon which conceivably could possess the attributes of a maturational process. But such withdrawal may be the outcome of a pattern of age-linked environmental stimulation and attitudes.

Another type of maturational or age-bound changes that is of great interest to the psychologist, is that which seems to be intrinsic to a particular psychological process or area. Examples within the area of emotional and personality development are those described by Freud and by Erikson, both of whom have stages for adult life and old age. It is somewhat difficult to define these stages in terms of a heirarchy and in terms of age limits on the basis of specific investigations on good samples of the population. There is a problem here in the use of the terms to describe stages, since it is not clear that there is a true heirarchy in the sense that individuals move out of the earlier into the later stages without retaining substantial remnants of earlier behavior. In a recent article, Kessen (10) has examined the significance of chronological age and of stage in the study of child development with particular attention to stages within a psychological process. He also points out the necessity of studying some of the age changes in the Linnean rather than the Galilean mode.

A good example of the stage concept within a psychological process is given by the Piaget studies of the development of logical thought in children. He describes (13) four stages: a) the sensorimotor period (0-2 years) in which action has not been internalized as thought; b) the stage of pre-operational thought (2-7 years) in which there is an absence of reversible operations; c) the stage of concrete operations (7-11 years) in which problems can be solved with objects present; and d) the stage of abstract thinking (12 years on) in which problems can be solved symbolically by propositional or formal operations. These stages constitute a heirarchy of complexity through which persons move as they develop. Some however remain permanently at lower levels.

There seems to be no comparable process in aging, even though some investigators think of aging as a reversal of development in which stages are peeled off successively. It seems unlikely that the down grading of responses is such a reversal because evidence exists of the retention of residuals of the former levels reached even in very deteriorated persons. We do know that Kay (9) found that older persons given problems of different levels of complexity involving learning did less well than did younger ones on the problems of greatest difficulty or complexity, while they gave approximately equivalent performances on the simpler problems.

LEARNING: TRANSITIONS AND TRANSFORMATIONS

When stimulated and motivated, the human being acquires various skills, knowledges and attitudes which affect subsequent behavior. Through practice and experience, the circuit between input and outgo becomes so organized that patterned action follows appropriate cues. The form of the learning curve and the principles of learning such as the distribution of effort, the effect of no practice, the efficiency of reward and punishment seem to hold at all ages, and to indicate that some phases of learning are not age-bound. There is some question about transfer and interference since some experiments show greater transfer and less interference in younger persons and less transfer and more interference in older persons. Moreover, there is evidence that it takes an older person a somewhat longer time and greater effort to reach the same level of performance as younger persons. Reference has already been made to a finding that older persons do less well on complex and difficult tasks than younger persons. Actually, however, the total body of research on learning in older human beings and animals is very limited and in no way comparable to that available for the child, youth and young adult. Because of its theoretical and practical implications this area could well be given much attention.

Here, however, we are not so much interested in the mechanics of learning nor even in the change in behavior that comes directly within a particular skill or pattern of knowledge, as with the effects of that skill or pattern in transforming the relations of the living person with his environment. A course of training, a new skill, the insight which comes from solving a series of problems may open up a large range of activities for a particular individual and change the direction of his life significantly. Powerful interests may appear that determine the amount and quality of practice and lead him on to new skills and knowledges. The individual's perception and confidence in himself may be changed, and his relations with the world may be modified.

For example, the acquisition of skill in reading which extends over a few years, however valuable it may be in and for itself, gives the child a tool which opens up a new world of stimulation and activity for him. Because instruction in reading in our society is located quite precisely within a narrow range in the age span and because of virtually universal education within our society, it is taken very much for granted and has almost the characteristics of a maturational process that is more closely based on constitutional factors. With older persons, specific patterns of instruction are far from universal. Nevertheless for a Grandma Moses, an acquired skill in painting had marked effects in many aspects of her remaining years of life. Here we have a significant event (training, experience, practice, etc.) that modifies the stream of subsequent practice and the relations of the persons to the environment, and sets in train, consequences that are out of all proportion to itself. Such choice points occur with high frequency in childhood and youth, and less frequently in the older ages. But much as do the maturational stages, and the heirarchies found within sequences in behavior, they operate to determine the course of subsequent events and to set in train sequences that determine what may be called the *shape*, the psychological shape of the living person.

It should be noted that an age-related principle is also involved. It concerns the manner in which earlier practice opens up greater possibilities for practice and hence subsequent cumulative effects than does later practice. A person who learns to swim or to read early in life will have more occasions on which to swim or read than will a person who learns later because he is sensitized to the opportunities within his environment and therefore more likely to use them. Although it is better in this sense to learn at twenty or forty than at sixty or seventy, nevertheless learning at sixty or seventy is desirable.

It would seem to be fairly obvious that substantial research on the secondary effects of the learning process are needed, particularly in a period when so many persons above the age of forty-five seem to need retraining because of automation and so many persons above the age of retirement find themselves with unfilled time on their hands.

INSULTS AND RESIDUALS:
TRANSITIONS AND TRANSFORMATIONS

Living organisms encounter insults in the form of illnesses and accidents that may affect development and aging. These range from phenomena such as reduced oxygen in the fetal period to the major illnesses and accidents of later life. Younger organisms seem to have a greater capacity for adapting to and recovering from insults than do older organisms. But major insults, such as blindness may also have greater effects upon the adaptation of the young organism than upon that of the older organism because the older organism has established a large number of habits which enable him to meet the insults more effectively. Sometimes a single limiting factor disastrously interferes with development and presumably with aging, no matter how many other factors are favorable. Usually however a circle of feedback is set up, related to the effects of the insult created upon other persons, which cumulates effects subsequent to the insult. Science seeks to determine the nature of insults, methods of curing and alleviating them, and ways of eliminating the factors that create them. In other words, it seeks the optimal conditions for unhampered development and for aging, the optimal environment for resisting decline or preserving physical and mental health.

In recent years, great strides have been made in medicine and in psychology in the development of rehabilitative techniques for many types of insults. Often there is involved both a curative process such as the repair of or the use of substitutes for crippled limbs, and a psychological process such as acquiring skill in the use of the repaired or substituted limbs. Greater strides will be made in the future. This is an area of very important research for those concerned with aging not only for the benefits conveyed to the older person as an individual but also for the benefits to society which finds the cost of the care of disabled persons to be several times that of the care of the rehabilitated person. And it must be remembered that society benefits from the rehabilitated person's own contribution.

ACCIDENTS OF FORTUNE AND IMPOSED CHOICES: TRANSITIONS AND TRANSFORMATIONS

Not dissimilar in terms of the factors involved are the accidents of fortune, imposed decisions, and the various single events that occur in life which may have either good or bad residuals, depending upon the effects which cumulate within the organism. Here we deal with such phenomena as inheriting money, making a good or bad marriage, the dictation of a training program or professional career by parents, and for older persons such events as mandatory retirement, the loss of spouses, the death of friends, confinement in an institution, etc.

This is an area in which our knowledge of the factors that determine outcomes is limited. If the same event happens to two different individuals, one may rise above it and the other may be snowed under by it. What antecedent factors determine outcomes? How is the outcome related to the current of subsequent stimulation and practice, to the feedback that comes from other persons in the environment, and the context in which the person perceives himself as functioning? There may be set up what has been called the "vicious circle" in the case of the delinquent who is not only punished for his action but is returned after punishment to the same environment with all the factors within it that produced his original difficulty. But the vicious circle has a converse in that "success breeds success," in other words both poor and good adjustment to situations set up trains of events that mold the person.

In the older person there are many of these outside events which impinge upon him; serious illness and accident which limit activity, the death of friends and associates that destroy many of his social relations, mandatory retirement which moves him out of the occupation about which most of his life has been centered, and perhaps even confinement to an institution. He has some advantage over persons at younger ages because, as a survivor, he has met and solved many problems of living in the past. Many older adults, therefore, adjust very well to the accidents of fortune. But others do not do so. Here as with younger persons, the basic question is how to break the vicious circle and thus set in train a series of feedbacks from self and environment that will make for desirable behavior.

Theoretically we may work either with the individual and change his attitudes, skills, and perception of himself, or we may work with the context and by changing it in significant places modify the feedback, or we may use some combination of both approaches. Formerly, very great emphasis was placed upon treatment of the individual, lately more emphasis has gone to improving environments. While there are some differences in the methods and techniques to be used with young and older persons—and much research still is needed in this area—in both we need to understand the ongoing living organism as he operates in a very complex environment of stimulation and feedback.

Cumming and Henry (5) have recently developed a disengagement theory for describing what happens to people as they age, and have supported it by substantial research. Essentially their theory concerns the rate and amount of withdrawal of older people from the activities of life, and of the progressive constriction of the life space. But they view disengagement neither as a product exclusively of internal changes nor of the cessation of environmental demand, but as the outcome of a combination of the two. Clearly if the person lives long enough and downward change continues, the cumulative effect will be withdrawal. Contrasted with this theory, from the practical point of view, is an activity theory which emphasizes the importance of maintaining a high rate of interchange with the environment by creating stimulating conditions and encouraging individuals to maintain their activity level and even to develop new interests. From our point of view even though some disengagement seems to be inevitable—in fact it starts very early in life as the person drops one activity and substitutes

another—those who are concerned with older people could well give
attention to the possibilities of enriched environments, the elimination of restrictive physical and mental conditions, and the encouragement of old or new interests in older people. In the meantime,
we not only need further research on the factors that lead to disengagement, but also research on the way to enrich environments in
order to provide opportunities for older persons whether in institutions or out in the community.

STABILITY AND CHANGE AS MEASURED BY INTER-AGE CORRELATIONS

Our discussion so far has been concerned with stability and
change as revealed in the plotting of averages against time, chronological age or some derivative of age. But another method of analysis is now coming to the fore, as longitudinal and follow-up studies
are made. Measures obtained at one age level are correlated with
the results of similar measures at another age level. For successive
measures, scores at various age intervals may be correlated in turn
with an origin such as the earliest age, or with a terminus such as
an adult age (in the case of children). When this is done, stability
and change appear as the coefficients decrease, increase, or remain
stationary. If done in follow-up studies the extent to which later
outcomes for individuals can be predicted from earlier ones is
revealed. Note, however, that when the level of functioning for the
group as a whole increases or decreases while individuals maintain
the same relative positions, means and standard deviations will
also be needed to interpret the long time effects.

In general, the results indicate that for childhood and youth
the correlations with initial status decrease and those with terminal
status increase in a systematic way that can be plotted. In some
degree, these phenomena are a function of the part-whole relationship in that with growth more and more of the earlier ability and
experience is included in the score for the later ages, as shown
by Anderson (3) and discussed in detail by Hofstaeter and
O'Connor (7). For example, Tuddenham and Snyder (16) who
present detailed tables showing the inter-age correlations at all
ages from two to eighteen years for a number of anatomical meas-

ures as well as measures of strength, report that for males, height at two years correlates .60 with height at eighteen years, while height at seventeen years correlates .98 with that at eighteen. Corresponding figures for the height of females are .66 and .99. For weight for males the figures are .32 for two years and .97 for seventeen years, with weight at eighteen years compared with .40 at two and .96 at seventeen for females. Although inter-age correlations drop somewhat with the onset of adolescence, they later resume their upward course. For psychological measures such drops are not likely. Progressive changes in inter-age correlations for intelligence have been found by a number of investigators. The effect occurs over and above that which occurs because of a tendency for correlation coefficients to decrease as time increases between measures. As far as I know, no similar technique has been used with data on older persons, perhaps because longitudinal data of the type needed for such study has not been available. But it is reasonable to assume that inter-age correlations will decline systematically with losses in various capacities and skills.

In a longitudinal study of children from birth to maturity Kagan and Moss (8) find interrelations for a number of personality characteristics and emotional traits for various periods of development. They point out the existence of *sleeper* effects which yield ambiguous relationships on the basis of cross sectional data at particular periods but which show positive relations and effects in a later period. Moreover, they find some evidence that characteristics of the child which on their face value might seem logically to be related to similar adult characteristics turn out not to predict them but to predict other adult characteristics. Anderson (2) in a follow-up study finds that the quality of physical and psychological care given in early childhood bears some relation to the adjustment and achievement of the same persons as adults some twenty-eight years later while characteristics of the child (except for intelligence) do not seem to. Stone and Onqué (15) present abstracts for a considerable number of longitudinal studies on the personality of children, in which various methods of handling data were used.

When we turn to studies of adults and older people we find very few in which longitudinal data was obtained and these mostly cover short periods of time. There are more follow-up studies, mainly in the field of intelligence of which perhaps the most widely known is that of Owens (12) who from a first test at eighteen years to a follow-up at fifty years did not find the drop in intelligence level that had been reported in many cross-section studies. He also obtained evidence of differential change in scores of the sub-tests of Army Alpha.

In general, we depend for much of our present knowledge of the age relations of psychological and behavioral functions upon cross-section studies, of which a great many are covered in the Handbook of Birren (4). In the future we may expect more longitudinal data because more agencies and institutions are now interested in aging research. Just as records of long standing are now coming under analysis in the research institutes in child development that were established in the period between 1925 and 1929, so records and data now being collected on older people may be followed up for some years to come. A beginning has been made in the development of manuals for the statistical analysis of longitudinal data by Goldfarb (6). Because his material is limited and at an elementary level, there is still need for an advanced treatment of the statistics and methods appropriate for use in longitudinal studies.

CONCLUSION

What we have done in the preceding pages is to take a brief excursion into a very large area of research, with emphasis primarily on the developmental aspects of the life of the person and on the types and kinds of changes that occur in him as he grows and as he ages. Although there has been much discussion of change, the reader should remember that the converse of change is stability. The living being maintains his own integrity and personality in the fact of the internal changes that occur and the external pressures which surround him. In the early part of his life changes are more abrupt, more striking, and more varied. This may result from the very rapidity with which the person moves from conception to maturity. In the later part of life change is more gradual, less striking, and probably less varied.

As we view the area of psychological and behavioral research on older people, we must not expect startling discoveries or breakthroughs. We deal with organisms that are far along in the developmental course in whom the main outlines of response have been already determined by genetic endowment and growth potential both of which have manifested themselves in large degree, and by a net of environmental stimulation, learning, organized habits, and defined attitudes that have stood the person in good stead over many years. He is after all in a select class of persons because he is a "survivor" of many of the vicissitudes of life.

But there still remains a substantial potential for living. It is this with which we are concerned in practically oriented research. But behind practical principles there are the more basic generalizations which research on aging has in common with all biological and psychological sciences. In the understanding of human beings, the comprehension of the life processes, the advancement of our knowledge of all living things, research on aging has an important role.

REFERENCES

1. Anderson, J. E.: Dynamics of Development; System in Process in Harris, D. B. (Editor): *The Concept of Development.* Minneapolis, University of Minnesota Press, 1957, 287 pp.

2. Anderson, J. E.: *Experience and Behavior in Early Childhood and the Adjustment of the Same Persons as Adults.* Minneapolis, Institute of Child Development, University of Minnesota. 1963, 42 pp.

3. Anderson, J. E.: The Limitations of Infant and Preschool Tests in the Measurement of Intelligence. *Journal of Psychology, 8:*351-69, 1939.

4. Birren, J. E. (Editor): *Handbook of Aging and the Individual: Psychological and Behavioral Aspects.* Chicago, University of Chicago Press, 1959, 939 pp.

5. Cumming E., and Henry, E. E.: *Growing Old: The Process of Disengagement.* New York, Basic Books, 1961, 293 pp.

6. Goldfarb, N.: *An Introduction to Longitudinal Statistical Analysis.* Glencoe, Ill. Free Press, 1960, 220 pp.

7. Hofstaeter, P. R., and O'Connor, J. P.: Anderson's Overlap Hypothesis and the Discontinuities of Growth. *Journal of Genetic Psychology.* 88:95-106, 1956.

8. Kagan, J., and Moss, H. A.: *Birth to Maturity: A Study in Psyschological Development.* New York, Wiley, 1962, 381 pp.

9. Kay, H.: Some Experiments in Adult Learning, in *Old Age in the Modern World.* London, E. and S. Livingstone, 1955, 647 pp.

10. Kessen, W.: Stage and Structure in the Study of Children. *Monographs of the Society for Research in Child Development, 27:* 65-86, 1962.

11. Ore, O.: *Graphs and their Uses.* New York, Random House, 1963, 131 pp.

12. Owens, W. A.: Age and Mental Abilities: A Longitudinal Study. *Genetic Psychology Monographs, 48:*3-54, 1953.

13. Piaget, J.: *Logic and Psychology.* New York, Basic Books, 1957, 48 pp.

14. Shuttleworth, F. K.: Physical and Mental Growth of Girls and Boys Age Six to Nineteen in relation to Age at Maximum Growth. *Monographs of the Society for Research in Child Development, 4:*281, Serial No. 22, 1939.

15. Stone, A. A., and Onque, G. C.: *Longitudinal Studies of Child Personality.* Cambridge, Mass., Harvard University Press, 1959, 314 pp.

16. Tuddenham, R. D., and Snyder, M. M.: Physical Growth of California Children from Birth to Eighteen Years. *University of California Publications in Child Development, 1:*183-364, 1954.

17. Welford, A. T.: *Skill and Age.* London, Oxford University Press, 1951, 161 pp.

Chapter 3

INFLUENCES OF EARLY DEVELOPMENT
UPON LATER LIFE

Alfred H. Washburn

I suppose it is self-evident that any living organism is the product of its own life history from the original unique characteristics of its gametes through all its life experiences to date. Many years ago, Frank Lillie once remarked that any biological organism is its own entire life cycle from gametes on. More recent studies serve only to strengthen such a statement. From this it would appear evident that if we hope to understand any living human organism in the latter part of its life cycle we must attempt to learn what has gone before. For a really complete understanding this would involve, ideally, some knowledge of the person's genetic endowment, of his human cultural inheritance, of the pattern of his development in utero and then during infancy, childhood and adolescence, and of his responses to many aspects of his environment during both his childhood and adult life. Unfortunately, adequate life cycle studies of even one human organism are practically nonexistent, in spite of the relative wealth of knowledge of the life cycles of a good many living organisms.

In view of this paucity of reliable information about human life cycles, the subject of this talk might well be "What observations on a given individual during his infancy and childhood may yield clues concerning his health and well-being in later life, especially in his old age?" I intend to raise questions and to speculate about answers rather than to present dogmatic conclusions about the influence of early development. Before doing so, I should mention the source of my material as well as the source of whatever modicum of wisdom you will conclude I have presented, as I finish.

For the past thirty-two years I have been a member of the staff of the Child Research Council of Denver. This is a small research institute dedicated to the following of individual human life cycles from birth to the end of life. Each person is enrolled during the early stage of his development in utero in order to give us the opportunity of following the mother's health, food intake, and course through pregnancy. This also gives us a chance to become familiar with the background and characteristics of the family in which this new edition of homo sapiens will grow and develop. From birth on each subject is seen at regular intervals by many members of the research staff, representing varied interests in human development. One may arbitrarily list these observations under the three general headings of physical growth, physiological development, and the development of psychological and personality traits.

The emphasis in most of the investigations is on the dynamic pattern followed by each child in the continuing process of becoming an adult. This holds true whether we are studying the changes in body structure, the food intake during growth, the constancy of the levels of proteins and lipids in the blood, the varying responses to such environmental hazards as acute infections, or the developing concepts of the world, leading to the individual's own unique style of response.

The institution started in 1927-28 with a small group of babies. Since 1930 five to six new babies have been added each year. During the past thirty years the case loss has been only 20 per cent. Thus, we have at present 200 subjects being followed, including forty who have passed their thirtieth birthday, with the remaining 160 distributed fairly evenly through the years from 0-30. Of those between zero and twelve years, forty-two are second generation children, one of whose parents is in the twenty-thirty-five year group of subjects. Babies are seen monthly, children up through the adolescent growth spurt every three months, and adults once a year.

The thoughts which I shall present today are the result of thirty-two years' association with this study of children in the process of becoming adults. Much stimulus to my thinking, as well as many fertile ideas, I have received from many other members of the research staff. For any speculation in which I indulge I must take sole responsibility. I must take the responsibility, also, for limiting myself to a rather superficial survey of many areas of interest. I hope, thereby, to stimulate questions, objections, or suggestions concerning what we ought to be investigating in early life in reference to the final aging process.

A few comments about inherited characteristics seem advisable even though I have little to contribute in this area. It certainly seems likely that gene-transmitted characteristics play almost as important a part in the individual differences in aging as they do in variations in the earlier years of life. From our own observations, as well as those of geneticists, it is apparent that one inherits quite specific isolated characteristics in both anatomical and physiological aspects of one's total make-up. For example, we have a boy who has apparently inherited from his father his rapid linear growth, his tall, very slender build and many of his facial characteristics. His father, however, has very heavy bone structure, verging on "marble-bone" in nature. In contrast, the boy has very delicate bone structure resembling that of his mother who is not tall or thin. In similar fashion we find strikingly similar blood levels of specific protein fractions running through members of some families. Thus, the gamma globulin levels may be very similar while beta and alpha 2 fractions may be very different. This is the more striking when one knows that there is 200-300 per cent difference in gamma globulin levels in different but apparently equally healthy youngsters. What is the significance of such startling difference for later health and resistance?

In speculating about such questions it is apparent that many of the variations between individuals are either due to or strongly influenced by genetic inheritance. However, the separation of genetic from environmental factors in a given person's structure or functioning is, more often than not, either difficult or impossible in the light of our present knowledge. I shall, therefore, make no further attempt to separate genetic from life-experiential factors in the discussion of the influences of early development on later life. I shall turn, then, to the matter of physique and the individual's pattern of change in structures during growth—the process by which he reaches his adult physique.

Although there are well-nigh endless variations in structure in our subjects, yet for a given child certain structures remain remarkably constant. A nice illustration of this is revealed in the x-ray films of the chest. By two and one-half to three years of age both heart shape and lung markings have become so stable that by enlarging the film taken at the age of three years one can make an almost perfect duplicate of a film taken at fifteen or twenty years on the same person. The change is simply one of growth, the pattern remaining constant. The features of the chest, revealed in the x-ray, are as characteristic as those of the face so that our radiologist recognizes each chest film as belonging to a particular person.

This raises fascinating questions. What is the significance for health in later life of the finding of lungs with very heavy markings as compared with one with very light markings? Do apparently large tortuous pulmonary vessels in a healthy child suggest the probability, or at least the potentiality of future trouble? We find a tremendous range in our healthy children, from very clear lungs, resembling an idealized text-book picture of "normal lungs," to markings so heavy that competent radiologists have labeled them pathological.

In similar quandary, we may ask what may be the future significance of some of the variations in the size and shape of the heart in apparently healthy children with no evidence of heart disease through years of follow-up examinations. We find hearts varying in size from one-third to over one-half the width of the chest. Moreover, the shapes which are revealed in these healthy children are so varied as to make one admire the courage of a text-book author who publishes a picture of a healthy child's heart. We can demonstrate hearts whose shape strongly suggests mitral disease as well as any of several congenital anomalies. What we don't know yet is whether any of these subjects with unusual heart shapes will develop any troubles with cardiac or circulatory disorders in middle life. We hope to learn the answer when we have followed these subjects on into later life. This is simply one of many illustrations one might give of our puzzlement and our excitement about the possible future significance of the many variations in structures observed during the childhood years.

In addition to the constancy of structure, just discussed, we have been interested in the patterns of change in structures which remain orderly although unique for any given individual. The late Dr. Jean Deming demonstrated the remarkable constancy in each person's pattern of growth, first during infancy and, second during adolescence. If one examines these data it is apparent that there are statistically significant differences between the sexes in infancy as well as in adolescence. Of equal interest is the fact that there is overlapping of the data for patterns of growth—some boys following that typical for girls with some girls following the more andric pattern. What, if any, may be the influence on future health and longevity of such findings? In the two most extreme cases we have observed both the less andric boy and the less gynic girl have presented some psychological and some health problems but each is married, each is in the early thirties and each has children. To illustrate how difficult it is to separate possible causal factors a few comments will be made about the boy.

In addition to his essentially gynic pattern of growth, especially in infancy, he had many feminine characteristics in behavior, as well as in body build, which lasted into adolescence. However, he also had an unusual pattern of change in his body build. He was a slender, delicate-looking, long-legged preschool boy but became, during later childhood and adolescence a relatively short-legged, long-trunked boy. By the middle of an early adolescence he was showing a top-heavy type of body build with too much fat on his trunk. By his mid-twenties, although he had taken off some weight, he looked like a big business executive with too much weight in his trunk, hair greying at his temples, and a rising blood pressure. I can only speculate on the possible association of the particular pattern of change in his body build, by which he reached his adult physique, with the early evidences of aging. Is it, perhaps, more likely that the mixture of andic and gynic characteristics is playing a major role? If so, one could wish that we had adequate studies of the balance of hormones in such cases. These few illustrations must suffice for raising sample questions about the possible influence of physical structures on later health. Let us turn now to some of the physiological, biochemical and medical observations.

Although the relation of food intake to both growth and health is generally accepted, the details of this relationship are far from clear. A careful recording of food intakes on our subjects reveals wide variations in the intakes of most of the essential nutrients, even in children whose growth and health appear to be good. I feel sure, however, that there are long-time effects which may not become manifest for years. In this connection I was much interested, a few years ago, in the observations of Dugald Baird in Aberdeen, Scotland. He found it necessary to go back into the childhood years in order to explain the striking differences between his underprivileged clinic mothers and those in his private practice. The inadequacy of childhood food intakes appeared to be a significant factor in the increase in complications of pregnancy and in the number of abnormal offspring in the underprivileged group. Studies of recent years, in many parts of the world, suggest that with both proteins and fats the effect on the individual may be manifested many years later. They also suggest the need for much greater knowledge about the different proteins and the different fats in the diet, as well as about the significance of the balance between the amounts taken in. How shall we learn about the long-time effects of high or low or unbalanced intakes except by following each of our subjects up into middle life and to old age if they survive

We have babies whose iron intake we believe to be excessively large. We can say that we can discover no beneficial result, but we also have to say that we have seen no deleterious result. We are speculating about the possibility of an ultimately harmful effect. This brings us to the whole question of the possible long-time influence of minerals, vitamins, antibiotics, vaccines, drugs, food additives, and environmental contaminants such as insect sprays or diesel fumes. This is, of course, an immense subject which deserves a whole separate paper. I shall make only a few comments.

The variety and amounts of drugs being consumed yearly by the American people is appalling. I am personally distressed by the ease and thoughtlessness with which many physicians prescribe all sorts of drugs. It is, I am sure, obvious to most of us that far too many vitamin and vitamin-mineral preparations are being given to American children. Although I lack adequate data I do have enough evidence to feel justified in the tentative prediction that the giving of antibiotics in childhood—except for the real life-threatening diseases—is resulting in lessening of their resistance to infections in later years. Moreover, I am convinced that the psychological effect of their coming to believe in rescue by a so-called "miracle drug," rather than their trusting the natural recuperative powers of their own organism, is most pernicious. And the administration of tranquilizers to babies makes me shudder!

In the life-long study of each of our subjects we shall have the opportunity, I hope, of finding the answers to at least some of the questions about the possible harmful effects of these agents.

There are also nearly endless unanswered questions concerning the future significance of the many deviations from the average which we find in various studies of the blood of each subject. The range of variation in healthy children is striking in the numbers and types of blood cells, in levels of cholesterol and alpha and beta lipids, in the amounts of circulating albumins and globulins, and in the levels of certain vitamins and enzymes. What does each individual's own unique pattern of levels of each of these substances signify about his future health? What, for example, will be the future health record of a child who seems able to maintain a persistently high level of gamma globulin, who produces plasma cells rapidly and who recovers quickly (without antibiotics!) from his childhood illnesses, as compared with that of one who has persistently low gamma globulin levels and sluggish recovery from illness?

In the area of simple physiological functioning the individual variations in test performance give us the same sort of unanswered questions. We have a battery of tests in the area of so-called "physical fitness." The differences between apparently healthy children are quite extreme. Although they do not appear to be related to the child's immediate health one suspects there may well be very significant differences in the later health record and physical performance between a child with a low score and one with a high score. Moreover, if one asks the simple question "Fit for what?," then it becomes obvious that we need to investigate very thoughtfully the aspects of fitness which give the best clues to fitness for a specific person in his own later life—not simply fitness for football or for Army service.

For some individuals the pattern of response to a stressing work-load on the bicycle ergometer is remarkably constant. For others it reveals striking variations which seem to depend on both physical or psychological factors. Although electrocardiographic patterns vary considerably, yet they tend to be remarkably constant in a given person through the years of his childhood development. Heart rate and blood pressure changes during growth show striking differences in different people. What is the difference in the future prospects of a twelve year old child with a persistent resting heart rate of 50 and of one with a resting rate of 90? If one considers what this means in terms of the total number of heart beats in a life time it seems as though there should be a difference in the future course run by these two individuals, but we don't have the answer to even so simple a question.

Since physiological and psychological functioning are so closely related we are naturally absorbed in the study of the psychological development of each subject whose life span we are following. There are many personality characteristics which are revealed early in life by appropriate tests and observations. Many are certainly well-established by the end of the preschool years. We have been interested in trying to learn how and how early the person's own unique characteristics emerge. At the same time we attempt to discover what environmental factors have been influential in a given child's psychological pattern of response to his world. Both of these aspects of our investigations hold possible significance for the person's mental health in later life. As many people have demonstrated, retrospect reconstruction of one's past history is often not a very reliable procedure. By a careful study in infancy and childhood, on subjects followed through to later life, we hope to answer some of the obvious questions. Perhaps one may think of this as a "control" for clinical psychiatry. Certainly we should be able to throw some light on the question of whether certain experiences in infancy or early childhood inevitably distort the development of a healthy personality. Or again, is mental illness in later life to be expected from characteristics in early life? If so, what can be done to prevent illness occurring? It seems probable that a knowledge of how the child has learned to deal with his world—his style of response—will be found to have real significance for his mental health and happiness throughout life. Possibly such knowledge will have even greater significance for that second childhood called old age.

This is hardly the kind of talk which lends itself to a neat summary. Instead I shall make a few final comments. I have tried to touch on many aspects of my subject in the hope that people in the audience who know lots more about geriatrics than I do would be stimulated to discuss some of the questions which have been raised. If there are some who want to ask questions about my material, or better yet, to object to my speculations or ideas, I hope they will feel free to do so. Since I am anxious to pick up any ideas on observations which the Child Research Council ought to be making I shall be most grateful for any criticisms or suggestions.

One final point needs stressing. There is the most urgent need for more studies of individual human life cycles. Ideally the investigation of the aging process should begin with the beginning of life.

SECTION B

Biological Manifestations of Growth and Aging

Chapter 4

THE DEVELOPMENTAL NATURE OF BONE CHANGES DURING AGING*

Stanley M. Garn, Christabel G. Rohmann,
and Philip Nolan, Jr.

With advancing years, there is a decrease in the mass of bone as measured in various ways. The radiographic density of finger bones measured *in vivo* becomes less (Balz *et al.*, 1957; Odland *et al.*, 1958). The weight of the skeleton decreases, as does the physical density (weight:volume) of individual bones, and the mineral content as measured by the percentage ash weight (Trotter and Peterson, 1955; Broman *et al.*, 1958; Trotter, 1960). The amount of cortical bone diminishes in rib cross-sections (Sedlin *et al.*, 1963; Sedlin, 1963). Density of iliac plugs similarly diminishes with age (Saville, 1960) as does the mineral content of femoral fragments removed in the treatment of hip fractures (Wray *et al.*, 1963).

These *in vivo* studies, investigations on skeletalized material and biophysical analyses of accident victims, elective surgery patients and fracture patients confirm the general clinical impression of an age-associated loss of bone material. They fit in with growing evidence that bone loss is a problem of major concern, like atherosclerosis widespread, and possibly of increasing prevalance and even severity. Viewed in this light "osteoporosis," as clinically defined, may be likened to the proverbial iceberg, the more visible smaller indication of a much larger general problem of aging.

* The present research was supported in part by Grant A-3816 from the National Institutes of Health.

41

Like atherosclerosis, bone loss must therefore be considered both from the standpoint of epidemiology, and in its developmental aspects. The epidemiology of bone loss itself poses a problem, that of adequate sampling from clinically normal subjects of all ages. The developmental aspects of bone loss would seem to be most difficult to unravel, both from considerations of sampling, and because of the obvious fact that the same bone can not be analyzed destructively at successive ages.

The present study, therefore, is unique in its approach to the problem of bone loss with age. It involves a simple non-destructive biophysical approach (radiogrammetry) that is highly replicable *in vivo*. The subject population involved is not only clinically normal, free living and ambulatory, but it approaches the ideal of a mendelizing population or breeding isolate. Moreover, this investigation offers, for the first time, sequential, longitudinal data on bone loss with age in an unselected normal group.

The present report, therefore, is concerned with the developmental aspects of bone change with age, in subjects who have completed long-bone growth, starting with age sixteen and terminating (in semi-longitudinal fashion) in the eighth decade. It documents the prevalence of bone loss, and provides for the first time an accurate measure of the rate of decrease in compact bone in individuals.

METHODS AND APPROACH

This study of bone change with age is based upon a total of more than 700 subject examinations of 462 clinically healthy long-term participants in the thirty-four year old Fels Longitudinal Program. All of the subjects were white, and predominantly of Northwest European extraction. The majority were Ohio-born and urban or semi-rural in residence. In body size they adhered closely to norms for similar populations (cf. Garn, 1957). As a group, they could be described as representative of the ambulatory normal well-nourished middle class, unselected with respect to metabolic or bone disease.

The prime radiographic data in each case consisted of postero-anterior hand radiographs taken at a uniform 36-inch tube-to-film distance on screen-type film, except for selected "runs" made on non-screen material for "bone density" evaluation. Attention was directed to the metacarpal bones, as largest of the tubular bones of the hand, and with the thickest areas of compact bone. After preliminary study, the second metacarpal was selected on the basis of size and morphological uniformity.

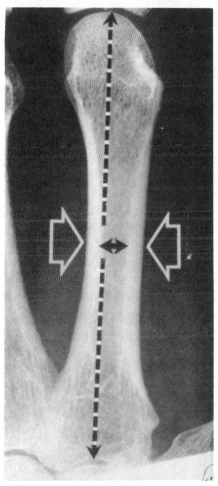

Fig. 1. Radiograph of a second metacarpal showing the three measurements taken in the present study. Metacarpal length was obtained with a semi automatic GOAT, while shaft width at mid-section and medullary thickness were measured with a ground-tip vernier caliper. Compare with Virtama and Mähönen (1960, Fig. 1).

The measurements involved, as pictured in Figure 1, included metacarpal length, total width of mid-section, and medullary width. Length was measured with the semi-automatic print-out GOAT (Gerber Instrument Company, Hartford, Connecticut), and shaft width and medullary width were measured with a ground-tip vernier micrometer. All measurements were recorded to 0.1 mm, the readout limits of the GOAT with metric gearing and the vernier caliper as well. Since radiographic enlargement was approximately one per cent (cf. Kemp, 1951) and close to constant, corrections for enlargement were neither made nor considered necessary.

Metacarpal length (L), metacarpal width (W) and medullary width (M) were thus obtained directly, and cortical width (C) by simple subtraction (C=W−M). Where serial radiographs were available, as in the sixteen-eighteen year groups and for certain of the older males in the forty-seventy-five age range, the separate radiographs were measured without reference to each other. The metric data were then transferred to standard 80-column punch cards and, after being verified, were separated into the following age groups: 16, 17, 18, 19-24, 25-34, 35-44, 45-54, 55-64, and 65-x for the final computer tabulations.

It should be noted that the population sample here considered was free-living, and non-selected with respect to any disease entity. Moreover, and in contrast to volunteers as ordinarily employed, it comes close to the ideal of a mendelizing population. More specifically, the adult males were espoused to the adult females, and the younger subjects (including all in the 16-18 age group) were the progeny of the older participants. This latter feature not only obviated the common problem of successive samplings, but made possible certain unique investigations into the family-line nature of bone structure and changes in the amount of cortical bone.

Finally, acknowledgment should be made to the earlier work of Virtama and Mähönen (1960) which suggested the practical possibilities inherent in the simple measurement of cortical thickness.

FINDINGS

At the beginning of the measuring program, and again at various times during the course of the data accumulation, sample radiographs were remeasured to test the replicability of all of the bony dimensions involved. Immediate replicability of cortical and medullary measurements (involving the same radiographs remeasured after several days) exceeded 0.98. Long-term replicability of the outer width and length measurements (involving separate radiographs taken 15 years apart, on the average) approximated 0.99.

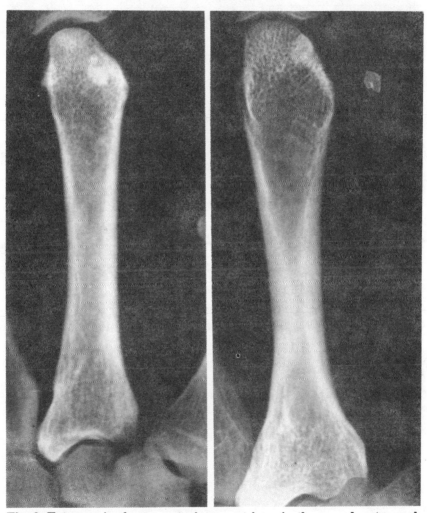

Fig. 2. Extremes in the amount of compact bone in the second metacarpal. *Left*, female subject No. 0153, age thirty-two, cortical thickness .38 mm. at mid shaft. *Right,* male subject No. 197, age twenty-four, cortical thickness 7.0 mm. Measurements uncorrected for radiographic enlargement which is less than 1 per cent under the conditions of this study (cf. Kemp, 1951).

Accordingly, all sources of error, including positioning and measuring errors, together accounted for but a small part of the large observed variance in the thickness of compact bone pictured in Figure 2.

Taking the bone length, cortical thickness and medullary size measurements by age and by sex, as shown in the first table, both age and sex trends were clearly discernible. To begin with, the males exceeded females in cortical thickness throughout the sixty-year age range considered. Here, the excess of compact bone was greater than the difference in metacarpal width alone. Second, there was a marked increase in the amount of compact bone between the sixteenth year and the middle of the third decade, in both sexes. Third, there was a decrease in the thickness of compact bone after the fifth decade in both sexes. However, the *rate* of decrease in compact (cortical) bone was far more pronounced in the women, as shown in Figure 3.

While the males tended to have more compact bone to start with, to gain more compact bone through the third decade, and to lose less compact bone after the fifth decade, the relative amount of cortical bone (cortex to total ratio) was actually greater in females up to the postmenopausal years. Female metacarpals were

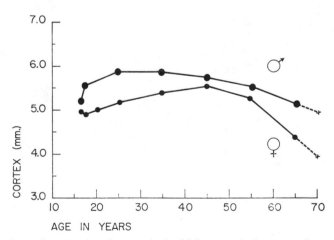

Fig. 3. Age changes in the cortical thickness of the second metacarpal (two-point moving mean). As shown, cortical thickness is less in the female at all ages and the amount of compact bone decreases at a faster rate in the female after the fifth decade.

TABLE 1

AGE CHANGES IN CORTICAL AND MEDULLARY THICKNESS
AND CORTICAL AREA AT MID-SHAFT

Age (yrs.)	Sex	No.	Length X	Length S.D.	Cortex X	Cortex S.D.	Medulla X	Medulla S.D.	Cortical Area
16	M	74	70.9	3.5	5.0	0.5	4.0	0.7	51.5
16	F	82	66.2	3.7	5.0	0.6	2.7	0.7	39.9
17	M	86	71.4	3.3	5.4	0.8	3.7	0.9	54.6
17	F	67	65.8	3.5	4.9	0.6	2.8	0.7	40.7
18	M	72	70.9	3.1	5.7	0.7	3.6	0.9	56.9
18	F	47	66.4	3.2	4.9	0.6	2.8	0.7	40.6
19-24	F	22	63.9	3.1	5.1	0.8	2.7	0.7	42.5
25-34	M	22	71.1	3.1	6.0	0.4	3.4	0.8	58.4
25-34	F	110	64.8	3.3	5.3	0.7	2.6	0.8	44.3
35-44	M	40	71.8	4.2	5.7	0.6	3.7	0.9	58.0
35-44	F	32	64.8	3.1	5.5	0.8	2.6	0.9	45.9
45-54	M	18	71.4	4.5	5.8	0.7	3.8	1.0	61.7
45-54	F	11	63.8	3.1	5.6	0.8	2.2	0.7	43.2
55-64	M	30	72.3	3.9	5.3	0.6	4.4	0.9	58.3
55-64	F	9	65.8	2.3	4.9	0.7	3.3	0.9	44.4
65-x	M	10	69.8	3.5	4.8	0.7	4.6	1.0	52.5
65-x	F	2	64.1	—	3.9	—	4.2	—	37.7

smaller in size and in volume than male metacarpals, and in terms of either cross-section area or total bone volume a greater proportion of the total was represented by compact bone.* However, with advancing age and the more rapid bone loss with age in females, the net effect was to reverse male and female ratios. Thus, as given in tabular form in Table 1 and graphed in Figure 4, the older women had smaller bones with greatly decreased structural strength.

With the considerable variability in the amount of cortical bone characteristic of any sex-age category, it was of interest to consider the extent of genetic involvement, even in this preliminary study. Since adult siblings were relatively few, parent-child similarities in cortical bone thickness were investigated, making use of sixteen-

---

* While the cross-section area (and hence the total bone mass) is less in the female, the much smaller medullary area leads to a high cortex:total ratio in women. This undoubtedly accounts for reports of higher radiographic bone "densities" in the female, where the "density coefficient" is obtained by dividing the mass coefficient of Mid V by a constant.

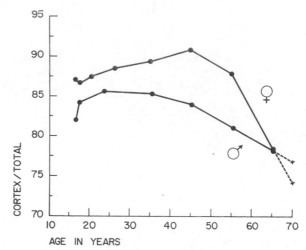

Fig. 4. Changes in the per cent of compact bone at mid-shaft in males and females aged sixteen to seventy-five. Expressed as a percentage of the total cross-section area, the female metacarpal has a larger percentage of compact bone during early maturity and a far greater decrease after the fifth decade. Compare these two-point moving means with Sedlin, Frost and Villanueva (1963, Fig. 2).

eighteen year old children and their adult parents, eliminating from consideration the older parents and possibly reduced amounts of compact bone. While father-daughter, father-son, mother-son, and mother-daughter correlations in metacarpal width tended to be low, positive but barely significant, the generally significant father-daughter correlations in the amount of compact bone (Table 2) were compatible with the hypothesis of X-linked inheritance (Garn and Rohmann, 1962).

While the cross-sectional analyses provided clear evidence for age-associated decrements in compact bone in both sexes, there was a very good question of whether the mass-data trends marked a generalized bony decrease characteristic of all aging individuals, or whether they were attributable to excessive bone loss on the part of the very few. Cross-sectional data alone could not resolve this problem. Accordingly, longitudinal data were employed, making use of fifteen-year follow-up radiographs on men forty and beyond at the time of the first radiographic examination. As shown in the third table, where the data are tabulated for all

TABLE 2

PARENT-CHILD SIMILARITIES IN COMPACT BONE

Parent-Child Correlation	Age 16 N	Age 16 r	Age 17 N	Age 17 r	Age 18 N	Age 18 r	Single Age[1] N	Single Age[1] r
Mother-daughter	33	0.04	22	0.05	17	0.01	34	0.02
Mother-son	34	0.06	37	−0.00	32	−0.10	41	0.06
Father-daughter	33	0.34*	22	0.29	17	0.36*	34	0.36*
Father-son	35	−0.08	37	0.08	32	0.18	40	−0.03
Mid-parent	—	—	—	—	—	—	75	0.15

[1] Cortical value for the youngest available of the ages given.
* Starred correlations significant at $p = .05$ or better.

individuals involved, decreased cortical bone was indeed the generality for males after the fifth decade. Out of a total of twenty-six
men studied, all but six decreased in the amount of compact bone
after forty, and only one (No. 0259) increased sufficiently in all
five metacarpals to suggest a major addition of compact bone in
the fifth decade and beyond. It may be concluded, therefore, that
bone loss is a general characteristic of aging in the male rather
than a unique characteristic of a proto-osteoporotic few.

While the fifteen-year follow-up studies confirmed the hypothesis of a generalized decrease in compact bone in the males, a

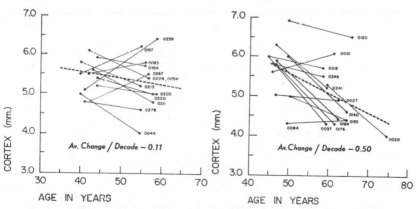

Fig. 5. Individual changes in the thickness of compact bone over two
overlapping fifteen-year periods. Between forty and fifty-five, the average
loss of compact bone is small. Between fifty and sixty-five, on the average,
compact bone decreases in the male approximately 10 per cent per decade,
For subject details see Table 3.

TABLE 3

LONG-TERM CHANGES IN CORTICAL THICKNESS
(MALES AGE 40-75)

Subject No.	Age (yrs.)	Cortex (mm.)	Age (yrs.)	Cortex (mm.)	Δ Cortex	Δ/Decade
0213	40	5.8	55	5.2	−0.6	−0.40
0197	40	5.5	55	6.2	0.7	0.47
0044	40	5.0	55	4.0	−1.0	−0.67
0259	41	5.1	59	6.4	1.3	0.72
0278	41	4.8	55	4.6	−0.2	−0.14
0028	42	6.1	57	5.4	−0.7	−0.47
0083	42	5.5	56	5.8	0.3	0.21
0054	42	6.1	57	5.4	−0.7	−0.47
0267	42	4.8	57	5.5	0.7	0.47
0211	43	5.6	58	4.8	−0.8	−0.53
0220	44	5.4	58	5.0	−0.4	−0.29
0354	44	5.9	56	5.7	−0.2	−0.17
0205	44	5.2	59	5.0	−0.2	−0.13
				Mean Change Per Decade		−0.11
0216	45	6.0	59	5.7	−0.3	−0.21
0037	45	6.0	60	4.3	−1.7	−1.13
0001	46	5.6	62	6.1	0.5	0.31
0346	46	5.8	59	5.5	−0.3	−0.23
0241	47	6.3	60	5.2	−1.1	−0.85
0186	47	5.9	63	4.4	−1.5	−0.94
0027	47	5.0	63	4.9	−0.1	−0.06
0176	47	5.8	62	4.3	−1.5	−1.00
0140	50	6.0	65	4.6	−1.4	−0.93
0084	50	4.3	65	4.4	0.1	0.07
0120	50	6.9	66	6.5	−0.4	−0.25
0153	50	5.0	65	4.4	−0.6	−0.40
0020	60	5.3	75	4.0	−1.3	−0.87
				Mean Change Per Decade		−0.50

further division of the data on the twenty-six individuals involved made it possible to pinpoint the timing of the individual decreases more accurately. For thirteen men initially studied at age forty to forty-four, and age fifty-five to fifty-nine at the time of the second examination, the mean change was −.11 millimeters per decade. Moreover, as shown in Figure 5, four of the thirteen individuals actually or apparently gained bone. In contrast, thirteen men forty-five years of age and over at the time of the first examination, and fifty-nine to seventy-five years of age at the time of the

second examination, evidenced a net cortical decrease of 0.50 millimeters per decade. This latter value, approximating a ten per cent
loss of cortical bone per decade, served to establish more accurately the timing of metacarpal bone loss in males. For practical
purposes it may be said to begin in the sixth decade.

Actually, decreases in the thickness of cortical bone and concomitant increases in the marrow space characterize all of the
metacarpals and not just the second metacarpal measured in the
present study, as shown in Figures 6, 7 and 8. Moreover, the

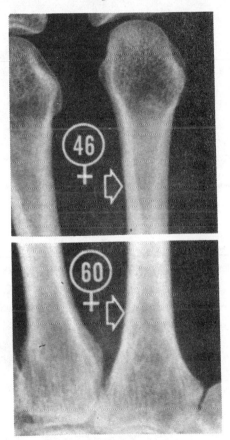

Fig. 6.   Age changes in compact bone over a fourteen-year period. *Above,*
second and third metacarpals of female subject No. 0001 at forty-six years
of age. *Below,* matching lower sections of the same bones of the same woman
taken sixteen years later. During this time period cortical bone has decreased
more than 14 per cent.

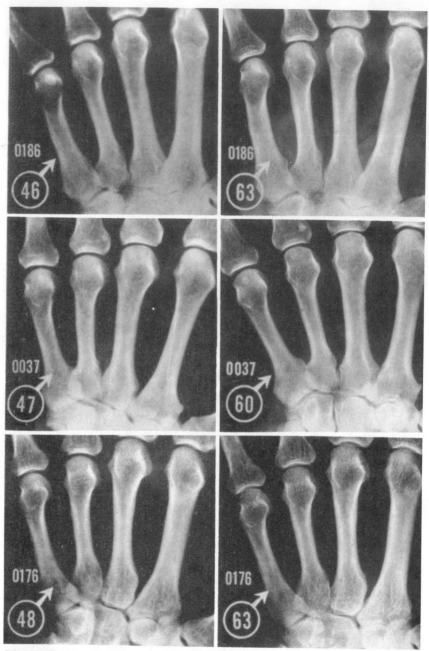

Fig. 7. Changes in compact and medullary bone of individual male subjects between the late forties and early sixties. As shown, there is an age-associated decrease in cortical bone in all four metacarpals. Individual changes in the amount of compact bone may be as high as 20 per cent over a fifteen year period

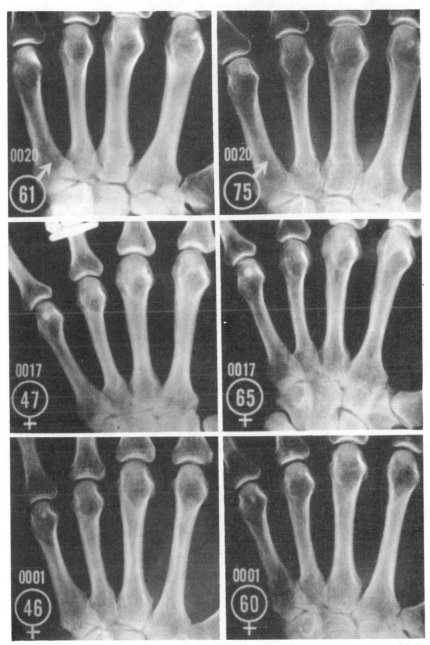

Fig. 8. Changes in cortical and medullary thickness in the second, third, fourth and fifth metacarpals in two women and one man. *Above,* a 24 per cent decrease in the cortical thickness of the second metacarpal. *Middle,* a 33 per cent decrease (2.2 mm) and *below,* a 0.7 mm (14%) decrease in the amount of compact bone at mid-shaft in the second metacarpal. Figures within the sex symbols refer to age.

decreases in cortical thickness appear more dramatic when examining serial radiographs of aging women. While this is partially attributable to a more rapid decrease in compact bone in the female, it represents an optical illusion as well. With a much smaller medullary space to begin with, a given decrease in cortical thickness may appear to be larger in the female, an illusion clearly shown in female subjects 0001 and 0017 in Figure 8. Notwithstanding this optical effect, the decrease in compact bone is quite apparent in serial longitudinal radiographs of aging individuals of both sexes. In sequential radiographic examination, attention should be directed to the cortical and medullary thicknesses rather than to the size and configuration of the trabecular pattern.

In the course of the radiographic examination, and during casual inspection of the data, there seemed to be some relationship between the amount of bone present and the rate of bone loss. This was confirmed by comparing the rate of bone loss per decade, as given in Table 3, and the initial thickness. The resulting correlation was then -0.41. As shown in Figure 9, then, there was good evidence that the rate of bone loss is indeed proportional to the amount of bone present in the fifth decade. Apparently a larger

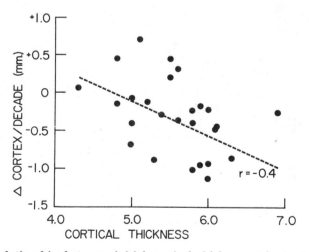

Fig. 9. Relationship between initial cortical thickness (abscissa) and loss of compact bone (ordinate). Between the fifth and seventh decades the rate of metacarpal bone loss in aging males is clearly related to the amount of compact bone initially present.

mass of compact bone or a larger mineral mass is more likely to slip into negative bone balance.

Now this latter suggestion, plus the resemblance between the developmental curve of bone growth and bone loss and published curves for steroid excretion led us to test the hypothesis that greater amounts of compact bone were associated with higher steroid excretion levels during the middle years. The rationale was that a higher 17-ketosteroid excretion level might support a thicker cortical mass during adulthood and therefore result in a greater loss of compact bone during the later period of steroid withdrawal. However, the data did not support this conjecture. Though there was a barely significant correlation between Lean Body Weight and total metacarpal thickness ($r = 0.26$ for 55 subjects) there was no significant correlation between cortical thickness and Lean Body Weight, twenty-four-hour creatinine excretion or twenty-four-hour 17-ketosteroid excretion. Accordingly, there was no reason to maintain that maximal thickness of cortical bone or the rate of loss of cortical bone was directly related to the amount of the neutral ketonic steroids excreted during the middle years.

In short, the present data clearly attested to the developmental nature of bony decreases with age, they confirmed the more rapid loss of compact bone in the aging female, and they documented the prevalence and specific timing of cortical bone loss in the male. However, the results failed to suggest specific hormonal mechanisms, though they did confirm the suggestion of a genetic factor controlling cortical thickness.

DISCUSSION

This preliminary investigation of changes in compact bone with age, employing a technically simple and non-destructive measurement, goes far toward demonstrating the amount of information on the normal aging of the human skeleton that can be acquired *in vivo*. The radiogrammetric approach is uniquely suited to long-term studies of bone in individuals, and can identify examples of extreme loss of compact bone in the process of happening. Though based on only one bone in the hand, the second metacarpal, there are excellent reasons for extrapolating the trends here observed to the remaining metacarpals, but not to the proximal, middle or distal segments of the digits, as will become apparent.

After the second metacarpal has become stabilized in external dimensions, there are continuing changes in internal architecture, as shown by an increase in compact bone and a decrease in marrow space well into the third decade and, in some individuals, even longer. As might be predicted, the amount of compact bone is considerably greater in the adult male, thus accounting for the higher physical density (weight:volume) and the greater radiographic "density coefficients." However, the cortical bone accounts for a higher percentage of the cross-section area or cross-section volume in the female, and is also true in the rib cross-section (cf. Sedlin, 1963; and Sedlin, Frost, and Villanueva, 1963). Though the female has less compact bone, the medullary space is disproportionately smaller, so the ratio (cortex to total area)is in consequence higher until the postmenopausal years, when the loss of cortical bone has become severe.

The age at which cortical bone reaches maximum in the second metacarpal, and the duration of the steady-state is still equivocal. In the male, maximum cortical width remains, on the average, from the third through the fifth decade. In the female, the maximum may well be attained after the third decade. But in both sexes cortical dimensions decrease after the fifth decade. The cross-sectional analyses indicate a rapid rate of bone loss thereafter.

In men, followed in true longitudinal fashion through the fifth, sixth, and seventh decades, loss of cortical bone is the rule. These longitudinal analyses show that decreased bone (as evidenced by massed-data trends) is not due to excessive bone loss in a selected few, but rather a generalized loss of cortical substance in the many. Since the decrease from forty to fifty-five is small, while the decrease from forty-five to sixty is relatively large, it follows that the greater bulk of bone loss in the males in the Fels Longitudinal Series occurs in the sixth decade. And here the relationship between the amount of bone loss and the initial amount of bone exemplifies a further application of the "law of initial value" (cf. Lacey and Lacey, 1962). If bone loss is viewed as an example of negative calcium balance, it must be viewed as negatively dependent upon the mass of mineral present as well.

Understandably, exact comparisons can not now be made between bone loss in the second metacarpal as here demonstrated, and bone loss in the rib, pelvis, femur, or in the middle segment of the fifth digit. There is the statistical problem of sample size, excluding for the moment juveniles included in certain of the studies. There is the further problem of sampling. Very little is known about the ante-mortem histories of the skeletons studied by Trotter and her associates (see references), the accident victims sampled by Saville (1960), or the "normal subjects" investigated by Balz *et al.* (1957). One may argue against the statistical normalcy of Wray's hip-fracture subjects (Wray, 1963), the elective surgery and autopsy cases used by the Henry Ford Hospital group, and so on. These strictures are not intended to minimize these contributions to our knowledge, but merely to emphasize the difficulties of literature comparisons involving generally disparate samples and generations.

Still, and with these *caveats* duly noted, there do seem to be anatomical or regional differences in the onset of bone loss. Decreased density of iliac plugs and decreased cortical area measurements of the ribs (Saville, 1960; Sedlin, 1963) seem to precede metacarpal losses by a decade or more. On the other hand, decreases in the radiographic "density" of the middle segment of the 5th digit seem to begin at a later age, as judged both from the earlier German data of Balz *et al.* (1957) and the later American data from the Western Regional Survey (Odland, 1958) and unpublished cooperative studies with Dr. Harald Schraer. The age-associated pattern of bone loss would thus seem to conform to the sequence observed in animal depletion data, i.e., first central, then appendicular, and finally peripheral (Benzie *et al.*, 1956). Trotter's skeletal data help to confirm our suspicion, namely, that the pelvis and ribs are first involved in bone loss, then the long bones, then the large tubular bones of the peripheries, and finally the small tubular bones.

In reviewing the bone changes described in this study, and recognizing the fact that bone loss may begin early in the axial skeleton and late in the peripheral bones, it is possible to reject at least some of the current explanations for pronounced bone loss with age. However applicable Nordin's low-calcium hypothesis may

TABLE 4

AGE CHANGES IN BONE FOR VARIOUS SITES AND SAMPLES

Author and Date	Sample and Technique	Findings
Trotter and Peterson (1955)	Long limb bones of 10 white male cadavers, complete skeletons of 7 additional, age range 41-89 years.	Slight age decrease in percentage ash weight in limb bones.
Balz, Birkner and Schmitt-Rohde (1957)	Radiographic densities of Mid V in 103 "normal" subjects 10-75 years.	Decrease after 6th decade in combined-sex "normal" data.
Odland *et al.* (1958)	Radiographic densities of Mid V of volunteers from seven Western States.	Decrement in bone density in females 49-81 years for Mid V center trace.
Trotter, in Garn (ed.) (1960)	Weight: volume ratios in 40 Negro and 40 White skeletons from Terry Collection.	Density (weight: volume) decreased with age in all four race/sex groups, more in female.
Saville, in Garn (ed.) (1960)	Iliac plugs from 139 accident victims 20-85 years.	Decreased density after 4th decade, data complicated by alcoholics.
Garn, Rohmann and Nolan (1963), and Garn (1963)	Thickness of cortex and total cortical area of Met. II in 462 normal subjects age 17-75.	Decrease in both sexes after 5th decade, 10% per decade in males, more rapid loss in females.
Sedlin, Frost and Villanueva (1963)	Rib cross-sections from 139 "relatively normal" subjects including 112 adults, primarily (75%) removed at surgery.	Decrease in cortical area after 3rd decade, approximately 25% in both sexes.
Wray, Sugarman and Schneider (1963)	Fragments of femoral cortex from 25 (age 62-93) hip fracture cases, 21 female, 4 male.	Decreased ash: dry weight ratios, averaging less than 50%.

be to some populations, the simple fact is that the group under study includes men who have lost bone on diets greatly exceeding 2000 mg/day. Further it is doubtful whether rib and iliac bone loss in rather young Americans can be attributed to a long-term calcium-deficient diet. And finally, the prevalence of bone loss with age (as shown by our longitudinal analyses) argues against the calcium-deficiency theory, since it would account only for occasional individuals habituated to an extremely low dietary calcium intake.

The exercise or activity-level hypothesis may also be rejected as an explanation for bone loss in the participants in the Fels Longitudinal Series, and particularly for the second metacarpal site. While there is no question that immobilization can account for loss of bone substance, the Fels sample included no bed-ridden subjects. The subjects were all ambulatory, and engaged in manual activities. So decreased physical activity does not explain bone loss in the present study.

Moreover, bone loss is by no means peculiar to the postmenopausal female. As our data and the other data cited show, bone loss takes place in both sexes, albeit at a greater pace in the aging female. Moreover, it would now appear that central or axial bone loss may actually begin as early as the third decade. There is a possibility, in fact, that a decrease in the compact bone of vertebrae, ribs and the iliac bones may begin before maximum compact bone has been attained in the hand and the foot! Whereas the massed-data trend line in the present study is reminiscent of published curves of 17-ketosteroids, the apparent temporal "spread" for bone loss at different sites makes it difficult to implicate particular steroids of either adrenal or gonadal origin.

It is safe to say, however, that bone loss with age appears to be a nearly universal phenomenon, with the individual who develops more compact bone likely to lose more bone during the process of aging. The female would appear to be more prone to the sequelae of bone loss, because of her more limited supply of compact bone to begin with, and her greater rate of bone loss with advancing years. It should be possible to identify osteoporosis-prone individuals before they exhibit the classical symptoms.

SUMMARY

1. Changes in compact and medullary bone were examined in the second metacarpal (Met. II) of 462 normal subjects sixteen to seventy-five years of age.

2. In both sexes, compact bone increased at the expense of marrow space through the third decade and then decreased after the fifth decade.

3. Throughout the age range considered, the volume of compact bone was less and the rate of bone loss after the fifth decade was greater in females.

4. From 575 parent-child comparisons, involving father-daughter, father-son, mother-daughter and mother-son correlations, there was an indication of X-linked inheritance of compact bone.

5. Longitudinal studies of bone change in older men revealed an individual decrease approximating 10 per cent per decade after the 45th year.

6. In these longitudinal comparisons, men with larger cortical volumes lost more compact bone than males with small cortical volumes.

7. With due consideration to sampling considerations, these findings confirmed other studies suggesting a later loss of bone in the appendicular skeleton than in the axial skeleton.

8. Attention was directed to the female with little compact bone as a likely candidate for clinical osteoporosis.

REFERENCES

1. Balz, G., Birkner, R., and Schmitt-Rohde, J. M.: Über calcipenischen Osteopathein und ihre Diagnostik mit Hilfe eines Besonderen Röntgenverfahrens, *Arztl. Wchnschr., 12:*209-213, 1957.

2. Benzie, D., Boyne, A. W., Dalgarno, A. C., Duckworth, J., Hill, R., and Walker, D. M.: Studies of the skeleton of the sheep. II: The relationship between calcium intake and resorption and repair of the skeleton in pregnancy and lactation, *J. Agric. Sc., 48:*175-186, 1956.

3. Broman, G. E., Trotter, M., and Peterson, R. R.: The density of selected bones of the human skeleton, *Am. J. Phys. Anthropol., 16:* 197-212, 1958.

4. Garn, S. M.: Roentgenogrammetric determinations of body composition, *Human Biol., 29:*337-353, 1957.

5. Garn, S. M.: An annotated bibliography on bone densitometry, *Am. J. Clin. Nutrition, 10*:59-67, 1962.

6. Garn, S. M.: Human biology and research in body composition, in Brozek, J., (Ed): Symposium on Body Composition, *Ann. New York Acad. Sc., 99*:000-000, 1963.

7. Garn, S. M., and Rohmann, C. G.: X-linked inheritance of developmental timing in man, *Nature, 196*:695-696, 1962.

8. Garn, S. M., Rohmann, C. G., and Nolan, P.: Ageing and bone loss in a normal human population, abstract presented at International Symposium on Gerontology, 1963.

9. Kemp, L. A. W.: *A Students' Radiological Mathematics,* Springfield, Thomas, 1951.

10. Lacey, J. I., and Lacey, B. C.: The law of initial value in the longitudinal study of autonomic constitution: reproducibility of autonomic responses and response patterns over a four-year interval. *Ann. New York Acad. Sc., 98*:1257-1290; 1322-1326, 1962.

11. Nordin, B. E. C.: Osteoporosis and calcium deficiency, *Proc. Nutrition Soc., 19*:129, 1960.

12. Odland, L. M., Warnick, K. P., and Esselbaugh, N. C.: *Bone Density Cooperative Nutritional Status Studies in the Western Region,* vol. 2, Montana Agricultural Experiment Station, Bozeman, Montana State College, 1958.

13. Saville, P.D.: Differences in fresh bone, in Garn *et al.* (Ed): *Transcript of the Workshop on Bone Densitometry,* Yellow Springs, The Fels Research Institute, 1960.

14. Sedlin, E. D.: The ratio of cortical area to total cross-section in diaphyseal bone. An histologic index of osteoporosis, *Clin. Orthop.,* 1963 (in press).

15. Sedlin, E. D., Frost, H. M., and Villanueva, A. R.: Variations in cross-section area of rib cortex with age, *J. Gerontol. 18*:9-13, 1963.

16. Trotter, M.: Sex differences and age changes in dry bone, in Garn, *et al.* (Ed): *Transcript of the Workshop on Bone Densitometry,* Yellow Springs, The Fels Research Institute, 1960.

17. Trotter, M., and Peterson, R. R.: Ash weight of human skeletons in per-cent of their dry fat-free weight, *Anat. Rec., 123*:341-358, 1955.

18. Virtama, P., and Mähönen, H.: Thickness of the cortical layer as an estimate of mineral content of human finger bones. *Brit. J. Radiol., 33:* Jan, 1960.

19. Wray, J. B., Sugarman, E. D., and Schneider, A. J.: Bone composition in senile osteoporosis, *J.A.M.A., 183*:118-120, 1963.

Chapter 5

RESPIRATORY ADAPTATIONS TO HIGH ALTITUDE AS RELATED TO AGE*

D. B. DILL, W. H. FORBES, JERRY L. NEWTON,
AND JAMES W. TERMAN

Our interest in the physiology of aging centers around responses to stress. In Robinson's cross-sectional study (Robinson, 1937), the stress imposed was muscular activity; in a recent study, the responses of two men to exercise in low and high temperatures were compared with their responses to the same stresses thirty years earlier (Dill and Consolazio, 1962). During the past summer the stresses of high altitude were studied.

TABLE 1

THE SUBJECTS: JULY, 1962

Name	Age Yr.	Height cm	Weight kg
Dill	71	178	72
Forbes	60	178	69
Hall	66	174	84
Keys	58	172	72
McFarland	61	192	97
Talbott	60	173	74

Note: All were members of the high altitude expedition to Chile in 1935. Dill and Talbott also took part in a high altitude study in Colorado in 1929. The weights given are the minimum values in the basal state during their stay at altitude.

* This study was supported by Contract FA-2049 with Federal Aviation Agency.

Attention in this report is directed to respiratory measurements in rest and exercise. The six subjects listed in Table 1 had taken part in the high altitude studies in Chile in 1935 (Keys, 1936) and most of them have been subject to experimentation at sea level over many years.* On four of the six, base-line observations were made at or near sea level some weeks or months prior to the summer study. On the other two, base-line observations were made three months afterwards. Our studies were carried out at the White Mountain Research Station; and locations and altitudes of its laboratories are given in Table 2.

TABLE 2

WHITE MOUNTAIN RESEARCH STATION

Laboratory	Altitude		Barometric Pressure
	ft	m	mm Hg
Big Pine	4,000	1220	660
Crooked Creek	10,150	3093	535
Barcroft	12,470	3800	485
Summit	14,250	4343	455

Note: The mail address of the Station is Big Pine, California, where the base laboratory is located. This is in Owens Valley which lies east of the Sierra Nevada and west of the White Mountain chain. The Crooked Creek laboratory is thirty-three miles northeast of Big Pine. Eleven miles north of Crooked Creek is the Barcroft laboratory and seven miles further north by road is the Summit laboratory.

PROCEDURE AND METHODS

The subjects arrived in pairs at about ten day intervals at the Crooked Creek Laboratory after a few hours travel from 1300 m or lower. Respiratory and other measurements were made before breakfast each morning at the Crooked Creek, Barcroft, and Summit laboratories. In addition, a measurement was made after a thirty minute rest late in the afternoon after arriving at the two

---

* Of that party, Edwards died in 1937 and Barron in 1957. Matthews could not come from England nor could Christensen of Stockholm who was spending the year in India.

upper laboratories. A 200-liter gasometer was used for collecting expired air over a ten minute period; the samples collected were analyzed on the Haldane. The schedule varied slightly from the goal, i.e., daily measurements for seven days including two at Crooked Creek, three at Barcroft, and two at Summit. In one case, delay was due to a snow storm, in another to illness, and in a third to an emergency that shortened the stay on the summit to one day. From one to many exercise experiments were carried out on four of the subjects at Barcroft.

RESULTS

The results in rest are shown in Figures 1, 2 and 3. The day-to-day movements for each subject are indicated by the line in each figure. For example, in Figure 1, Dill and Forbes reached the first station in a few hours and basal observations were completed within one-third day after leaving Las Vegas, Nevada, altitude less than 1 km. Keys and Talbott arrived by the same route and the same schedule of observations was begun. Hall and McFarland arrived

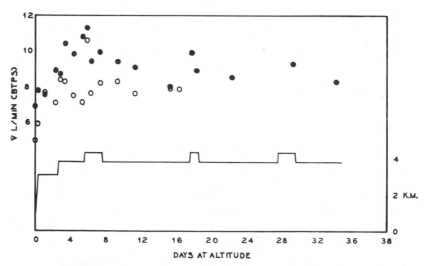

Fig. 1. Observations on Dill and Forbes in rest. Respiratory minute volume, $\dot{V}$, at body temperature, ambient pressure and saturated, BTPS, in relation to the days at altitude and the altitude. Solid circles, Dill; open circles, Forbes.

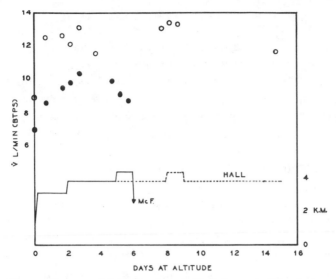

Fig. 2. Observations on McFarland and Hall in rest. Respiratory minute volume, V̇, at BTPS in relation to days at altitude and altitude. Solid circles, McFarland; open circles, Hall.

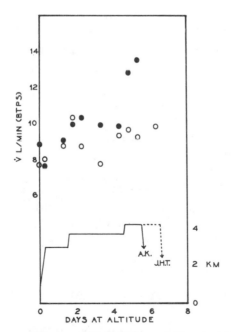

Fig. 3. Observations on Keys and Talbott in rest. Respiratory minute volume, V̇, at BTPS in relation to days at altitude and altitude. Solid circles, Keys; open circles, Talbott.

from Big Pine in the late afternoon so there was a delay of twelve to fifteen hours in starting measurements.

The minute volumes for each individual were higher than at sea level when calculated to body temperature and pressure, saturated,—BTPS. There was only one exception to this generalization: on the first morning at Crooked Creek Key's minute volume was lower than at sea level.

Two factors affected the day-to-day measurements,—acclimatization and increasing altitude. Enough observations were made on Dill to partially separate these responses. The averages of observations on him are:

Sea Level	Crooked Creek	Barcroft		Summit	
January 7.1	June 28-30 8.1	June 30-July 3	10.0	July 3-5	10.2
		July 7-13	8.4	July 15-16	9.4
		July 20	8.5	July 27	9.3
		August 1	8.3		

These results indicate that values for V, respiratory minute volume, at the two upper stations had stabilized within ten days after arrival at Crooked Creek. During the week of acclimatization there may have been a greater increment in volumes with altitude than would have been observed if the stay at each station had been lengthened. The average percentage increase of V over its average at sea level during the first week was as follows:

Barometric Pressure, *mm Hg*..	535	485	455
Δ V, %	20	34	44
Δ V, %, range	−8 to +40	11 to 53	24 to 72

The average V has an inverse relation to 0.21 (B-47) where 0.21 is the proportion of oxygen in air and (B-47) is the barometric pressure less the pressure of water vapor in the lungs. This relation for each of the three altitudes is:

$$1.20(0.21 \times 488) = 123$$
$$1.34(0.21 \times 438) = 123$$
$$1.44(0.21 \times 408) = 123$$

This would not apply to altitudes nearer sea level: the upper, nearly flat portion of the oxygen dissociation curves makes possible a large decrement in barometric pressure with but little effect on arterial oxygen and hence on $\dot{V}$. The relation revealed above indicates that within the range of 3.1 to 4.3 km the average pulmonary ventilation in these six subjects tended to adjust to the partial pressure of oxygen in the air as it reached the alveoli. Additional light will be shed on this topic by our findings on alveolar and arterial gas tensions and on the oxygen saturation of arterial blood. Those resules are being prepared for publication.

Individual variations in response to stress are as interesting to clinical investigators as to physiologists. Without taking body height and weight into account Hall had the highest ventilation at all stations. This does not mean that he was best adapted; he seemed to be most handicapped by dyspnea on exertion, by headache, by Cheyne-Stokes breathing at night and associated loss of sleep. On this account we delayed his summit trip for four days. By that time he was well enough acclimatized to be moderately comfortable at the summit. If one calculates the respiratory minute volume in liters/min/m², Keys had the largest at the summit, 7.12, and McFarland the smallest, 3.89. This measurement on Keys was made about 5 AM; arterial blood obtained a few minutes later was 80 per cent saturated. About three hours earlier he was awakened by what he rated as the most severe headache he had ever experienced. It was persistent, not improving until later in the morning when he was well on his way to the valley. Talbott, the next morning, had a respiratory minute volume at the summit about five-sevenths as great as that of Keys, an arterial saturation of 69 per cent and no headache.

These observations do not allow us to attribute severe headaches to the oxygen saturation of blood reaching the central nervous system. Two possible explanations come to mind: one might be given in terms of the state of the circulation. The other involves the assumption of a prolonged period of low pulmonary ventilation and associated deep hypoxia during sleep. Cheyne-Stokes breathing which we all experienced at night during the first week to some degree is evidence that in sleep the respiratory regulating mechanism is less sensitive to oxygen deficiency.

Exercise experiments were carried out on Dill, Keys and Talbott at 3.8 km. The results are plotted as open squares in Figures 4, 5 and 6. The records obtained on the same subjects in Chile

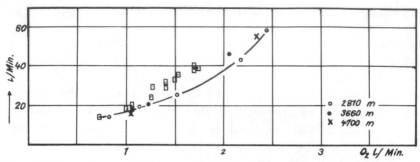

Fig. 4. Observations on Dill in exercise. The curve relates respiratory minute volume at standard conditions, STPD, to rate of oxygen consumption at three altitudes in 1935 (Christensen, 1937). The open squares represent his responses at an altitude of 3.8 km in 1962.

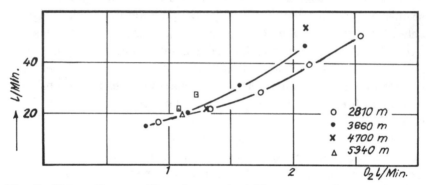

Fig. 5. Observations on Keys in exercise. The curves relate respiratory minute volume at standard conditions, STPD, at four altitudes in 1935 (Christensen, 1937). The open squares represent his responses at an altitude of 3.8 km in 1962.

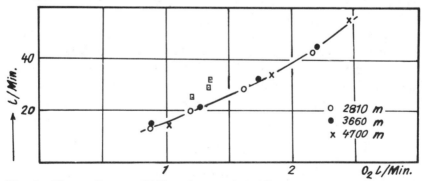

Fig. 6. Observations on Talbott in exercise. The curve relates respiratory minute volume at standard conditions, STPD, at three altitudes in 1935 (Christensen, 1937). The open squares represent his responses at an altitude of 3.8 km in 1962.

(Christiansen, 1937) are shown in the same figures. Although few measurements were made on Keys and Talbott during the past summer, their response was quite like Dill's in the range of oxygen consumptions of 1 to 1.3 liters/min. All three had values for V at STPD, about 5 liters/min greater than in Chile at about the same altitude twenty-seven years before. Keys and Talbott were handicapped by incomplete acclimatization last summer: they were subjects only two days after reaching 3.09 km and one day after reaching 3.8 km while Dill had had five weeks to acclimatize. The measurements on Keys and Talbott and some of those on Dill were made during an ergometer ride at 50 rpm with minute-by-minute increments in brake load up to near-exhaustion. The final R. Q. values reached or exceeded unity so it is likely that maximum aerobic work capacities at the time were reached. A summary of the results is shown in Table 3.

TABLE 3

Best Work Performance at 3.8 km

	Dill		Keys		Talbott		McFarland
	1935	1962	1935	1962	1935	1962	1962
V̇, STPD, *liters/min*	46	39	47	28	45	32	27
V̇, BTPS, *liters/min*	90	75	92	54	88	63	53
V̇ O₂, *liters/min*	2.06	1.73	2.09	1.21	2.20	1.40	1.30

Note: As pointed out in the text, Keys and Talbott were subjects within two days of arrival while Dill had had five weeks to acclimatize. The values for 1935 were possibly sub-maximal since an attempt was made to attain a steady state. There are no comparable observations on record for McFarland

DISCUSSION

The measurements of respiratory minute volume during the first week at altitude indicate moderately rapid respiratory adaptation. The minute volume was considerably increased within a few hours after arriving at the Crooked Creek laboratory. The average respiratory minute volume at each of the three stations was inversely proportional to the barometric pressure less the pressure of vapor in the lungs, i.e., to the partial pressure of oxygen in air reaching the alveoli. There were few observations of this sort on these six men during their high altitude expedition twenty-seven years before; conditions did not permit day-to-day measurements such as was possible at the White Mountain Station. There are records on young men in the literature, however, that are pertinent. Thus Luft (1941) has described an experiment he conducted at 3.45 km on the Jungfraujoch with Becker-Freyseng, Loeschcke and Opitz. Within a few hours V at BTPS had increased from 7 to 9 liters/min. These observations were in accord with the following expression:

$$\frac{pCO_2 \text{ at sea level}}{pCO_2 \text{ at altitude}} = \frac{\dot{V} \text{ at altitude}}{\dot{V} \text{ at sea level}}$$

Substituting our observed average values for V at BTPS in this expression and assuming a pCO_2 at sea level of 40 mm Hg it follows that the mean alveolor pCO_2 at each station would be 32, 30 and 28 mm Hg, respectively. As will be seen in a paper soon to be published these are within the range of our observations. In another such study (Rahn and Otis, 1949), alveolar pCO_2 and V at BTPS were observed on three subjects at sea level and during eighteen days at 9500 ft where the barometric pressure averaged 536 mm Hg. The alveolar pCO_2 in the acclimatized state was 30.9 mm Hg but strangely enough the V dropped from 8.68 at sea level to 8.51 at altitude. A large body of data on men in the third and fourth decades has been obtained by Chiodi (1957). His values for V at BTPS in liters/min/m² follow, the number of subjects in each group is in parentheses.

Duration of Residence	*Sea Level*	3.99 km	4.52 km
Years	3.8 (8)	4.5 (5)	4.9 (20)
14 to 54 days		5.2 (9)	
4 to 8 days		5.4 (7)	
4 days			5.6 (2)

Our values for six men averaging about thirty years older are in good agreement. Expressed in the same terms the averages for our observations are:

Sea Level	3.8
2 days at 3.09 km	4 5
2 days at 3.8 km	5.1
2 days at 4.3 km	5.5

On the basis of the above observations, particularly those of

Chiodi, it is concluded that the respiratory response to altitude of our group was about the same as that of young men. It does not follow that this would be true at altitudes above 4.3 km.

The respiratory responses to exercise at 3.8 km were quite different than twenty-seven years before. While easy work on the bicycle ergometer was accomplished with the same minute volume as before, this was not true in harder grades of work. Keys and Talbott near their peak work capacity after only two days to acclimatize had respiratory minute volumes only about three-fifths as great as in 1935 at the same altitude. The oxygen consumption was correspondingly lower. Dill who had had a month to acclimatize attained a respiratory minute volume and oxygen consumption within about 15 per cent of the maximum 1935 values at about the same altitude (Christensen, 1937). There is other evidence of the difference in degree of acclimatization attained by Dill and Talbott. Their maximum oxygen intake at sea level was measured earlier in the year. Dill was able to reach 75 per cent of his sea level oxygen consumption and 102 per cent of his $\dot{V}$ value at BTPS while the corresponding figures for Talbott were 54 and 56 per cent respectively. Another fact of probable significance is that Dill was having some difficulty with asthma when his sea level performance was measured in January, 1962. This cleared up completely while at altitude.

Finally, a comparison can be made of the maximum performances on the ergometer of Dill and Talbott in 1962 and 1935 with observations made in a high altitude study in 1929 (Dill, Edwards, Fölling, Oberg, Pappenheimer and Talbott, 1931).

Year	*Barometric Pressure*	*Maximum $\dot{V}$ in Exercise, BTPS*	
	mm Hg	*liters/min*	*liters/min*
		Dill	Talbott
1929	760	93	103
1929	535	89	121
1935	543	73	54
1935	489	90	88
1935	429	128	128
1962	760	75	115
1962	485	75	63

These comparisons indicate that in exercise on the bicycle ergometer Talbott is able to reach as high a respiratory minute volume
at sea level as in 1927, whereas Dill cannot do so at sea level nor
at altitude. It is noteworty that both reached their highest value
at a barometric pressure of 429 mm Hg in 1935.

SUMMARY

The adaptation of six men to high altitudes has been compared
with their responses to altitude twenty-seven years ago. In this
report special attention has been given to respiratory adaptations in rest and exercise. The respiratory minute volume in rest
increases about as rapidly and to the same extent as in young
men. Nevertheless, several of the six were slower to acclimatize
than before as indicated by dyspnea on exertion, headache,
Cheyne-Stokes breathing and associated loss of sleep. In exercise
easy work on the ergometer was performed with the same respiratory minute volume as in 1935. As the grade of work was increased
the minute volume increased more than in 1935; the oxygen consumption in peak performance was much less than in 1935. In
general, it appeared that adaptation was slower than when we
were twenty-seven years younger but that this was not due to the
respiratory system.

ACKNOWLEDGMENT

We are pleased to acknowledge our great indebtness to Nello
Pace, Director, Raymond J. Hock, Resident Physiologist, and the
members of the permanent staff of the White Mountain Research
Station.

REFERENCES

1. Chiodi, H.: Respiratory Adaptations to Chronic High Altitude Hypoxia.
   J. Applied Physiol., 10:81-87, 1957.

2. Christensen, E. H.: Oxygen Intake and Respiratory Function in Great
   Heights. *Scand. Arch. Physiol., 76*:88-100, 1937.

3. Dill, D. B., Edwards, H T., Fölling, A., Oberg, S.A., Pappenheimer, Jr.,
   A. M., and Talbott, J. H.: Adaptations of the Organism to Changes in
   Oxygen Pressure. *J. Physiol., 71*:47-63, 1931.

4. Dill, D. B., and Consolazio, C. F.: Responses to Exercise as Related to Age and Environmental Temperature. *J. Applied Physiol., 17*:645-648, 1962.

5. Keys, A.: The Physiology of Life at High Altitudes. The International Expedition to Chile, 1935. *The Scientific Monthly, 43*:289-312, 1936.

6. Luft, U. C.: High Altitude Adaptation. *Ergeb. Physiol. biol. Chem. exptl. Pharm., 44*:256-314, 1941.

7. Rahn, H., and Otis, A. B.: Man's Respiratory Response During and After Acclimatization to High Altitude. *Am. J. Physiol., 157*:445-462, 1949.

8. Robinson, S.: Experimental Studies of Physical Fitness in Relation to Age. *Arbeitsphysiol., 10*:251-323, 1938.

Chapter 6

METHODS IN THE NATIONAL HEALTH SURVEY: AGE PATTERNS IN MORBIDITY AND MEDICAL CARE

PHILIP S. LAWRENCE

The organizational title, The National Health Survey, implies collection of data which are nationwide in scope and this is, in fact, one of the basic characteristics of our activities. Yet the title also gives the erroneous impression that this is one-time door-to-door survey of illness conditions.

The National Health Survey actually consists of several quite different continuing programs and techniques, each designed to measure a different aspect of illness, disability, or medical care.

One source of data about the health of the population consists of records from places where people receive medical services, for example, hospitals, nursing homes, physicians, or clinics. Studies in which this source is used, conducted by the Health Records Survey, are in the early stages of development in our program.

A second source of data comprises clinical tests, measurements, and physical examinations applied directly to samples of persons in the population. These techniques are used by the phase of the survey known as the Health Examination Survey.

The third source of data, the people themselves, by means of direct health interviews recorded on questionnaires, is used in the Health Interview Survey.

The fact that each of these three sources has particular strength, or inherent weaknesses, not possessed by the others, has emphasized the need for a multiple approach to the task of providing general purpose statistics about the health of our population. Each of these methods will be described briefly in the hope that you may see in one or another of them a resource that can be called upon to provide data or techniques which will be useful in relation to your own work.

HEALTH RECORDS SURVEY

The Health Records Surveys are a family of studies for which the first stage of sampling is the establishment, or facility, which provides medical, personal, or residential care. The basic source of data is from existing records of the facility, or records designed for the purpose of the survey. The central objective is to obtain statistics on the numbers and types of institutions and health facilities in the United States, on their staff, on services provided, and on the personal and health characteristics of the patients or resident population.

Planning and initial stages of development for the Health Records Surveys have been in progress for about one year. The first step has been the creation of a master list of all hospitals, nursing homes, and other residential institutions in the United States—currently in the neighborhood of 40,000. Each of these establishments was sent a questionnaire to obtain data on the number, type, size, ownership, geographic distribution, and numbers of persons who can be served. In addition to providing significant data about the institutions themselves, the master list provides a frame which can be stratified and sampled to obtain further data about the resident population.

The first of the national sample surveys to be undertaken concerns residents of nursing homes. Among the topics included will be public welfare status, professional services available, bed status, ambulatory status, hearing, vision, continence, mental awareness, age, sex, race, and length of stay. The questionnaire for this study has been developed and pretested and data will be collected on a national sample in 1963.

Another facet of the Health Record Surveys has also started. This is to be a continuing survey of short-stay hospitals to determine sizes and types, methods of financing care, and detailed information about the patients' illnesses and types of care received.

Although the Health Interview Survey also obtains information about hospitalizations and their socio-economic correlates, an interview can not provide satisfactory data about details of diagnosis and services. Nor does the interview include the hospital experience of persons who have died during a given interval. These data will be obtained through the Health Record Surveys.

HEALTH EXAMINATION SURVEY

You will appreciate that neither an interview nor records can provide data which require direct physical examinations or clinical and laboratory tests on a representative population group. This is the purpose of the Health Examination Survey—to obtain data on the medically defined prevalence of specific diseases and dental conditions, and to obtain distributions of the population with respect to physical and physiological measurements.

The Health Examination Survey has two specially designed mobile examination centers. These consist of trailers which, when set up, are connected by corridors. Each unit has on hand an experienced staff of professional and allied medical personnel. During the past two years, these units have located in forty-two areas of the country and have examined about 6,500 adults of ages eighteen through seventy-nine. A medical history and physician's examination was directed primarily toward cardiovascular disease, arthritis and rheumatism, and diabetes. In addition, the first cycle on adults included an electrocardiogram, three blood pressure readings, a glucose tolerance test for blood sugar, a serological test, a full size chest x-ray, x-rays of the hands and feet and a serum bentonite floculation test for arthritis, measurement of serum cholesterol level, and a microhematocrit determination.

Dentists on the mobile units conducted a standardized examination to determine the absence or condition of individual teeth, and examined the mouth for periodontal disease, oral hygiene, and malocclusion. A screening test was conducted for near and far vision, with and without glasses. Hearing thresholds were charted with a pure tone audiometer in a soundproof booth.

From these examinations and tests it will be possible to provide data not only for cases already under treatment, but also on previously undiagnosed, unattended, and non-manifest chronic diseases.

Physical measurements of height, weight, skinfolds and about a dozen other anatomical dimensions were taken. These, together with the physiological tests, should provide valuable benchmarks on the distribution of such characteristics in the general population, and differences in physical and physiological levels throughout the range of adult ages.

A great deal of research has been devoted to standardization of physical examinations and equipment, validation of measurements, and other aspects of quality control. Likewise, much attention has been given to problems of sampling response, resulting in an overall examination rate of about 86 per cent, and a number of locations in which the response was 97 or 98 per cent. Research and validation have been conducted not only to improve the quality of this particular survey, but also to contribute to knowledge of methods which should benefit other workers in the field of clinical assessment of health status. Reports will be published, not only on the substantive findings, but also on the methods employed.

THE HEALTH INTERVIEW SURVEY

Health examinations and laboratory analyses are expensive, particularly when employing mobile equipment and staff on a nationwide sample. The cost limits the sample size to such an extent that national estimates can be produced only for diseases of high prevalence and for a limited number of interrelationships. Furthermore, it is apparent that lengthy or embarrassing examinations would reduce cooperation, and the resultant nonresponse would affect the validity of the data.

Because of the need for information which can not be obtained adequately from examination or record sources, data are derived from the Health Interview Survey. The purpose is to provide information on morbidity, medical care, and other health related topics. Health interviews do not enumerate certain types of disease conditions completely nor with diagnostic refinement. Rather, they measure the social and demographic dimensions of health—

the impact of illness and disability, and actions taken as a result of these conditions, in various population groups.

Information is obtained from a probability sample of households throughout the nation. Interviewing goes on continuously, week after week, covering about 140 thousand persons each year. Since the samples each week and each year are independent, certain data are cumulative with time, resulting in a total to date of about three-quarters of a million persons. Information is now being consolidated to provided four years of data on chronic illnesses and limitations of older people.

The interview includes a basic core of questions which are continued from year to year. These are the demographic items on age, sex, marital status, family composition, occupation, education, and income, as well as questions on morbidity conditions, disability, and hospitalization for which annual trend data are desired. In addition, other items are inserted at intervals of three to five years on topics such as physicians visits, dental care, and health insurance coverage. Beyond this, questions of timely or specialized interest are included on an ad hoc basis. Example of these topics are: health and personal care received at home; recuperation time following surgery; the volume of visits for medical X-rays; the proportion of the hospital bill paid by insurance; and the duration of chronic limitation of activity.

During the past year the Health Interview Survey has incorporated two new devices to increase the scope and range of detail. One of these is the use of self-enumeration questionnaires left with the respondent when the basic interview is completed. These are mailed in, with nonresponse follow-ups conducted by letter, telephone, or by personal visit. Data on expenditures for health care are currently being obtained by this method.

The second device developed by the Health Interview Survey is the use of a follow-up questionnaire. Users of data often require more detail about persons with a particular health problem than can be included within the time or space of a reasonable interview. Persons with the characteristic can be indentified on the basic interview and may then be sent a second questionnaire to obtain the additional detail. This method is in current use to learn more about the problems of persons with impairments of hearing. Similar techniques for obtaining information about persons with defective vision, and persons with diabetes are now being pretested.

An advantage of the interview survey is that information on a wide range of personal characteristics may be obtained, on a large sample of the population, at the same time that data are obtained on health and medical care. Age is perhaps the most important single variable in the health spectrum. Space does not permit discussion of many of the interesting relationships that have been found in the health interview survey, but examples of a few of the age patterns may suggest certain areas where more detailed studies are needed.

UTILIZATION OF MEDICAL SERVICES

During the interval from July 1957 through June 1959, persons of all ages made about 5.0 visits to the doctor each year. Figure 1, which shows the age distribution, reflects the changing

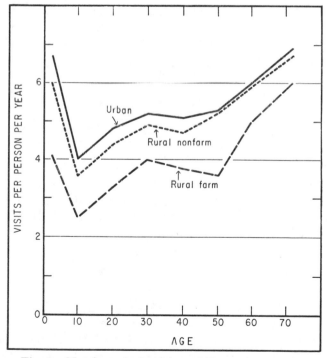

Fig. 1. Number of physician visits per person per year by residence and age.

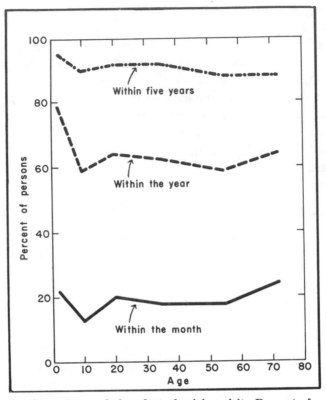

Fig. 2. Interval since last physician visit. Percent of persons whose most recent physician visit was within the month, within the year, or within the five years prior to interview by age.

patterns of medical care resulting from the acute illnesses of child-hood, maternity in early adult ages, perhaps some neglect in middle ages, and finally the increasing toll of chronic disease among older persons. Other National Health Survey data indicate that the low rate of visits among rural farm residents is not due to less ill-ness in this segment of the population. Further study is needed to determine whether the low rate results from a difference in education, income, or distance from medical facilities. All of these factors and others probably play a part. For example, among all persons in families with less than $2,000 annual income, there were 4.6 visits to the physician in the year, whereas among persons in families of $7,000 or higher income, the rate was 5.7 visits. For persons above age sixty-four the rates were 6.5 visits in the lower income group and 8.7 visits in the higher income group.

Approximately 75 per cent of the total visits to physicians, and 83 per cent of visits of older persons, were for purposes of diagnosis or treatment. This constitutes necessary medical care, but the striking thing is that among older persons, only one visit in every nine, or slightly more than one visit every two years, was for general check-up and other preventive care services.

The average volume of medical visits, as presented above, fails to show the distribution of visits with time. Figure 2 reveals that about 40 per cent of the adult population failed to talk to a doctor for any purpose within a year. This was quite constant from age to age. Even among the oldest ages, over 10 per cent of the persons had not seen a doctor in more than five years. It hardly seems probable that such large segments of the older population are without need for some sort of medical treatment or preventive service within these time intervals.

The National Health Survey has collected no data on medical visits since 1959. Within the coming year similar data will again be obtained with an additional dimension—the extent of utilization of services of various types of medical specialists.

Although some features of medical care may be considered elective, it is probably most true of dental services. As a result of this attitude, there are marked gradients in the rates of dental visits by family income and education of the family head. Figure 3 shows that dental visits were three times as frequent among persons whose family income was over $4,000, and education greater than eight years, than in lesser income and education classes. These socio-economic differences in dental care utilization existed within every age group. Although the average volume of dental visits was twice as high among younger people (1.6 visits per year) as among persons sixty-five and older (0.8 visits per year), the higher income and better educated older persons obtained dental care at two to three times the rate of lower income and education groups of their ages.

The elective nature of dental care and extent of dental neglect is further pointed out by differences in the proportion of dental visits for preventive care. In the population of all ages, those with less than $2,000 family income had 12 per cent of their dental visits for examination or cleaning of teeth in contrast to 22 per cent of those with $7,000 or more family income. Among persons over age sixty-four, the contrast was even greater—8 per cent and 38 per cent for the low and high income groups, respectively. On the other hand, the proportion of visits for extractions and denture work was considerably higher among persons of low family income. These observations concerning the relative proportion of visits for preventive care by income also hold true with respect to education of the head of the family.

The low proportion of preventive services and high proportion of extractions (about 35 per cent of the visits) in the lower income

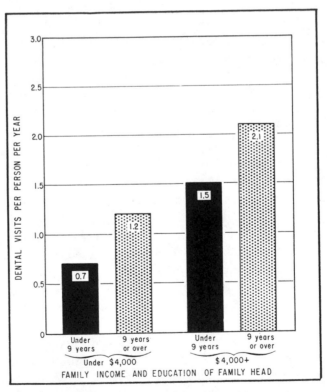

Fig. 3. Number of dental visits per person per year by family income and education of family head.

and education groups, leads one to believe that loss of teeth provides a measure of dental neglect. Figure 4 shows that more than half of the population over sixty-four years of age is edentulous. In all, about 22 million people in this country are without any natural teeth. Lack of teeth and oral discomfort, since they are not fatal, often fail to get their share of attention among the prob-

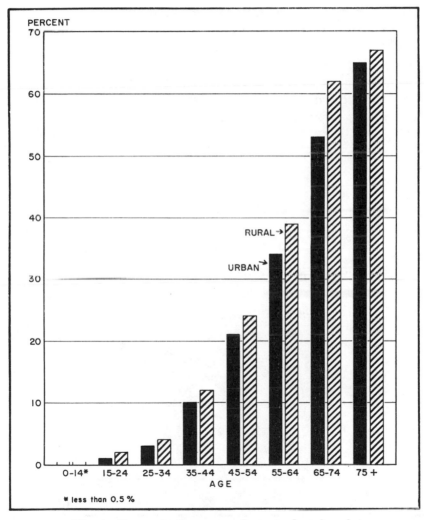

Fig. 4. Per cent of persons who are edentulous by residence according to age.

lems of older persons. However, among the many facets of health, this is one where people who are concerned with the problems of the aged must start with the young.

Unfortunately, many of the current dental problems of older people reflect their relative educational and economic disadvantage, and the earlier lack of techniques that are today considered good dental practice. Although dental health of the elderly should improve in future decades, improvement can be hastened through health education and provision of adequate facilities.

In recent years there has been an increasing interest in the rate of hospital utilization by persons of all ages but, because of the social and economic circumstances of older people, the spotlight has focused on this group. Figure 5 shows clearly the high rate of hospitalization of women in the reproductive years of age,

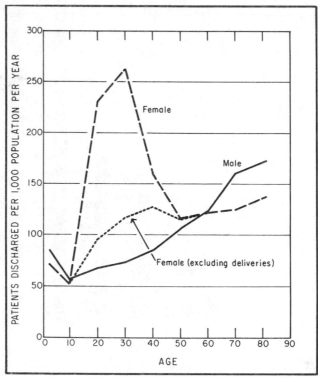

Fig. 5. Average number of patients discharged per
1,000 population per year by sex and age.

and reveals the higher rate for men than for women in the older years of life. However, the interviews from which these data were derived included information on only the living population. In terms of total patients, living and dead, using inpatient hospital facilities in a year, the rates at older ages (65 and above) should be increased by perhaps 30 per cent. The National Health Survey, in cooperation with the National Vital Statistics Division, is now completing a national sample study which follows back from death certificates to obtain data on hospitalizations in the terminal year of life. In the future these data will be used in the adjustment of interview data to estimate total hospital utilization. Furthermore, the Health Records Survey program is now developing a national sample of hospitals to obtain details of patient care for persons who have died as well as for those still living.

Length of hospital stay depends, of course, on the type and seriousness of the patient's condition. But it depends also upon a constellation of social and economic situations, one which is illustrated in Figure 6. At younger ages, under forty-five, people who live alone may stay in hospitals longer because there is no one at home to care for them. On the other hand, the group under forty-five living with relatives contains large proportions of children and women hospitalized for deliveries, whose hospital stay is generally short. At older ages those persons who have continued to live alone tend to be a physically select group with fewer serious conditions requiring hospitalization, or who recover more rapidly than their cohorts who are less select. Furthermore, older people who live alone who do develop a serious disease or disability are often placed in long-stay hospitals or nursing homes. The data shown in Figure 6 did not include the institutional population.

Figure 7 illustrates the proportion of hospital discharges for which some part of the bill was paid by insurance. This is not the same as the extent of hospital insurance coverage in the population as a whole, but the age pattern is similar. Hospitalized young people, in their late teens and early twenties, had a relatively low proportion of their bills paid by insurance as a result of discontinuance of family coverage. Payment by insurance reached its peak among workers and wives of workers, then dropped off rapidly in the older age groups. More detailed data show that about 30 per cent of persons over age sixty-four had three-fourths or more of the hospital bill paid by insurance in contrast to 58 per cent of persons of ages forty-five to sixty-four. In other words, for older people, the extent to which the bill was paid was less, as well as the proportion of persons for whom any part of the bill was paid. It should be pointed out, however, that the figures did not take into consideration people whose hospital expenses may have been covered by other sources such as free service, welfare, or veterans' programs.

Measurement of the extent of hospital utilization and patient

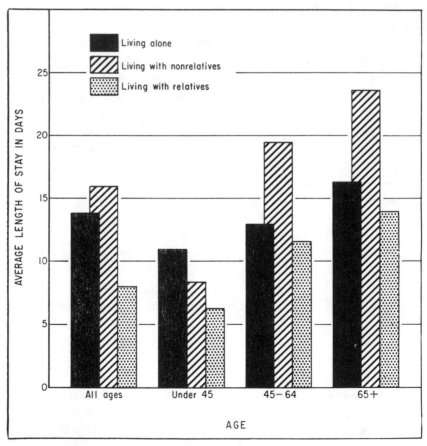

Fig. 6. Average length of hospital stay for patients
discharged by household composition and age.

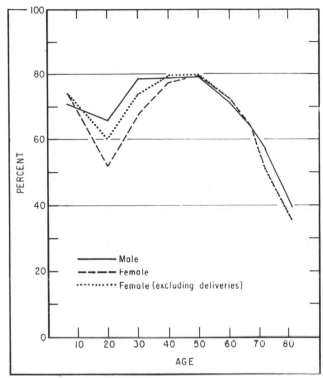

Fig. 7. Per cent of hospital discharges with some insurance payment for the hospital bill by sex and age.

care is a difficult and challenging task because of the multitude
of medical and demographic interrelationships that enter the picture. Much needs to be learned through intensive studies to supplement the broad baseline data developed by the national surveys.

MORBIDITY AND DISABILITY

The health interview of the National Health Survey has collected data on acute illnesses continuously throughout every year.
The age patterns shown in Figure 8 were for the year July 1960
through June 1961. The data included acute illness and injuries
which resulted in medical care or required the person to reduce
his normal daily activities. Acute illnesses of this severity occurred
at a rate of about 125 episodes in the year among every 100 persons
of ages sixty-five and over.

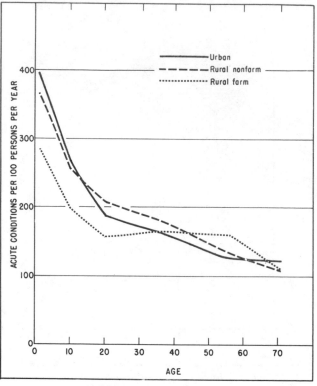

Fig. 8. Incidence of acute conditions per 100 persons
per year by residence and age.

Although older persons had a lower rate of occurrence of acute
conditions than did younger people, the age pattern of disability
due to these conditions was quite different, as shown in the table
below.

RESTRICTED ACTIVITY DAYS AND BED
DAYS PER 100 PERSONS PER YEAR

	Restricted Activity Days	Bed Days
All ages	857	332
Under 15	955	404
15-24	724	293
25-44	787	297
45-64	759	256
65+	1130	405

In a population of about 15½ million non-institutionalized persons over age sixty-four, there were 175 million days on which they had to restrict their normal activities and 63 million days spent in bed due to acute conditions alone. In terms of degree of impact the acute conditions constituted a more serious problem among the elderly than among younger persons.

The days of restricted activity and bed days due to acute illness and injury comprised about one third of all of the days of

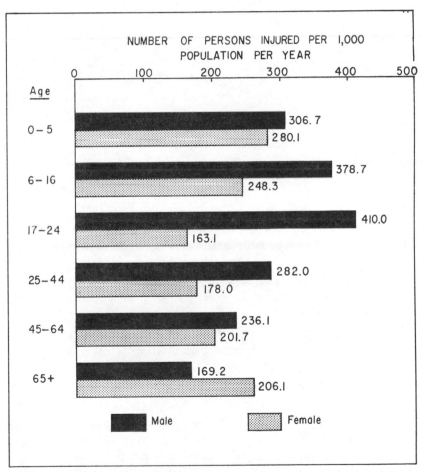

Fig. 9. Number of persons injured per 1,000 population per year, by sex and age.

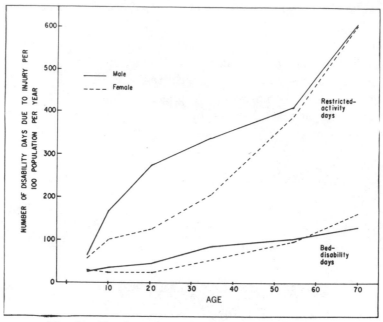

Fig. 10. Number of restricted-activity and bed-dis-
ability days due to injury per 100 population per
year, by sex and age.

disability among persons over age sixty-four, the balance being
due to chronic diseases. Although the chronic diseases are largely
responsible for long-term limitations and death, the impact of
acute conditions can not be overlooked as a contributor to the
problems of the aged, and probably also as a contributor to
senescence.

The age pattern of acute conditions varies widely by type of
condition. Space does not permit examination of all of these relationships, but accidental injuries may be singled out among the
conditions which present special hazards for older people. Among
women the rate of persons injured per 1000 population was higher
for those sixty-five and over than for any other adult age group
(Fig. 9). Although the rate was lower for males, still about one in
every six older men was injured each year to an extent that
required medical care or reduction in normal daily activities. The
older men, of course, were not subject to as high risk as younger

men from injuries in motor vehicles, sports, or industrial accidents, but in home injuries men over age sixty-four exceeded in rate all other adult age groups.

The increased rates of bed days and restricted activity in older years were very pronounced, as shown in Figure 10. These high rates reflect the severity of the types of injuries to which older people are subject. Fractures and dislocations occurred annually to about 48 of every 1000 persons over age sixty-four—a rate higher than for any other age group and twice as high as for persons five to fourteen or forty-five to sixty-four years of age.

About 62 per cent of injuries to persons over age sixty-five occurred in or about the home, and 20 per cent on the street, again higher than for other ages. It is worthy of note that in these places there has been relatively little done toward construction design or control of safety geared to the problems of hearing, vision, and locomotion which are concomitants of aging.

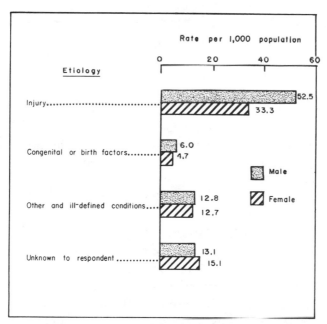

Fig. 11. Average prevalence of impairments (except paralysis and absence) of limbs, back, trunk per 1,000 population by etiology and sex.

Not only are injuries which occur in later years a problem but the residual effects of injuries which occurred earlier in life add a tremendous burden as age increases.

Figure 11 shows the rate of persons who have impairments of the limbs, back, or trunk, due to injury and due to other causes. The chart includes persons of all ages, and indicates a rate of about forty persons with residual impairments of the limbs or back due to injury in each 1000 population. Among persons over sixty-five the rate was even higher, 94 per 1000, exclusive of disc conditions.

Similar figures may be shown for other types of impairments. Among persons of all ages, about 16 per cent of visual impairments and 70 per cent of absence of major extremities resulted from injury. Prevention of accidents among young people should be part of the thinking of those who are concerned about problems of the elderly.

It was indicated earlier that interviews do not measure the prevalence of chronic conditions completely, nor with diagnostic precision. Deviations from normal which are detectable to the clinician or by laboratory test may be unknown to the interview respondent, or have so little impact on his way of life that he fails to report them. Interview results can not be expected to reproduce the prevalence of conditions as determined by clinical diagnoses. Nor can clinical and laboratory findings, important as they are for diagnosis and prognosis, measure the social impact of illness on individuals—how it effects them and what they do about it. The two methods measure illness on two different axes, and it is for this reason that the Health Interview Survey emphasizes not the total prevalence of chronic conditions by diagnosis, but rather the prevalence of conditions which cause disability.

Even among young adults of ages fifteen to forty-four, over 40 per cent had at least one chronic condition of sufficient impact to have been reported on interview (Fig. 12). By ages sixty-five and over, the vast majority of persons had such a condition, and over half reported multiple chronic conditions. Many of the conditions reported had associated disability. About 500 million person-days were spent in bed each year by the non-institutional population of the United States because of chronic illness. One-

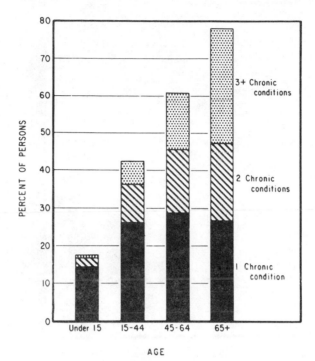

Fig. 12. Per cent of persons with chronic conditions
according to age.

third of these days were accounted for by persons over age sixty-
four.

Figure 13 indicates the extent to which chronic conditions
limited usual activities—the ability to work, do housework, go to
school, or otherwise engage in normal pursuits of life. At ages
forty-five to fifty-four, about 13 per cent of the population was
limited in activities. But above these ages the proportion rose
rapidly to 55 per cent at ages seventy-five and over. In the latter
age group, 32 per cent of the population living at home was limited
in mobility. That is, they were either confined to the house or were
unable to get around outside without the help of another person.

Not only does the prevalence of chronic conditions increase
with increasing age, but the severity soars in terms of the limitations which these conditions impose. Great efforts are being made
to find the causes and means of prevention of chronic conditions,

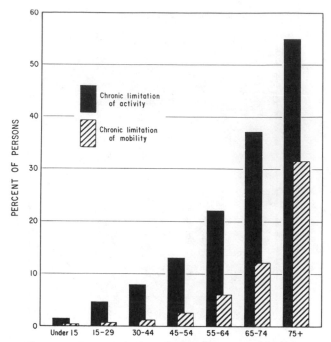

Fig. 13. Per cent of persons with any degree of
chronic limitation of activity and mobility according
to age.

but equal efforts are needed to find methods, and provide services,
for prevention and reduction of disability once disease has occurred.

CONCLUSION

The data and charts presented here show only a few broad
aspects of the age patterns of medical care and morbidity. All of
the information was derived from National Health Survey reports
which contain a great deal more detail about the age and sex
distribution of health variables by demographic characteristics of
the population. Titles of the reports used are shown below for
reference purposes.

As in the case of the Health Records Survey and Health
Examination Survey, a substantial part of the staff and budget of
the Health Interview Survey is devoted to methodological research.
This research includes development of new or improved methods,
quality control, pretesting, and evaluation. Improvement of tech-

niques in collection of health information has a long way to go, yet a great deal has been learned within the past few years. Although all of our surveys are geared to obtaining data on national samples, some of the methods employed are applicable to state and local studies. It is also true that many of the data collection techniques now used nationally were initially developed on a community level. It is hoped that not only will the National Health Survey serve as a resource, but that it will be the recipient of knowledge which others have gained as to methods of increasing the scope and reliability of health statistics.

REFERENCES

1. Acute Conditions, Geographic Distribution, United States — July 1960-June 1961. Series B-No. 34. PHS Publication No. 584-B34. Public Health Service. Washington, D.C.

2. Acute Conditions, Incidence and Associated Disability, United States — July 1958-June 1959. Series B-No. 18. PHS Publication No. 584-B18. Public Health Service, Washington, D.C.

3. Chronic Conditions Causing Limitation of Activities, United States — July 1959-June 1961. Series B-No. 36. PHS Publication No. 584-B36. Public Health Service, Washington, D.C.

4. Disability Days Due to Injury, United States — July 1959-June 1961. Series B-No. 40. PHS Publication No. 584-B40. Public Health Service, Washington, D.C.

5. Dental Care, Preliminary Report on Volume, United States — July-September 1957. Series B2. PHS Publication No. 584-B2. Public Health Service, Washington, D.C.

6. Dental Care, Volume of Visits, United States — July 1957-June 1959. Series B-No. 15. PHS Publication No. 584-B15. Public Health Service, Washington, D.C.

7. Health Examination Survey, Plan and Initial Program. Series A-No. 4. PHS Publication No. 584-A4. Public Health Service, Washington, D.C.

8. Health Household-Interview Survey, Concepts and Definitions, Series A-3. PHS Publication No. 584-A3. Public Health Service, Washington, D.C.

9. Hospital Discharges and Length of Stay: Short-Stay Hospitals, United States — 1958-1960. Series B-No. 32. PHS Publication No. 584-B32. Public Health Service, Washington, D.C.

10. Limitation of Activity and Mobility Due to Chronic Conditions, United States—July 1957-June 1958. Series B-11. PHS Publication No. 584-B11. Public Health Service, Washington, D.C.

11. Older Persons, Selected Health Characteristics, United States — July 1957 - June 1959. Series C-No. 4. PHS Publication No. 584-C4. Public Health Service, Washington, D.C.

12. Persons Injured, by Detailed Type and Class of Accident, United States — July 1959 - June 1961. Series B-No. 37. PHS Publication No. 584-B37. Public Health Service, Washington, D.C.

13. Physician Visits, Preliminary Report on Volume, United States — July - September 1957. Series B-1. PHS Publication No. 584-B1. Public Health Service, Washington, D.C.

14. Physician Visits, Volume, United States — July 1957 - June 1959. Series B-No. 19. PHS Publication No. 584-B19. Public Health Service, Washington, D.C.

15. Proportion of Hospital Bill Paid By Insurance, Patients Discharged from Short-Stay Hospitals, United States — July 1958 - June 1960. Series B-No. 30 PHS Publication No. 584-B30. Public Health Service, Washington, D.C.

16. Selected Impairments, by Etiology and Activity Limitation, United States — July 1959 - June 1961. Series B-No. 35. PHS Publication No. 584-B35. Public Health Service, Washington, D.C.

SECTION C
Changes in Psychological Functions

Chapter 7

THE PSYCHOLOGY OF AGING IN RELATION TO DEVELOPMENT

JAMES E. BIRREN

The present purpose is to discuss some aspects of the psychology of aging in relation to development, with particular attention to implications for research on early life correlates of late life characteristics. There has been a dramatic trend toward earlier physical development of children in Western Countries, and perhaps in other areas as well. Possibly less dramatic but none the less real is the trend toward increased average length of life. Other characteristics of older adults may also be changing and merely await systematic observation. Their study can be regarded as part of a search to identify the conditions which promote optimum biological, psychological, and social development throughout the life span.

Development and *aging* may be studied separately and in their own scientific context without regard to the continuity of the individual from early to late life, a continuity of a social, psychological, and biological nature. Accepting the fact that there are both continuities and discontinuities in processes over the life span, it may be of scientific advantage to study some of the early and late life relations. Prearmed with suspicion that behavior over the life span is likely more complex than we can now imagine, but with the confidence that there is order to be discerned, examination of early and later life relationship may contribute to an empirically oriented life-span developmental psychology. A certain bias must be admissible in the selection of what aspects of aging

are to be examined in relation to early development for just as one
cannot know all of the literature on development one cannot know
all research about aging. Bias also arises from interests and training. Irving Lorge once remarked that physicians are most likely
to see the sick elderly, social workers the destitute elderly, and
the clergy older persons with religious concerns. Generalizations
from any of these samples to what older adults are like are biased.
Laboratory research on aging is also biased in terms of methods
and variables studied. Furthermore, if one studies persons aged
seventy years, generalizations must be qualified by the fact that
over half of the original peer group or cohort has already died.
Any generalization about aging from observations of seventy year
olds applies to only half the population, those who survive to that
age. Even in a longitudinal study, mean curves based upon
individuals must be systematically biased by subjects dropping out
because of ill health and death. To be relevant to aging of the
whole population, the curves of longitudinal studies have to be
corrected for possible survivorship bias. The question may be
asked however what significant differences are there in early-life
biological and psychological characteristics of those who survive
and of those who fail to survive to the half way mark.

HEREDITY AND THE PSYCHOBIOLOGY OF AGING

Species tend to live characteristic lengths of life (Ciba Col-
loquia, Rockstein, 1959) and show a remarkably constant force
of mortality over the life span (Jones, 1959). There are two different implications here: 1) that early development does not
influence the rate of aging, and 2) favorable early development
is of great practical significance as it provides the base on which
the mechanisms of aging act. Since within the human species,
longevity is associated with parental and grandparental longevity
(see Jones, 1959), we are led to the rather inescapable conclusion
that longevity is to some extent under hereditary control. This
early conclusion has recently been further elaborated in the human
twin studies of Kallmann and his associates (Kallmann and Jarvik, 1959). The point of interest is that the organism at birth has
some characteristic for longevity, a characteristic which may be

called the *potential for senescence*. Not to be confused is the somewhat different question of the relative amounts of hereditary and environmental determination of longevity. At present, environmental conditions appear to be of greater importance for the population. Since organisms at birth have some degree of potential for longevity there is a basic question about the evolution of control over length of life as late life characteristics are not readily explained as consequences of selection. Because late-life characteristics do not appear until long after the age of reproduction, such characteristics can not themselves be subject to selection. In fact, the later in life a characteristic appears the less likely it could have been directly subjected to selection. The question is how did or does heredity become established as a determiner of longevity and of other late life characteristics including that of physical appearance and behavior.

I have called inferences regarding the origin of hereditary control over late life characteristics a *counterpart theory* (Birren, 1960). This merely says that if heredity plays a part in determining a late life characteristic it must appear as a counterpart of some characteristic which was subject to pressures of selection in early life. Animal strains survive which have optimum characteristics at age of reproduction and there is a decreasing probability of elimination of undesirable characteristics after the age of reproduction. Medawar has called this a precession of favorable gene effects and a recession of unfavorable effects (Medawar, 1957, p. 39). The longer individuals live past the age of reproduction the greater the possibility of their expressing an unfavorable characteristic which was not subject to elimination by selective pressures, and the lower the possibility that the trait will be eliminated from the population.

While having long lived ancestors gives some advantage to one's expectancy for long life, it does not follow that this is a large gain compared with the secular trend for greater longevity in the population or that inbreeding for longevity will necessarily lead to large improvement in length of life. Evidence reviewed by Comfort (1956) for lower animals suggests that heterozygosity rather than homozygosity is associated with greater longevity. Crossing of highly inbred lines of mice have produced unusually long lived and vigorous animals. "Super-mice produced by heterosis develop precociously, reach a large size, and remain in active reproduction much longer than their parents, thereby exhibiting a combination of rapid growth with increased longevity..." (Comfort, 1956, p. 127). Comfort concluded, "Heterosis should be regarded, in all probability as the restoration of 'wild vigour,' whether by restoring heterozygy or other processes, in lines which have lost that vigour through inbreeding" (p. 130). At least there is this one example in mice where heterozygosity is related to favorable early and late life characteristics.

Maternal age has been discussed most commonly in relation to characteristics of the newborn, e.g., mongolism, and less frequently longevity and late life characteristics. However, a 1954 symposium devoted to this subject does establish the point that there are both early and late life characteristics which relate to parental age (Miner, 1954).

Particularly in complex organisms, vertebrates, behavior at the age of mating is an important determinant of which animals will mate and survive. Individuals who have shown vigor, endurance, speed, memory and learning among other behavioral capacities, have mated and their progeny have survived. It would seem highly probable that the nervous system, being the likely register of the successful early life behavior, would hold key to many late life characteristics.

SOME SECULAR TRENDS IN DEVELOPMENT AND AGING

It has long been known that there are appreciable sex differences in longevity which leads to the question whether the age of sexual maturation is also related to length of life. This would seem to be a timely question since pubescence now occurs significantly earlier than in previous generations with possible acceleration of behavioral changes as well. The trend toward earlier menarche is so large to almost amount to a biological revolution in human development. The general comparative position about different species has been that if reproductive life begins early it ends early. One may well wonder in humans if the female with a late menopause would not also have been a late adolescent developer

with a late menarche. While from the point of view that the reproductive life is fixed in length it would be expected that the contemporary trend toward earlier pubescence would be accompanied
by an earlier menopause, available data do not support this view.
Less clear are the psychological issues although we may not have
to wait very long for information since Dr. Bernice Neugarten and
her colleagues at the University of Chicago are carrying out
psychological studies of the menopause.

Data was collected on 3075 women and girls born between 1923
and 1933 in Finland (Simell, 1952). In 1950, the average age at
menarche was 14.25 years ± .03. "Since the year 1882, the
menarche age in Finland has fallen by 2.37 years, and since 1919
by 1.70 years ± .03."

Menarche age for Swedish speaking girls was 13.85 ± .09 and
for Finnish speaking girls, 14.28 ± .08: other differences follow.

Children of intellectual workers .... 14.03 ± .04

manual workers .... 14.39 ± .04

Town children .... 14.08 ± .03

Rural .... 14.46 ± .04

The percentage occurring in the month of birth was 11.96 ±
0.46. The author concluded, "According to my material psychic
factors seem to have a great influence on the age at which menarche
appears" (p. 74). If by this a psychosexual stimulating effect of
the environment is implied, Tanner (1961) would disagree. "The
opinion that menarche has been hastened due to earlier psychosexual stimulation and the freer climate of adolescent sex experience is sometimes put forward by teachers and other. There is
absolutely no evidence to support this view, and a great deal
against it . . ." (Tanner, 1961, p. 118).

Tanner (1962) has reviewed the literature on the trend in age
at menarche and shows an average decline of about four months
per decade over the period 1830-1960. Data from Norway show
that the age at menarche has changed in almost a linear decline
from about seventeen years in 1844, to about 13.5 years in 1950.
Similar trends are seen in the data from Germany, Finland,

Sweden, Great Britain and the USA. For the USA, data show about a year and a half drop in age at menarche from 1905 to 1955.

Tanner notes significantly that, "There is little evidence at present that the trend has stopped, or that girls are now maturing at something like the earliest possible time" (p. 154).

A review by Hauser *et al.* (1961), of the relation between age of menarche and at menopause, contrasted data from Switzerland, Finland and Israel. Of importance, is the fact along with earlier development no evidence for a declining age at menopause was found, rather a slight tendency to later menopause.

It should not be assumed from the previous discussion of the secular trend in age at menarche that age at menarche does not also show a clear genetic factor. Two studies have shown a significantly smaller mean difference at age of menarche in identical twins compared with fraternal twins (Petri, 1935; Tisserand-Perrier, 1953). Perhaps age at menopause would also show a genetic factor if studied, however important environmental forces are implicated.

Some limited evidence collected by Jolly (1955) indicates that girls with precocious sexual development need not have an earlier menopause. He cites the instance of a woman who began to menstruate at the age of two, had a stillbirth at the age of nine, menopause at fifty-two, and died at age seventy-five. Another history showed regular menstruation beginning at age two and one-half until age fifty-three, with eight pregnancies. Still another case showed menstruation beginning at thirty months continuing to age fifty-three with nine pregnancies. Such startling exceptional cases suggests that early onset of reproductive life in the female has little relation to total life span and certainly need not be accompanied by earlier menopause.

Jolly in commenting about interest in the opposite sex by a group of cases of puberty occurring before the age of ten, "A surprising feature of sexual precocity is the fact that sex interest is but rarely awakened in these children, even in those in whom a true puberty has occurred. This is particularly so among girls, and of all the fifty examples only one showed any real interest in the opposite sex" (Jolly, 1955, p. 7). This suggests that pacing of heterosexual interests in adolescents is under the control or influence of factors other than gonadal hormones.

Extreme examples of precocious sexual development may also be examined for evidence of parallel changes in mental development. Jolly feels that slight mental retardation is a more common finding rather than acceleration, however he points out that the greater physical maturity is often accompanied by a greater expectancy by others and may lead to secondary problems. Furthermore one would have to separate the cases of relatively "normal" or constitutional acceleration from those cases in which pathology is dominant, e.g., tumors.

Verzar (1963) has reviewed the evidence of the effects of castration on longevity and finds that it has little effect on the life span. The implications seem to be that sexual maturation and functioning are not important in the processes of aging. However, in the psychological domain, early or late development may have considerable secondary or tertiary effects on adjustment throughout the life span (Jones and Mussen, 1958; Mussen and Jones 1957). The psychological and social consequences of such an instance as that of the Peruvian girl who bore a child at the age of six and one half years are inestimable. Accelerated sexual development and physical growth of children must be accompanied by psychological consequences, particularly if the children are growing up in the culture paced by concepts of maturation laid down in past generations.

In the USA, the average age at marriage for females is now around age twenty or slightly lower. This relatively young age compared with past decades may appear less striking if analyzed as years since menarche. However the previously cited cases of precocious development makes one skeptical that the hormonal changes of pubescence are pacing the early interest in marriage.

For both height and body weight there is also a clear trend toward acceleration of the processes of development. This results in a rather marked increase in the final adult size. Were it only the adolescent growth spurt that occurred earlier, then the final heights and weights of children would be less now than in previous years. In fact, children throughout the school years are taller and heavier than they were in past generations. In height there has been an average increase about an inch per generation. The secular trends in adult height and weight do resemble those of the adolescent growth spurt and age at menarche, in that children achieve their adult physical form, size, and physiological functions at an earlier age. There is no doubt that children are developing faster, giving us some important issues to explore for consequences in aging but others as well. One of broader issues, to be mentioned only in passing, is the possibility that an educational system may need adjustment to keep in step with the faster growth rates of children. This would be of considerable importance if psychological correlations existed with the trends in height and weight which result in children of nine today being equivalent to those of age ten-thirty years ago (Tanner, 1962, p. 152). The end is not yet in sight for the potentiation of physical development of children.

The question may be raised whether the trend toward earlier development in man is an example of an evolutionary trend. The fact that the trend has appeared over such a short interval makes it unlikely that to an important degree selective mating by height and weight has taken place. Rather the explanation would seem to lie in the direction of environmental potentiation of the characteristics of the species. With increasing control and homogeneity of the environment, genetic factors in development will eventually reveal themselves more clearly. A similar statement may be made about the age trends in mortality. Spiegelman (1960, p. 306), in his review of factors in human mortality concluded, "The level of the age curve of mortality is the resultant of the interplay of environmental and biologic, including genetic factors. With increasing control over the environmental factors in mortality, the resultant age curve of mortality reflects, increasingly, the effects of genetic factors in mortality. However, since there is some interdependence between the environmental and the genetic factors, it seems unlikely, in the present state of knowledge, that a stage will be reached where the age curve of mortality will reflect purely the genetic factors."

Mortality curves may well express the present influence of collections of factors which also prevent individuals from reaching their potential upper limit of size, form, and function.

MENTAL ABILITY

From the data on accelerated physical growth one is led to expect a secular trend toward accelerated mental growth. If children of nine today are equivalent physically to those of ten, thirty years ago, one might also expect to find higher mean I.Q.'s in contemporary ten year olds. The issues here are even more complex than those involved in physical growth. So many factors change in school populations that isolation of a relatively pure secular trend of intelligence is a difficult task, albeit one with rather large significance. One aspect of mental ability and age will be singled for comment; the relation between reasoning and the expanding repertory of information one acquires with advancing years. Most studies using measures of vocabulary and information show a continuing increase over the adult years. At first it was thought that this only was to be found in longitudinal studies (Bayley and Odin, 1955; Owens, 1953; Kallmann and Jarvik, 1959). More recently the same trend appears in cross sectional studies wherein educational level is controlled (Birren and Morrison, 1961). How does the nervous system cope with the increased storage of information from childhood through old age and maintain normal communication. By analogy, if one searches a large file at the same rate as a small file more time will be required to find a sought for item (excluding the additional possibility of being distracted by some interesting item uncovered in passing). Since the rate of speech is not much influenced by advancing age, search time with a larger vocabulary is not much increased. One unlikely possibility might be that along with a larger vocabulary association and selection time becomes faster with advancing age. Evidence seems convincing that association time becomes longer with advancing age (Birren, 1961; Riegel and Birren, 1962). If the search rate is slower and yet verbal output remains high, some change is implied in the organization of stored information. One way the organization of information might change is through the use of broader concepts which embrace previous discrete elements. Such a hypothesis would be consistent with the expectation that adults cope with their expanding information by the use of abstractions. An alternative possibility is that the associative material is placed in longer chains of discrete information and reflected in rambling garrulous speech in which one word leads to another. The first hypothesis leads us to expect a more abstract level of speech with advancing age whereas the latter explanation leads us to expect a more concrete and simple associative type of speech. An empirical check on the alternatives would be found in the frequency of superordinate words in verbal associations as a function of age. The point of interest is the frequency of use of superordinate terms from the school years over the adult years. This frequency serves as an indicator of a tendency with increased age to embrace larger amounts of information under broader concepts. Data relevant to this issue was presented at a symposium "Changes in Verbal Association During the Life Span," arranged by Klaus Riegel at the 1962 meeting of the American Psychological Association.

Results from the 1910 Kent-Rosanoff word association test, and from recent studies, show an age factor in the nature of the word associations. While there is likely a significant factor of a secular trend or "changing times" effect on word association, Riegel's pilot work found, "The age of Ss was found to be the more important determinant for the agreement in primary responses than the time of testing (changing times)" (Riegel, 1962). It would be rather simple if the age trends in word associations were all in the direction of increasing use of superordinates thus confirming the hypothesis that the individual in organizing the increasing mass of verbal information he acquires with age uses broader concepts or superordinate categories. Unfortunately the evidence is not straightforward. Palermo gathered data on subjects from the fourth grade through college level, using not only the Kent-Rosanoff list but an additional list of 100 words of a wider range of types of word forms. One primary finding is that the frequency of the most commonly associated words (popular responses) increases with age for both men and women. This is in accord with the notion that with age one becomes more experienced with relative word frequencies: it follows that older subjects show a higher proportion of agreement in word association. However, there remains the matter of the type of the word associated; earlier it was pointed out that there might be expected a trend toward increased use of superordinates. Palermo found the opposite, however, superordinates increased from fourth to sixth grade followed by a decline thereafter; males tending to give more superordinates than females. Older subjects tended to give word association of the same class as the stimulus word. On this matter of an age decline in use of superordinate associations, Palermo differs from Riegel, the latter's results showing an increase. Possibly there is a difference in task attitude or set the different experimenters established in their subjects. In the case of a word association test, one has only to give a word quickly, uncomplicated by purpose. Mostly, however, we associate for some purpose; we search among the words of our repertory and select to best advantage.

The data indicate that young children give more unique responses on word association tests than do adults. Since children know fewer total words the results may not be so much an indication of sheer novelty of association as it is a reflection of the amount of experience with the word frequencies in speech and print. Another factor, timing of associations has to be added to this picture of association processes. Normal conversation flows at a rather fast continuous rate and a thought not put into words quickly enough is lost. There is the common experience of losing a thought which was not inserted into the conversation rapidly. Such instances are perhaps a manifestation of the decay of associations. There is also time involved in the formation of the association, that is, some amount of time that elapses during the emergence of the association. This production time is assumed to increase with the complexity of the instructions and with the number of possible or alternative associations.

In a preliminary formulation, Riegel and Birren (1962) referred to *emergence time* and *selection time* in word association, such time factors being thought to be differentially affected by age. Earlier work had shown that advancing age is accompanied by slower word associations but it was not clear whether the slowness was not the result of an increase in the number of words known. Increased probabilities of certain word associations and increased total word knowledge, do not appear to be sufficient to explain the differences with age in verbal behavior, i.e., speed of emergence and selection of associations. It may prove necessary to regard control factor or set which gives direction to the mind or associations as a relevant variable in aging; the intensity of the purposive nature of associations may independently change with age. One is beginning to see, although very vaguely at the moment, how such factors as the size of the repertory of associations, variations in associative strength as a function of the frequency of use, the intensity of the purpose governing emergence and selection of associations, as well as association speed, interact to yield complex verbal behavior. The output of such a system with age in quantity and novelty is obviously a complex function, not to mention the additional factors of unique experience and temperament. However present concepts and methods of study of language seem useful in describing lifelong trends in verbal behavior.

PROBLEM SOLVING ORIENTATION

Jerome (1960) has reported pilot studies of logical problem solving in young and aged subjects in which the performance of the older subjects was strikingly different from the young. In particular he noted a high redundancy in the older subject's seeking of information necessary to solve the problems. Of the possible explanations of the behavior, it seems as though the older subject often fails to have a strategy and a clear goal, hence behavior may fluctuate from one aspect of the task to another. During our school years we develop a high order of skill in solving problems which in part may consist of an orientation to solve problems as well as specific skills and strategies. With the passage of time since school, this orientation to solve problems may decay in what Jerome describes as ". . . facility for recognizing situations for the application of heuristically controlled behavior." Needed are studies to determine the extent to which a problem solving orientation can be reestablished in older adults in place of a more associationistic kind of behavior.

PSYCHOLOGY OF AGING AND VASCULAR DISEASE

A series of previous studies seemed to point to the fact that the loss in psychomotor speed with age was primarily a function of the central nervous system (Birren *et al.*, 1955). It was not established whether or not this was related to possible cerebral vascular disease. Although in the rat a slowing response speed with age was also observed (Birren, 1955) and that species has little naturally occurring vascular disease. However, the issue with regard to humans was unsettled. Recently measurements of psychomotor speed were made in healthy elder men and a reduction in speed was found which would seem to lie outside the explanation of a vascular antecedent (Birren *et al.*, 1962). The finding was puzzling since Spieth (1962) had indicated that men with cardiac disease were slower than control subjects the same age and Simonson (1941) had shown perceptual and psychomotor changes in men with cardiovascular disease. An attempt to clarify this relation was carried out by Birren and Spieth by intercorrelating psychomotor speed, age and selected physiological measures related to vascular disease, blood pressure and serum cholesterol. The data based upon 161 men between the approximate ages of twenty-five and sixty years, indicated that psychomotor speed was more highly correlated with chronological age than was either blood pressure or serum cholesterol (Birren and Spieth, 1962). At the present stage of our knowledge it appears that the age changes in psychomotor speed reflect predisposing constitutional differences or age changes in the central nervous system which may also dispose the individual toward the development of vascular disease. Once vascular disease develops to a significant degree, further psychomotor slowing may be expected. This latter point seems necessary and important to add since individuals with significant cerebral vascular or cardiovascular disease do show marked slowing of behavior, e.g., hypertensive patients show significant psychomotor slowing compared with control subjects of the same age.

The association of slowness of reaction and hypertension suggests the relevance of studies of young adults before elevated blood pressure is found. One possibility which suggests itself is that those mechanisms of the sympathetic nervous system and adrenal glands which prepare the organism for fight or flight, are antagonistic to rapid discrimination of incoming signals and rapidity of psychomotor responses. The organism aroused to effect action may not be the organism best able to make fine and rapid discriminations.

This line of reasoning leads to the work of Lacey which has been directed at the study of differential speed of response in subjects he classifies as "cardiac labiles" and "cardiac stabiles." A cardiac stabile is an individual who shows relatively little spontaneous moment to moment variation in heart rate whereas the labile shows variability in heart rate. Labile subjects are found to be significantly faster in reaction time than stabile subjects. This work establishes some degree of association between cardiac functioning and response speed in young subjects in whom vascular disease would not yet seem a likely contributing factor. Lacey's review of the literature suggests that sympathetic arousal may be antagonistic to cortical excitability or rapid discrimination responses. This would seem to contradict common sense, for one would think that anger or anxiety would facilitate quick responses. However, one is not necessarily aware of small differences in discrimination speed of the highly aroused person compared with the relaxed individual who may be best able to anticipate or differentiate incoming signals and effect rapid responses.

Recently, we carried out a study relating speed of response to phases of the cardiac cycle (Birren, Cardon, Phillips, 1963). Perhaps the important point to be made at this time is that variability in the capacity for making rapid simple reactions is associated with the phases of the heart cycle. Not all subjects show the same pattern and important individual differences in physiological responsivity may well exist. The extent and pattern of arousal which, if studied in young adults, may relate to individual differences in reaction time and may be related to subsequent development of cardiac or other vascular disease.

There is enough evidence in the literature to indicate that cardiovascular disease is an area of research with implications for the psychologist, the sociologist as well as the physiologist and internist. One of the curious features about such information is the fact that cardiac disease seems to affect mostly the prototype of the American man. Masculinity, high activity or drive, productivity, and responsibility, appear positively related to the development of cardiac disease. The overtone of constitutional factors represented in body build, temperament, and perhaps physiological and psychological reactivity suggest that some of the precursor factors might be distinguishable in youth. Since so many factors are usually interacting in the general population, trends are likely to be obscure, but perhaps studies of college populations, in whom adequate initial mental and physical data were available as well, as follow-up possibilities, would prove useful.

Transient influences may also operate and even within an occupation cycle of demand may relate to physiological and psychological events. A study of accountants showed a significant and striking rise in plasma cholesterol corresponding to peak periods of stress (Rosenman and Friedman, 1959, p. 287). In another context, Korchin (1962), has portrayed the intellectual and responsible individual to be most affected by psychological stress. The environmental effect depends upon the magnitude of the psychological stress and the characteristics of the "host." A community study of cardiovascular disease was undertaken by the Public Health Service, known as the Framingham study, to control for many of the previous biases in study populations and also provide longitudinal data. Of interest is the fact that willingness to participate in the study is related to the likelihood of cardiovascular disease (Gordon *et al.*, 1959). In this case non-respondents had a higher mortality rate than respondents. The authors also pointed out another kind of hazard which they called the *silent partner*. For example, if anxiety were to some extent positively related to hypertension then the resultant picture might be different depending upon whether anxiety increased or decreased likelihood of participating. Retrospective studies of cardiovascular diseases are susceptible to further selective factors, and indeed a cardiovascular crisis itself may lead to changes in temperature or personality.

An example of a significant social-psychological variable has been found to be widowhood. The young widowed appear to have a significantly higher risk of mortality than the married (Kraus and Lilienfield, 1959). "This excess risk in the widowed under age thirty-five, compared to the married, was greater than tenfold for at least one of the specific age-sex groups involved for several leading causes of death, including arteriosclerotic heart disease and vascular lesions of the central nervous system" (p. 217). The significant relation between mortality and young widowhood, reminds one of the long known fact that the single, divorced and widowed tend to occupy a disproportionate number of institutional beds. There is probably a mixture of long standing influences as well as consequences arising from the death of the spouse. The authors suggests three hypotheses, mutual selection of poor-risk mates, joint unfavorable environment, and effects of widowhood. The authors had intended their analysis as provocative and suggest that further study of the young married in contrast to the young widowed group might lead to important facts about the etiology of the diseases most affected. One might expect that the death of a spouse, and events before and after, would be a stimulus for some kinds of bodily response and not other, e.g., those leading to hypertension but not neoplasms. The findings tend to support this in that the death rates from malignant neoplasms were about double in the widowed, compared with the married, whereas vascular lesions of the nervous system and arteriosclerotic heart disease were about 4.2. As might be expected if a psychological component were involved, suicide is higher in the widowed: results showed a ratio of 9.3 in the widowed compared with the married in the age range, twenty-twenty-four; 6.9 in twenty-four-thirty-four; and 3.5 in thirty-five-forty-four. To put these data in perspective it might be said that in general the relations between mortality rates and socioeconomic class are considerably smaller than the relation to mortality and widowhood.

The Framingham study corrborates the fact that young women show much less coronary heart disease than young men (Dawber and Kannel, 1962). The substantial increase in cardiovascular diseases in widows must therefore be given some significance. The fact that young widows show higher death rates than young married men suggests that the physiological consequences of the social psychological components of widowhood are more significant than the sex difference in mortality from heart disease. This leads to several suggested areas of research, one concerned with psychological sustaining factors and the physiological concomitants of grief. The psychological and physiological vulnerability of the host to grief should be studied. While for sometime it has been thought that older persons might be precipitated into a psychotic episode by a crisis, like that of the death of a spouse, the young have been thought less vulnerable, and perhaps they are, but only relatively so. The greater dependence of the older person upon his immediate environment as well as his health may make him more vulnerable to severe consequences of bereavement, although the data on death rates in young widows and widowers suggests that grief may be a potent variable in any age group.

A study of a small sample of healthy older men carried out at the National Institute of Mental Health suggested that bereavement and other forms of social loss was related to physiological variables (Birren, Butler, Greenhouse, Sokoloff and Yarrow, 1963). One cannot avoid the implication that bereavement and other significant psychological losses initiate bodily responses with long term consequences for the health and well being of the individual.

With advancing age there tends to be an association of deficit states with amplification of consequences when more than one state exists in the individual. On the subject of medical impairments, Spiegelman has commented, ". . . persons with more than one impairment generally experience an excess mortality greater than the sum of the extra mortality associated separately with each of the impairments" (1960, p. 301). From the literature one gathers, e.g., that the high mortality from cardiovascular disease results from a confluence of many factors, diet, urbanization, occupational strain, body type, heredity, and still others. Some of these imply origins in early life, pubescence or earlier and suggest that we should continually broaden the search for the factors and conditions which potentiate optimum biological, psychological, and social development throughout the life span.

SUMMARY

This discussion was not intended to be comprehensive but rather illustrative of some important problems of human development in which biological, psychological, and social forces interact. In all three of these aspects individuals are dynamic. There is no doubt that a major biological trend has been taking place in the earlier development of children, a trend which began at least in the early part of the 19th Century and which has proceeded to such an extent as to outweigh socioeconomic class differences in height and weight, and in age at pubescence. As yet the implications of the changes in rate of development have not been much explored with particular regard to school and familial customs. Astonishing is the fact that this major trend is largely unexplained beginning as it does before the period of modern rational medicine and social science. Earlier development may reflect a set of factors which also influence improved life expectancy although it may bring with it certain specialized liabilities, e.g., increased disposition to cardiovascular disease.

While not much can be said about the specific factors which optimize development in Western societies they are very likely associated with urbanization and upper social class for these have in the past been related to early development. After mature growth has been reached the same optimizing factors for growth may have relatively deleterious effects for adults and aging. While urban children develop earlier, rural people tend to live longer.

We clearly see a genetic thread running through the life span. Identical twins seem to age physically and psychologically more alike than fraternal twins or siblings. Modulating this genetic potential are presently manifest powerful social and psychological influences. Widowhood is associated with marked deleterious physiological and psychological states and a higher death rate.

Psychology began in the 19th Century as an offspring of physiology, later it was influenced by the growth of the social sciences until now it is properly looked upon as the bridge discipline between the biological sciences on the one hand and the social sciences on the other. A life span developmental psychology concerned with personal values and attitudes which give life its meaning as well as with the interactions of biological and social conditions which make human life possible is a fruitful context for research.

REFERENCES

1. Bayley, Nancy, and Oden, Melita H.: The maintenance of intellectual ability in gifted adults. *J. Geront., 10*:91-107, 1955.

2. Birren, J. E.: Behavioral theories of aging. In, *Aging.* N. W. Shock, ed., Washington, AAAS, 1960, 305-332.

3. Birren, J. E., Butler, R. N., Greenhouse, S. W., Sokoloff, L., and Yarrow, Marian R. (Eds.): *Human Aging: A Biological and Behavioral Study.* Washington Government Printing Office, 1963.

4. Birren, J. E., Cardon, P. V., and Phillips, Shirley L.: Reaction time as a function of the cardiac cycle in young adults. *Science, 140*:195-196, 1963.

5. Birren, J. E., and Morrison, D. F.: Analysis of the WAIS subtests in relation to age and education. *J. Geront., 16*:363-369, 1961.

6. Birren, J. E., Riegel, K. F., and Morrison, D. F.: Age differences in response speed as a function of controlled variations of stimulus conditions: evidence of a general speed factor. *Gerontologia, 6*:1-18, 1962.

7. Birren, J. E., and Riegel, K. F.: Age differences in word associations and word completions in discrete and continuous, timed and untimed tasks. Presented at, American Psychological Association, August 31, 1962.

8. Birren, J. E., Riegel, K. F., and Robbin, J. S.: Age differences in continuous word associations measured by speech recordings. *J. Geront., 17*:95-96, 1962.

9. Boyne, A. W.: Secular changes in the status of adults and the growth of children, with special reference to changes in intelligence of 11-year-olds. In, *Human Growth, 3,* J. M. Tanner, ed., London, Pergamon Press, 1960, 97-120.

10. Brun, G.: *Changes in the Lipid Contents of Serum in Patients with Manic-Depressive Psychosis.* H. K. Lewis and Co., London, 1940.

11. Comfort, A.: *The Biology of Senescence.* Routledge and Kegan Paul, London, 1956.

12. Dawber, T. R., and Kannel, W. B.: Atherosclerosis and you: pathogenetic implications from epidemiologic observations. *J. Amer. Geriat. Soc., 10*:805-821, 1962.

13. Dunbar, Helen F.: *Emotions and Bodily Changes.* Columbia University Press, New York, 1935.

14. Forssman, O., and Lindegard, B.: The post-coronary patient. *J. Psychosomatic Res., 3*:89-169, 1958.

15. Gertler, M. M., and White, P. D.: Coronary Heart Disease in Young Adults. Cambridge, Massachusetts, Harvard University Press, 1954.

16. Gildea, E. F.: Special features of personality which are common to certain psychosomatic disorders. *Psychosomatic Medicine, 11*:273-281, 1949.

17. Gildea, E. F., Man, E. B., and Biach, R. W.: Serum protein, non-protein nitrogen and lipoids in schizophrenic and manic-depressive psychoses. *Arch. Neurology & Psychiatry, 43*:932-947, 1940.

18. Goldsmith, G. A., and Williers, F. A.: Body build and heredity in coronary thrombosis. *Ann. Int. Med., 10*:1181-1186, 1937.

19. Gordon, T., Moore, F. E., Shurtleff, D., and Dawber, T. R.: Some methodologic problems in the long-term study of cardiovascular dis-

ease: observations on the Framingham Study. *J. Chronic Dis., 10:* 186-206, 1959.

20. Gressel, G. C., Shobe, F. O., Saslow, G., DuBois, P. H, and Schroeder, H. A.: Personality factors in arterial hypertension. *J.A.M.A., 140:* 265-272, 1949.

21. Hall, K. R. L., and Stride, E.: Some factors affecting reaction times to auditory stimuli in mental patients. *J. Ment. Sc., 100:*462-476, 1954.

22. Hauser, von G. A., Obiri, J. A., Valaer, M., Erb, H., Müller, T Remen U., and Vanäänen, P.: Der Einfluss des Menarchealters auf das Menopausealter. *Gynaecologia, 152:*279-286, 1961.

23. Hewitt, D., and Hillman, R. W.: A note on adult stature in relation to rate of maturation. *Vita Humana, 5:*177-181, 1962.

24. Jenkins, J. J.: Cultural and age influences on word associations. Presented at, American Psychological Association, August 31, 1962.

25. Jolly, H.: *Sexual Precocity.* Springfield, Thomas, 1955.

26. Jones, H. B.: The relation of human health to age, place, and time. In, *Handbook of Aging and the Individual.* J. E. Birren, ed., Chicago, University of Chicago Press, 1959, Chapter 11, 336-363.

27. Jones, Mary C., and Mussen, P. H.: Self-conceptions, motivations, and interpersonal attitudes of early-and late-maturing girls. *Child Development, 29:*491-501, 1959.

28. Kalis, Betty L., Harris, R. E., Sokolow, M., and Carpenter, L. G.: Response to psychological stress in patients with essential hypertension. *Am. H. J., 53:*572-578, 1957.

29. Kallmann, F. J., and Jarvik, Lissy F.: Individual differences in constitution and genetic background. In, *Handbook of Aging and the Individual* J. E. Birren, ed. Chicago, University of Chicago Press, 1959, Chapter 8, 216-263.

30. Kannel, W. B., Dawber, T. R., Kagan, A., Revotskie, N., and Stokes J : *Annals, Int. Med., 55:*33-50, 1961.

31. Keys, A.: Diet and the epidemiology of coronary heart disease. *J. Amer. Med. Assoc., 164:*1912-1919, 1957.

32. Korchin, S.: Some psychological determinants of stress behavior (In press).

33. Kraus, A. A., and Lilienfeld, A. M.: Some epidemiologic aspects of the high mortality rate in the young widowed group. *J. Chronic Dis., 10:*207-217, 1959.

34. McFarland, R. A., and Goldstein, H.: The biochemistry of manic-depressive psychosis. A review. *American Journal of Psychiatry, 96:*21-58, 1939.

35. Medawar, P. B.: *The Uniqueness of the Individual.* London, Methuen and Co., 1957.

36. Miles, H. H. W., Waldfogel, S., Barrabee, Edna L., and Cobb, S.: Psychosomatic study of 46 young men with coronary artery disease. *Psychosomatic Medicine, 16*:455-477, 1954.

37. Miner, R. W.: Parental age and characteristics of the offspring. *Annals New York Acad. Sc., 57*:451-614, 1954.

38. Mussen, P. H., and Jones, Mary C.: Self-conceptions, motivations, and interpersonal attitudes of late- and early-maturing boys. *Child Development, 28*:243-256, 1957.

39. Newman, M.: Coronary occlusion in young adults. *Lancet, 2*:409-411, 1946.

40. Ostfield, A. M., and Lebovits, B. Z.: Personality factors and pressor mechanisms in renal and essential hypertension. *A.M.A. Archives Int. Med. 104*:43-52, 1959.

41. Owens, W. A., Jr.: Age and mental abilities: a longitudinal study. *Genet Psychol. Monogr., 48*:3-54, 1953.

42. Palermo, D. S.: Cross-sectional comparison of word-association norms collected from fourth grade to college. Presented at, American Psychological Association, August 31, 1962.

43. Peete, D. C.: *The Psychosomatic Genesis of Coronary Artery Disease.* 1955. Springfield, Thomas, Chap. IV.

44. Petri, E.: Untersuchungen zur Erbbedingheit der Menarche. *Z. Moph. Anthr., 33*:43-48, 1935.

45. Pickering, G.: *The Nature of Essential Hypertension.* New York, Grune and Stratton, 1961.

46. Riegel, K. F., and Riegel, Ruth M.: Cross-sectional comparisons of word associations collected from the age levels, 17-19, 55-64, and 65 and over. Presented at, American Psychological Association, August 31, 1962.

47. Rockstein, M.: The biology of ageing in insects. *In, The Lifespan of Animals.* G. E. W. Wolstenholme and Maeve O'Connor, eds. Boston: Little, Brown and Co., 1959, 247-264.

48. Rosenman, R. H., and Friedman, M.: The possible relationship of the emotions to clinical coronary heart disease. In, *Hormones and Atherosclerosis,* G. Pincus, ed. New York, Academic Press 1959, Chapter 21, 283-300.

49. Saslow, G., Gressel, G. C., Shobe, F. O., DuBois, P. H., and Schroeder H. A.: A possible etiologic relevance of personality factors in arterial hypertension. *Res. Pub. Assoc. Nerv. Ment. Dis., 29*:881-899, 1949.

50. Simell, Greta: Über das Menarchealter in Finland. *Acta Paediatrica, 41,* Suppl. 84, pp. 82, 1952.

51. Spiegelman, M.: Factors in human mortality. In, *The Biology of Aging.* B. L. Strehler, ed. Washington, Amer. Instit. Biol. Sc., 1960, 292-308.

52. Tanner, J. M.: *Education and Physical Growth.* London, University of London Press, 1961.

53. Tanner, J. M.: *Growth at Adolescence.* Oxford, Blackwell, 2nd edition. 1961.

54. Thaler, M., Weiner, H., and Reiser, M. F.: Exploration of the doctor-patient relationship through projective techniques. *Psychosomatic Medicine 19*:228-239, 1957.

55. Tisserand-Perrier, M.: Etude comparative de certains processus de croissance chez les jumeaux. *J. Genet Hum., 2*:87-102, 1953.

56. Verzar, F.: *Lectures in Experimental Gerontology.* Springfield, Thomas, 1963.

57. Walker, A. R. P.: Some aspects of the endocrinologic picture of the South African Bantu — a population relatively free from mortality from coronary disease. In, *Hormones and Athersclerosis,* G. Pincus, ed. New York, Academic Press, 1959, Chapter 28, 385-401.

58. White, P. D.: *Heart Disease,* 3rd Ed. 1944. New York, MacMillan Co.

Chapter 8

STABILITY AND CHANGE IN
HUMAN CHARACTERISTICS

B. S. BLOOM

I have for the major part of my career been interested in evaluating the effectiveness of educational curricula in producing significant changes in the ways in which students act, think, and feel. It has been clearly evident in this work that there is increased resistance to change with increase in age. In order to understand this phenomena more clearly, I have posed it as a problem of stability and change in human characteristics.

After several attempts at attacking this problem, I decided it would be most worthwhile to bring together the results of all the longitudinal studies I could find in this country and abroad. These studies, as you know, follow a given sample of individuals over a period of time and attempt to secure repeated observations and measurements on each individual. There are about 1000 such studies that I was able to find—some for periods as long as forty years and others for periods of a year or two.

Although I had begun my search with educational problems in mind, I soon began to see advantages in a study of other human characteristics than those affected directly by the schools. It became apparent that the longitudinal studies of physical characteristics might help me to understand ways of treating other longitudinal evidence.

In particular, I became intrigued with height measurements which had almost perfect reliability in the more careful longitudinal studies. Such high reliability is, of course, rarely achieved in our measurements of achievement, interests, personality characteristics, etc. Furthermore, extensive research had been done on skeletal growth in humans and animals. It seemed to me that it would be very useful to begin with height growth and then to proceed to studies of the growth and development of other characteristics.

While there were a large number of longitudinal studies of height growth which followed the same individuals for one to three years, there were only about half a dozen studies which followed a group for ten years or more. When these major studies are compared with each other with regard to the magnitude of correlations among the different age measurements, the differences are relatively small. For the most part, these differences can be explained by the differences in the variability of the samples.

The comparability of the correlations reported by the different studies for height measurements appears to be a general phenomenon in longitudinal research. For each behavioral characteristic, the different longitudinal studies which had comparable subjects and which used similar measurements and similar instruments, reported correlational matrices which were very similar — especially when corrected for the differences in the variability of the samples.

I am not entirely clear as to how this phenomenon can be explained but the "lawfulness" of these relationships found in studies done in this country and abroad over the past fifty years enables us to see an order in the behavioral sciences which had hitherto been found only in the physical sciences. One implication of this finding is that a small number of carefully designed longitudinal studies may yield a definitive picture of a particular characteristic or of a specific area of investigation.

Since the usual data reported for longitudinal studies were the correlations and measures of central tendency and variability, I worked with this type of data and attempted to analyze them further. The correlation tables for various characteristics tended to show very similar trends. The highest correlations were usually those for the shortest intervals of time and the lowest correlations were usually those for the longest intervals of time.

However, there was another very interesting and somewhat perplexing trend in these correlation tables. As the age of the subject increased, the correlations tended to become higher and *not* to decrease with the length of the retest intervals. That is, the correlations showed different patterns for the early and late measurements in a longitudinal series. Why should the length of the test-retest interval be so important in determining the magnitude of the correlations in the early years but have so little effect on the correlations in the later years?

In an attempt to understand this phenomenon I began by studying the correlations between the gains in particular test-retest intervals and the initial and the final measurements. Characteristically, the correlations between the gains and the initial measures were very low — usually averaging very close to zero, while the correlations between the gains and the final measures were moderate to high. Interesting was the finding that the correlations between the gains and the *final* measures tended to increase with the length of the test-retest intervals, although the length of time *did not* appear to affect the magnitude of the relation between the gain and the initial measure.

The increasing correlations between the initial and retest measurements makes it evident that there is increasing consistency or stability in the measurements for the individuals in the sample. There is an increase in the proportion of the retest variance which is accounted for by the earlier test variance. This can be interpreted as merely demonstrating that the rank order of a sample of individuals is becoming less and less changeable, although nothing is known about whether the entire sample is increasing, decreasing, or remaining at the same level on the measurement scale.

However, the fact that the gains correlate approximately zero with the earlier measurements, leads us to attempt to explain the relation between initial and retest measurements in terms of a kind of part-whole relationship. Thus, if height at age three is unrelated to the gains in height from age three to eighteen, then the correlation between height at age three and height at age eighteen must be attributed to the proportion of the height at age eighteen which has been attained by age three. In this type of reasoning we are seeking to explain stability not only as increasing consistency but also as decreasing change in some absolute sense.

Anderson's (1939) Overlap-Hypothesis seems to yield an excellent approximation to these relationships. Anderson has suggested that the square root of the ratio of the means of the two measurements will equal the correlation between the two measurements. We find that the Overlap-Hypothesis works very well when the measurements are perfectly reliable, when the scale of measurements approximates an absolute scale with equal units and an absolute zero, and when the variance of the sample on which the means is determined is approximately the same as the variance on the sample on which the correlations are determined. The use of the Overlap-Hypothesis permits us to relate cross-sectional data to longitudinal data and to estimate with considerable accuracy, in advance, the relationships that are likely to be found in a longitudinal study which may take twenty years to complete. The use of this hypothesis also permits us to explain increasing consistency of relationships in terms of increases in absolute development. Thus, increasing stability as indicated by correlations is interpretable not only as increasing consistency of rank order relationships but also as increases in the proportion of the criterion development accounted for by the earlier measurements.

It is this last use of the Overlap-Hypothesis which enables us to describe the development of particular characteristics in terms of both correlations and level of development. Where we have both scales (correlations and percent of mature development) they agree to a very high degree. Where we have only the correlational data, we may begin to infer the nature of a developmental scale from the correlational matrix.

In a forthcoming book, we will describe the developmental features of selected behavioral characteristics. Perhaps the most striking generalization to be drawn from these developmental curves is that growth and development is not in equal units per unit of time. An extreme example of this is height growth where the child on the average gains 30 per cent of his mature height from conception to birth, 15 percent of his height from birth to age one, and 8 per cent from age one to two. Thereafter, he gains 2 to 3 per cent per year except for larger spurts during adolescence. The point of this is that an individual may gain as much height in nine months as he will gain in nine years. Although this is the most common pattern, not all characteristics show this rapid early growth followed by increasingly slower growth.

In the book we have attempted to relate a large number of longitudinal studies to the Overlap-Hypothesis. In each case, we have used the developmental curve for a particular characteristic to determine the theoretical correlation to be expected between measurements at any two ages, hypothesizing that the development in the particular cross-sectional study is what normally occurs between the specific ages in a longitudinal study. Since our measuring instruments are not perfectly reliable, we apply the reliability of the particular instrument to determine the theoretical value reduced for unreliability of measurement. When the variability of the sample differs significantly from that observed in a population, we have made allowances for this in our theoretical estimates. When these factors of time, reliability, and specific sample characteristics are taken into consideration, the majority of the observed correlations in longitudinal studies of one year or more fit very closely the values derived from our theoretical curves.

Perhaps the most profound implication of this is that we can use theoretical values in the behavioral sciences and that the deviations of observations from these theoretical values can be explained by appropriate analyses. For example, from our absolute scale of school achievement development we estimated the theoretical correlation between achievement indices (teacher grades general achievement as measured by a test, etc.) at the twelfth vs. the thirteenth years of school to be about $+ .95$. However, the correlations between high school grades and college freshman grades are usually of the order of $+ .50$. The search for the explanation of the difference between the two values led us to question the equivalence of grades from different schools or colleges and to the development of techniques for equating grades from different educational institutions. The corrected or scaled grades at the high school and college level correlate about $+ .80$ (Bloom and Peters, *1961*). However, the difference between $+ .80$ and $+ .95$ still needs to be explained. We found most of the difference in these two values to be accounted for by the unreliability of the high school and college grades. Highly reliable achievement test batteries administered to students during high school and then again at the end of one or two years of college reveal correlations of approximately + .92 which is very close to the theoretical value derived from the absolute scales.

While more precise work is needed to secure better absolute scales and more accurate theoretical values than are at present available, we believe that behavioral science research in education and psychology will profit greatly if research problems arise from the need to explain differences between theory and observation and differences between theortical and observed values.

A somewhat more significant outcome from the developmental curves and their agreement with longitudinal data is the description of growth and development over time for each characteristic. Where is the period of most rapid development and where are the periods of least rapid development? We believe this has great relevance for attempts to influence the development of particular characteristics. If a particular personality characteristic is largely developed in the age period one to five, what are the appropriate conditions for its "optimal" development during that period? What, if anything, can be done to alter it at later stages in the individual's career? We have hypothesized that a particular characteristic can be affected by environmental conditions to a greater degree in the period of least stability and most rapid change and that it can be affected least by environmental conditions in the period of greatest stability and least rapid change.

There is some theoretical as well as empirical support for this hypothesis. First, we do find that although there is little relation between gains or changes in a particular characteristic and initial measurements, there are relatively high relations between these changes and estimates of the qualities of the environment as they relate to the specific characteristic. Thus, gains in height are larger for individuals living under good nutritional and health conditions than for individuals living under relatively poor nutritional and health conditions. Reading comprehension *gains* from grades two to eight are highly related to home and school conditions, while gains in general intelligence are related to motivational and other conditions in the home.

Further support for this hypothesis is found in Kirk's (1958) study in which institutionalized mentally retarded children between ages four and five were able to make significant gains in general intelligence if given a special nursery school experience while a control group of children became progressively lower in general intelligence under the usual institutional conditions. Lee's (1951) study of Negro children who moved from the South to Philadelphia at various ages from six to thirteen showed significant gains in general intelligence if they moved to Philadelphia at age six, somewhat smaller gains if they moved north at later ages, with almost no gains if they moved at age thirteen. Although this research, as yet, has not followed these individuals beyond age fifteen, the shape of the curves suggests that the largest part of the gain was made in the year or two immediately after moving north and that it is unlikely that the individuals who moved north at the later ages will make significant gains.

Other support for this hypothesis may be found in personality and learning theory—Hebb (1949), Erickson (1950), and McClelland (1951)—which emphasize the importance of early environment and the increasing resistance to change at later ages.

One implication of this view and of the longitudinal data already available on physical characteristics, intelligence, school learning, interests, attitudes, and other personality characteristics is that the home and the school environments have their greatest effect in the early years. The first three or four years of life are crucial for later developments and the first three or four years of school are of greatest significance for later learning not only in the schools but throughout the life of the individual. Much must be learned about the ways in which the environment affects the individual in these very critical stages in development. What constitutes "healthy" and desirable environments at these stages and what are the characteristics of unhealthy, undesirable, or deprived environments? This approach requires that the behavioral scientist be able to distinguish between desirable and undesirable development, between healthy and unhealthy types of development, and between good and less good. The scientist has always hesitated to become involved in value considerations and has defended himself by claims that his primary interest is in descriptive and relational inquiry. Perhaps the research workers on gerontology may help us distinguish between the good and the less good. Studying individuals toward the end of their careers, they may be able to help us understand what made for satisfaction and dissatisfaction, what ennobled man and what reduced him to something less than man, what constituted health and what constituted less than health. I am suggesting that the investigators of child development and the investigators of old age may have much to give and receive from each other.

There are many implications for the behavioral sciences from longitudinal research on stability and change in human characteristics. I will confine my attention to a few for the workers in gerontology.

The agreement between data derived from cross-sectional and longitudinal studies suggests that our research designs can be far more productive and fruitful in the future. A series of short longitudinal studies (two to five years) can be planned in such a way as to yield significant findings over a twenty or thirty year span. Absolute scales based on cross-sectional samples can be used to verify longitudinal findings.

We have repeatedly found that the greatest amount of change appears to take place when individuals enter a new environment which is in sharp contrast to the environment from which they came. Furthermore, most of the change appears to happen in the first year or so, rather than in the later years. Thus, our studies of college students suggests that more change takes place during the freshman year than in the remaining three years of college. In Lee's (1951) study of changes in intelligence with movement of Negro children from the South to the North, the greatest portion of the change took place in the first year in the new environment. Similar findings could be cited from studies of changing conditions in nutrition, school learning and attitude formation. If these findings are verified at later ages, it would suggest that the introduction of an individual to a new environment is a very critical period that must be thoroughly understood for theoretical as well as practical reasons. Furthermore, if change in individuals is desired, we must recognize that much of the change will be determined by the nature of the environment into which the individual is put.

The astonishingly high level of predictability which is found in longitudinal research has implications for this field. First, the analysis of the data helps us to understand that our correlations between an initial and a later measurement represent the proportion of the later measurement which was already present at the time of the initial measurement. The future is built on the past and it can be predicted on the basis of the evidence already available in the past.

Second, if we wish to use tests or other instruments to predict the future, we must contrast the use of such instrumentation with historical or other data derived from the past of the individual. The longitudinal data will enable us to determine the level of prediction to be sought from other types of instrumentation and appropriate analysis will suggest the characteristics which the instruments must sample if they are to predict as well as other types of evidence.

Third, the levels of prediction available from longitudinal data should enable those working with the aged to anticipate the behaviors and reactions of individuals to a high degree and to use these as a basis for working with these individuals.

Finally, we must recognize the large part that environmental differences play in determining individual differences. Most of our work in testing has been directed to the measurement of individual difference. Environmental differences have been thought to be sources of error in our measurements rather than sources (and causes) of individual differences. The definition of specific environment variables as related to specific individual variables is likely to be a major emphasis in the near future. When longitudinal data on the individual is related to specific environmental measures, our predictions begin to aproach unity. An equation which is fundamental for human characteristics might be written as

$$I_2 = I_1 + f(E_{2-1})$$

When I = Individual Characteristic at times 1 and 2 and E = the Environment for that characteristic during the period time 2-1

REFERENCES

1. Anderson, J. E.: The limitations of infant and preschool tests in the measurement of intelligence. *J. of Psychol.*, 8:351-379, 1939.

2. Bloom, B. S., and Peters, F. R.: *The Use of Academic Prediction Scales for Counseling and Selecting College Entrants*. New York, Free Press of Glencoe, 1961.

3. Erickson, E. H.: *Childhood and Society,* New York, Norton, 1950.

4. Hebb, D. O.: *The Organization of Behavior.* New York, Wiley, 1949.

5. Kirk, S. A. *et al.: Early Education of the Mentally Retarded.* Urbana, Univ. of Illinois Press, 1958

6. Lee, E. S.: Negro intelligence and selective migration: a Philadelphia test of the Klineberg hypothesis. *Amer. Sociol. Rev., 16*:227-233, 1951.

7. McClelland, D. C.: *Personality.* New York, William Sloane Assoc., 1951.

The informaticn which follows was used in the original symposium presentation to illustrate the principles contained in the body of the text. This material has been included since it is thought that it will be of particular interest to those who heard the original presentation as well as to those who wish to follow in some detail the implications of the text.   (Editor)

TABLE, 1

CORRELATIONS BETWEEN HEIGHT AT EACH AGE AND HEIGHT AT MATURITY (AGE 18)

(Tuddenham and Snyder, 1954)

Age	2	4	6	8	10	12	14	16	18
2	....	83	77	75	72	67	61	62	60
4	....	....	93	91	88	82	73	74	75
6	....	....	....	97	95	88	77	79	81
8	....	....	....	....	98	92	82	83	85
10	....	....	....	....	....	96	86	88	88
12	....	....	....	....	....	....	94	89	83
14	....	....	....	....	....	....	....	....	79
16	....	....	....	....	....	....	....	....	93

CORRELATIONS BETWEEN HEIGHT AT EACH AGE AND HEIGHT
AT AGE 18
(Tuddenham and Snyder, 1954)

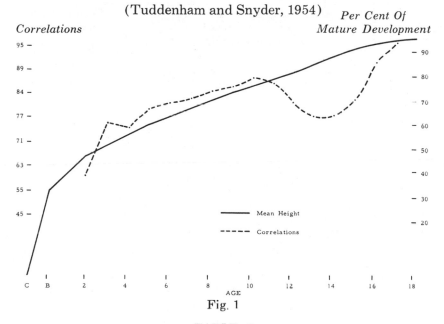

Fig. 1

TABLE 2

CORRELATIONS BETWEEN INTELLIGENCE AT EACH AGE
AND INTELLIGENCE AT AGE 17*
(Bayley, 1949)

	Months					Years			
Months	13	18	24	36	48	7	9	11	17
6	63	35	08	13	09	−12	04	−07	−04
13	..	60	47	41	23	13	13	02	002
18	..	..	50	54	41	33	14	11	20
24	..	..	..	74	47	60	43	43	41
36	..	..	..	..	64	53	55	48	56
48	..	..	..	..	..	71	76	69	71
Years									
7	..	..	..	..	..	..	79	74	79
9	..	..	..	..	..	..	..	90	84
11	..	..	..	..	..	..	..	..	92

* Tests administered were: California First Year Scale (1-15 mos), Calitor-
nia Preschool Tests (18-48 mos) and Stanford-Binet (7 to 17 years). Reliabilities: California First Year Tests (.80), California Preschool Tests (.85
est.), Stanford-Binet (.90)

CORRELATIONS BETWEEN INTELLIGENCE AT EACH AGE AND
INTELLIGENCE AT AGE 17 (BAYLEY, 1949)
CONTRASTED WITH THORNDIKE'S ABSOLUTE SCALE OF INTELLIGENCE

(Thorndike, 1927)

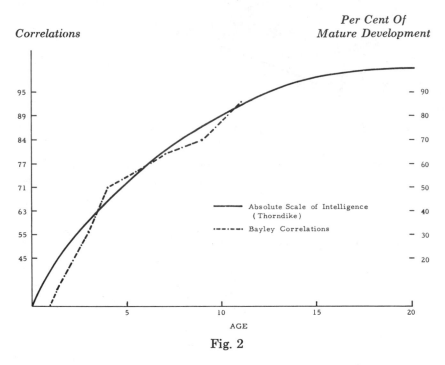

Fig. 2

TABLE 3

CORRELATIONS BETWEEN ACADEMIC ACHIEVEMENT

IN GRADES 4, 9, AND 12*

Grades	9	12
4	.72	.68
9	..	.91

* Grade 4 Test — Iowa Tests of Basic Skills
  Grade 9 and 12 Tests — Iowa Tests of Educational Development
  Reliability = .95

CORRELATIONS BETWEEN ACHIEVEMENT AT EACH AGE AND
ACHIEVEMENT AT AGE 18 (GRADE 12)
CONTRASTED WITH VOCABULARY DEVELOPMENT

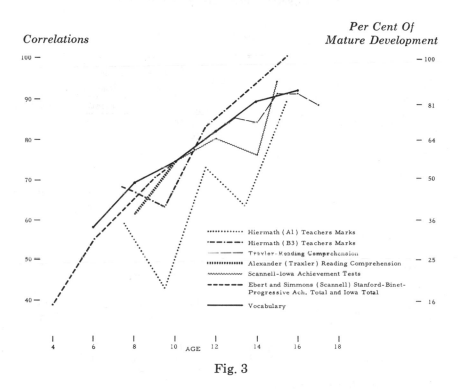

Fig. 3

TABLE 4

SELECTED LONGITUDINAL STUDIES OF INTERESTS, ATTITUDES

AND PERSONALITY CHARACTERISTICS

Ratings

				Correlations		
Characteristic	*Author*	*Sex*	*Ages*	*Observed*	*Theoretic-ally Expected°*	*Theoretical Reduced by Actual Reliability*
Aggression ..	Tuddenham	.... M	16-36	.68	.90	.68
	(1959)	F	16-36	.07	.90	.68
Indirect	Kagan and Moss	M	3-14	.00	.61	.49
Aggression	(1962)	M	6-14	.64	.73	.58
to peers		M	10-14	.71	.87	.70
		F	3-14	.53	.61	.49
		F	6-14	.56	.73	.58
		F	10-14	.60	.87	.70
Aggression to	Kagan and Moss	M	3-24	.02	.52	.42
Mother vs.	(1962)	M	6-24	.39	.64	.51
Adult Anger		M	14-24	.77	.87	.70
Arousal		F	3-24	.19	.52	.42
		F	6-24	.10	.64	.51
		F	14-24	.24	.87	.70
Sociometric	Bonney	M&F	8-9	.84	.96	.77
Position	(1943)	M&F	10-11	.67	.96	.77
	Cannon	M&F	15-18	.84	.92	.74
	(1958)	M&F	17-18	.83	.97	.79

* When test reliability is perfect.

TABLE 5
Inventories

Characteristic and Instrument	Author	Sex	Ages	Observed	Theoretically Expected°	Theoretical Reduced by Actual Reliability
Artistic-	Rosenberg	M&F	15-18	.65	.92	.82
Kuder	(1953)	M&F	18-22	.77	.96	.86
Preference ..	Herzberg ...... et al. (1954)					
Engineer-	Van Dusen	M&F	18-21	.85	.97	.92
Strong	(1940)					
Voc. Int.	Burnham	M	18-22	.78	.97	.92
	(1942)					
	Strong	M	22-27	.84	.99	.94
	(1934)					
Chemist-	Corring	M	15-18	.65	.92	.87
Strong	et al. (1941)					
Voc. Int.						
Religious-	Todd (1941) ...	M&F	18-20	.46	.97	.81
Alport-	Whitely	M	19-22	.66	.99	.83
Vernon	(1938)	M	20-22	.78	.99	.83
Values	Kelly (1955) ...		25-45	.60	.97	.81
Conservatism-	Nelson (1954) ..		19-33	.57	.98	.82
Radicalism						
Lentz						
Opionnaire ..						
Self-	Farnsworth	M	19-20	.77	.99	.80
Confidence-	(1938)	M	19-22	.66	.99	.80
Bernrenter	Kelly (1955) ...	M&F	25-45	.61	.97	.82
Personality ..						

Tests

Characteristic and Instrument	Author	Sex	Ages	Observed	Theoretically Expected°	Theoretical Reduced by Actual Reliability
Field	Witkin (1962) ..	M	10-17	.50	.80	.77
Dependence		M	14-17	.87	.92	.87
		F	10-17	.79	.80	.77
		F	14-17	.94	.92	.87
	Flugel (adapted from Witkin, 1962)	M	17-20	.85	.94	.89
Sophistication of body concept	Witkin (1962) ..	F	10-17	.63	.80	.72

* When test reliability is perfect.

Theoretical Curves for the Development
of Selected Human Characteristics

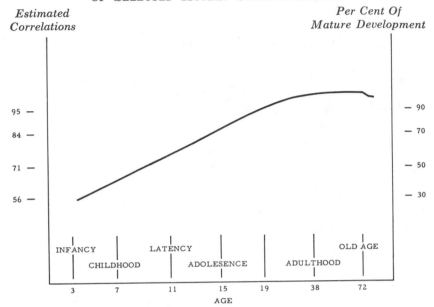

Estimated Correlations

Per Cent Of Mature Development

*The numerical values have been
added to Sanford's developmental curve.

Fig. 4

Development of Ego
(Adapted from Sanford, 1962)

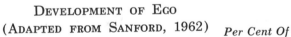

Per Cent Of Mature Development

Correlations

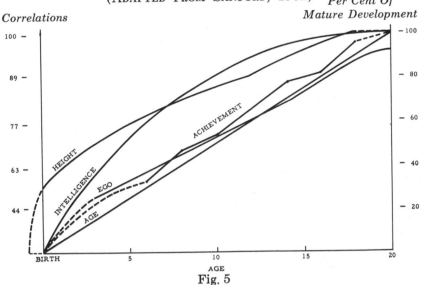

Fig. 5

BIBLIOGRAPHY

Physical

Tuddenham, R. D., and Snyder, M. M.: Physical growth of California boys and girls from birth to eighteen years. *Child Develpm., 1*: No. 2, Berkeley: U. of Cal. Press, 183-364, 1954.

Intelligence

Bagley, N.: Consistency and Variability on the growth of intelligence from birth to eighteen years. *J. Genet. Psychol., 75*:165-196, 1949.

Thorndike, E. L.: *The Measurement of Intelligence.* New York, Teachers College, Columbia Univ., 1927.

Achievement

Alexander, M.: Relation of an environment to intelligence and achievement. Unpublished Master's Study. University of Chicago, 196.

Ebert, E., and Simmons, K.: The Brush Foundation Study of child growth and development. I. Psychometric *Tests Monogr. Coc. for Res. in Child Develpm., 8*: No 2, 1-113, 1943.

Hiermath, N. R.: Relation of teachers' grades to environment: a longitudinal study. Unpublished Master's Study, University of Chicago, 1962.

Scannell, D. P.: Differential prediction of academic success from achievement test scores. Unpublished Ph.D. Dissertation, State University of Iowa, 1958.

Smith, M. K.: Measurement of the size of general English vocabulary through the elementary grades and high school. *Genet. Psychol. Monogr., 24*: Pt. 2, 311-345, 1941.

Traxler, A. E.: Reading growth of secondary school pupils during a five year period. Ach. Test Program in Ind. Schools and Supp. Studies. *Ed. Rec. Bureau,* Bull. 54, 1950.

Personality

Bonney, M. E.: The relative stability of social, intellectual and academic status in grades two to four and the inter-relationship between these various forms of growth. *J. Ed. Psychol., 34*:88-102, 1943.

Burnham, P.: Stability of interests. *School and Society, 55*:332-335, 1942.

Cannon, K. L.: Stability of sociometric scores of high school students. *J. Ed. Res., 52*:43-48, 1958.

Carring, L., Taylor, K. Van F., and Carter, H. D.: Permanence of vocational interests of high school boys. *J. Ed. Psychol., 32*:481-494, 1941.

Farnsworth, P. R.: A genetic study of the Bernrenter Personality Inventory. *J. Genet. Psychol., 52*:3-13, 1938.

Herzberg, F., Bouton, A., and Steiner, B. J.: Studies of the stability of the Kuder Preference Record. *Ed. and Psych Meas., 14*:90-100, 1954.

Kagan, J., and Moss, H. A.: *Birth to Maturity.* New York, Wiley and Sons, 1962.

Kelly, E. L.: Consistency of the adult personality. *Amer. Psychol., 10*:659-681, 1955.

Nelson, E. N. P.: Persistence of attitudes of college students fourteen years later. *Psychol. Monogr.,* Vol. *68,* No. 2, Whole No. 373, 1954.

Rosenberg, N.: Stability and maturation of Kuder interest patterns during high school. *Ed. and Psych. Meas., 13*:449-458, 1953.

Strong, E.: Permanence of vocational interests. *J. Ed. Psychol., 25*:336-344, 1934.

Todd, J. E.: Social views and the behavior of college students. Teachers College Bureau of Publications, Columbia Univ., 1941.

Tuddenham, R.: The constancy of personality ratings over two decades. *Genet. Psych. Monogr., 60*:3-29, 1959.

Van Dusen, A. C.: Permanence of vocational interests. *J. Ed. Psychol., 31*:401-424, 1940.

Whitely, R. C.: The constancy of personal values. *J. Abnorm. and Soc. Psychol, 33*:405-408, 1938.

Witkin, H. A. *et al.: Psychological Differentiation.* New York, Wiley and Sons, 1962.

Chapter 9

CHANGE AND CONTINUITY IN DEVELOPMENT*

JEROME KAGAN

Contemporary psychological thought is being influenced by new insights and exciting discoveries cmanating from a varicty of disciplines — including behavioral genetics, neurophysiology, comparative psychology, and ethology. The last two disciplines are giving considerable attention to the notion of critical periods in development. Stated most simply, this notion implies that the varied processes that punctuate development are being established at different rates during different time periods. The time during which a behavior is growing at its most rapid rate can be regarded as a critical psychological period. It is implied that external interference or disruption during the critical period will have a maximal effect—malevolently or benevolently—on the response in question. Identical interference at another time may have no effect on the response. There are many illustrations from biology that indicate the usefulness of this construct. In behavioral development, however, it has been more difficult to find clear cut examples of critical periods. Scott's (1958) work on social behavior in puppies and Hess' (1959) work on imprinting are two excellent examples of the importance of this idea for behavior.

This paper summarizes the findings of a recent study of a group of seventy-one adults between twenty and thirty years of age on whom we had extensive longitudinal data from birth

* This research was supported in part by Research Grant M-1260 from the National Institute of Mental Health, United States Public Health Service.

139

through adolescence. The relationships between selected behaviors during different childhood periods and adulthood were studied in an attempt to look for partial answers to three questions. First, is there stability between selected responses displayed during childhood and those manifested during the adult years. Second, for what responses does stability occur. Finally, during what critical periods does one see evidence of the establishment of strong predispositions that preview the future behavior of the individual.

PROCEDURE

The procedure involved quantitative assessment of two independent sets of data—ratings of adult behavior based on five to six hours of interview with each of seventy-one subjects who were between twenty and thirty years of age, and independent ratings (by a second psychologist) of the child's behavior during four developmental periods, 0-3, 3-6, 6-10, and 10-14 years of age. The childhood ratings were based on behavioral observations in the home, nursery school, day camp, public school, and interviews at the Institute. The major behaviors studied included aggression, dependency, passivity, intellectual achievement, social interaction anxiety, heterosexual behavior, and sex typed activities. Further, four kinds of maternal practices were assessed from the longitudinal data: maternal restrictiveness of the child, maternal criticism of the child, maternal protection, and maternal acceleration of the child's cognitive and motor development.

Independent ratings of both the longitudinal and the adult interview material produced satisfactory inter-rater reliabilities. The average reliability for the longitudinal data was in the high 70's; the average reliability for the adult interview variables was in the 80's, with 87% per cent of the coefficients over .70. Several of the variables from the longitudinal and adult interview schedule were omitted because they did not furnish adequate inter-rater reliabilities. The analysis of the data involved correlation between each of the childhood variables, for each of the four developmental periods, with the behavior variables derived from the adult interview.

RESULTS

Considering the space limitations, we can only summarize briefly the major results that emerged from this analysis. The complete study is presented elsewhere (Kagan and Moss, 1962).

STABILITY OF BEHAVIOR AS A
FUNCTION OF SEX TYPING

The most dramatic finding was that many of the behaviors displayed during the period six to ten years of age were relatively good predictors of phenotypically similar behavior during early adulthood. For example, passive withdrawal from stressful situations, dependence on one's family, ease of anger arousal, involvement in intellectual mastery, social interaction anxiety, adoption of sex typed activities, and heterosexual behavior in adulthood were each related to reasonably analogous behavioral dispositions during the school years. However, the degree of stability of each of these responses was intimately dependent upon its congruence with traditional standards for sex role characteristics. For example, passive and dependent behavior was stable from childhood to adulthood for females but not for males; whereas aggressive and sexual behavior were stable from childhood to adulthood for males but not for females. Intellectual achievement, on the other hand, which is culturally sanctioned for both sexes displayed continuity for both men and women. The differential stability of passivity, dependence, aggression, and sexuality emphasizes the importance of cultural rules in determining behavioral change and stability. Passive and dependent behavior are subjected to consistent cultural disapproval for men but not for women. This disapproval is communicated to the male through direct rewards and punishments issued by peers and adults, as well as through the characteristics associated with ideal role models—be they real or the fantasied product of the public media. Thus a dependent ten year old will gradually inhibit blatant expression of dependency in order to avoid rejection and live up to his ego ideal.

A low threshold for anger, direct aggressive retaliation, or sexual behavior are disproportionately punished among females. Males were given greater license in these areas. The data revealed that childhood rage reactions predicted adult aggressive behavior for men but not for women; early adolescent sexual behavior predicted sexual patterns in adulthood for men but not for women. It is suggested that aggressive girls gradually inhibit open display of this behavior for it conflicts with their standards and leads to social rejection.

Intellectual mastery is positively sanctioned for both sexes and both of these behaviors showed a high degree of continuity for males and females from the early school years to adulthood. In selected instances even preschool behavior was related to a similar disposition in adulthood. For example, the preschool girl's involvement in achievement tasks predicted her concern with intellectual mastery in adulthood ($r = .44$, $p < .05$).

Even the children who were reared by families who did not consciously attempt to mold the child in strict concordance with traditional sex role standards responded to the pressures of the extra-familial environment. The aggressive girls learned to inhibit direct expression of aggressive behavior; the dependent boys gradually placed inhibition upon urges toward dependent overtures to others.

Moreover, the occurrence of derivatives of child behavior was related to the sex role appropriateness of the childhood response. Passivity among young boys predicted non-competitiveness, sexual anxiety, and social apprehension in adult men, although it did not predict direct dependent overtures to social objects. A tendency toward rage reactions in young girls predicted intellectual competitiveness, masculine interests, and dependency conflict in adult women, but was not related to direct expression of aggression in adulthood. It would appear that when a childhood behavior is congruent with traditional sex role standards it will be predictive of phenotypically similar behavior in adulthood. When it conflicts with sex role standards the relevant motive is more likely to find expression in theoretically consistent substitute behaviors that are socially more acceptable than the original response. Stated pithily, the individual's desire to mold his overt behavior in concordance with the culture's definition of sex appropriate responses is a major determinant of the patterns of continuity and discontinuity in his development.

It should be noted that not all childhood responses displayed long-term continuity. Compulsivity and irrational fears during childhood were not predictive of similar responses during adulthood. Moreover task persistence and excessive irritability *during the first three years of life* showed no relationship to phenotypically similar behaviors during later childhood or adulthood.

Our interpretation of the data from this study rests heavily upon sex role identification. A sex role standard is a cognitive representation of the attributes, behaviors, and attitudes that are associated with the concepts male and female in a given culture. A sex role standard summarizes the culturally appropriate characteristics for males and females. The significance of a sex role standard rests with its governing influence on the initiation and maintenance of a broad band of behaviors, including the stability of behavior over long periods of time. We suggest that the child wishes to believe that his behavior is consistent with the standard that represents the ideal boy or girl. There will be a core of communality in this concept among all members of a culture, but there will be differences from child to child depending upon the particular familial milieu in which he was raised. Many behavioral choices are made in the service of maintaining the child's belief that his behaviors, feelings, and thoughts are congruent with those of the perfect male or female. Correlatively many behavioral choices are governed by the desire to avoid elicitation of the thought, "I am not behaving in a way congruent with my biological sex." One of the important implications of these data for gerontological work relates to the differential occurrence of conflict at time of the menopouse. It may be that the ease with which a woman passes through this critical period will be related to her sex role identification. The degree to which the standard feminine attributes prescribed by the culture (i.e., attractiveness, nurturant relation to children, acceptance by men) are critical for a woman's self concept may influence the degree to which she will suffer anxiety and tension during this period. It would be of interest to do a prospective study in which measures of sex role identification obtained on women in their thirties were related to the degree to which psychopathology evidenced itself 15-20 years later.

THE EARLY SCHOOL YEARS AS A CRITICAL PERIOD

In general, the continuity between child and adult behavior became manifest during the first four years of school. This relation was clearest for withdrawal tendencies, involvement in task mastery, social spontaneity, and adoption of traditional sex typed interests. The poorer predictive power of responses during the preschool years suggests that developments during the period 6-10 induce important changes in the child's behavioral organization. The primary events in this period include (a) identification with the parents and a concomitant attempt to adopt the values and overt responses of the parent, (b) the realization that mastery of intellective skills is both a cultural requirement as well as a source of satisfaction and (c) the encounter with the peer group. The latter experience forces the child to accomodate, to some degree, to the values and evaluations made by peers. For some children, peer experiences strengthen patterns of dominance, social spontaneity and positive self-evaluation. For others, peer rejection and a perception of marked deviation from peer valued attributes lead to social anxiety, submission, and a sense of ineffectiveness. Some children in the latter group develop compensatory domains of confidence that do not involve peer interaction. But those who are unable to do so continue to anticipate failure when faced with task or social challenges. For a large group of children the first four years of contact with the school and peer environments crystallize tendencies that will be maintained through young adulthood.

THE SLEEPER EFFECT

One of the major characteristics of psychological phenomena is their long time course. The bombardment of atomic nuclei or chemical reactions usually leads to effects that are immediate— sometimes too fast to measure. In psychological development, however, the effects of specific early experiences are often not evidenced for long periods of time. There may be a lag between a cause and open manifestation of the effect. One way to detect a time lag between cause and effect is to uncover a stronger relation between a variable measured early and one measured late in development than between similar variables measured contemporaneously or more contiguously in time. We have called this set of statistical circumstances the "sleeper effect." The phrase "sleeper effect" is purely descriptive, for such an effect could occur for a variety of reasons.

We noted this effect twice in our data. In one instance, passivity and fear of bodily harm during the first three years of life were better predictors of love object dependency in adult men than later assessment of these childhood responses. It is possible that manifestations of passivity and fear of harm in a young boy are less disguised during the preschool and school years. During the later age periods the boy learns to inhibit open expression of passivity and fear for these are immature reactions that are subject to disapproval. Thus, assessment of passivity or bodily harm anxiety from behavioral observation at age six may be less sensitive than an evaluation of these tendencies during the third year of life. During this earlier period the child's defenses are weaker and he is less able, or less highly motivated, to prevent the anxiety-based reactions from gaining direct expression. However, a latent predisposition to passivity may be present during the school years and may find expression in adolescent and adult derivative reactions.

A second set of phenomena we have called the "sleeper effect" occurred when selected maternal practices during the first three years of life turned out to be more sensitive predictors of pre-adolescent and adult behavior than evaluations of similar maternal practices later in childhood. For example, a hypercritical maternal attitude toward a daugther during the first three years predicted adult achievement behavior (r= .59, p <.01). However, maternal criticism of daughters during ages three to ten showed a negligible relationship with achievement behavior in adult women. Similarly maternal protection of daughters during the first three years predicted adult withdrawal from stress (r= .52, p <.01); whereas protection during age three to ten showed no relation to adult withdrawal. One explanation for these results rests on the assumption that the reciprocal nature of the mother-child interaction changes with time. The child's ability to provoke relatively permanent changes in specific maternal reactions toward him increases with age.

A six year old is more likely to produce a major alteration in the mother's characteristic behavior toward the child than is a two year old. The mother-child dyad is a feed-back system, and the degree to which the child's actions have the power to change the mother's behavior increases with development. During infancy the child's personality is ambiguous and the discrepancy between her standard and what she perceives in her child is necessarily small. The mother sees the child as she would like to see him, and he is an object primarily to be acted upon. The form and content of many maternal behaviors toward an infant are not as contaminated by the effect of the child's behavior on her as her behavior toward a ten year old. To illustrate, a mother's concern with the intellectual achievement of her two year old is more likely an index of her basic needs and values than is her degree of concern with the performance of her ten year old who might be failing in school. Many mothers change their expectations as the child develops, and a mother's lack of concern with the school achievement of her ten year old daughter who is failing could be a recently acquired defensive maneuver to protect the mother from disappointment. Similarly encouragement of independence or over-protection of a ten year old may be newly developed reactive measures to a child's excessive dependence or fragile defenses respectively. These findings suggest that the elucidation of cause-effect relations in human development may require, for selected questions, a longitudinal design.

This conclusion also applies to research on individuals in the last three decades of life. It is not unreasonable to assume that the quality of the relationship a young mother has with her child and the degree to which the young thirty year old parent derives satisfaction from the child will be more predictive of the stress the mother might experience during the menopause than a mother's behavior with the child when it is a young adult. The point we are trying to make is that significant psychological conflicts or strengths are established at maximal intensity during certain times. These processes may lie dormant until crises occur, ten, fifteen, or twenty years later. Complete understanding of the etiology of the crisis reaction may not be possible if one does not know the behaviors that occurred twenty years before.

SUMMARY

This paper has summarized the results and implications of a much larger study of a group of young adults on whom extensive longitudinal data were available. The major conclusions were that stability of behavior during the adolescent and adult years is intimately dependent upon congruence with sex role standards. It was suggested that the construct of sex role identification—(i.e., the desire of an individual to match his behavior to a sex role standard) continues throughout life and may be an important variable to study in investigations of differential vulnerability to psychopathological reactions during the fourth and fifth decades of life.

A second conclusion emphasized the importance of the "sleeper effect." The phrase "sleeper effect" refers to the occurrence of higher correlations between two variables measured far apart in time, than similar variables measure contemporaneously. It was argued that the answers to selected psychological questions demand a longitudinal design in order to elucidate the true cause-effect relationships.

REFERENCES

1. Hess, E. H.: Two conditions limiting critical age for imprinting. *J. comp. physiol. Psychol.,* 1959, 52.515-518.

2. Kagan, J., and Moss, H. A.: *Birth to Maturity*. New York, John Wiley, 1962.

3. Scott, J. P.: Critical periods in social behavior in puppies. *Psychosom. Med., 20*:42-54, 1958.

Chapter 10

PERSONALITY AND OTHER CORRELATES OF IQ CHANGE IN WOMEN*

LESTER W. SONTAG AND MARY O. KIBLER

This paper deals with the phenomenon of *IQ* change in adult men and women. We will concern ourselves with two questions: is there a significant change in the mean *IQ* of a sample of our population over a seventeen year period, and are there meaningful correlates of these changes? We do find provocative personality, perceptual, and physiological characteristics associated with *IQ* change among the women. These characteristics were derived from psychiatric interviews, perceptual-conceptual tests, and autonomic measurements. All of the data are a product of the longitudinal study at The Fels Research Institute.

It is often assumed that performance on mental tests declines after the age of twenty (19, 26). It is also generally believed that this decline continues with advancing years. On the other hand, some investigators have found *IQ* increases with age (1, 10, 18) in some studies up to the age of sixty. Advocates of both views have suggested a variety of explanations for the observed changes. For many reasons—problems of matching cross-sectional samples, the difficulties inherent in comparing scores of different *IQ* tests, and a general decline in speed of performance—a convincing explanation of the problem is difficult to obtain. There is great individual variability in score, a fact that is well substantiated by both longitudinal and non-longitudinal studies.

* This research was supported in part by Research Grant M-1260 from the National Institutes of Health, United States Public Health Service.

CORRELATES OF CHANGE IN IQ —
NON-LONGITUDINAL STUDIES

A variety of studies have explored and attempted to explain the basis for *IQ* changes. Howell (9) compared the performance of fifty men and fifty women on six subtests of the Wechsler Bellevue Intelligence Test. His groups were equated for age over a range of sixty to eighty-nine years, and there were no significant sex differences in the decline which he found. In addition, the decline was independent of educational achievement and level of intelligence. Doppelt and Wallace (4) studied a relatively homogeneous sample of men and women from Kansas City, aged sixty to seventy-five, and found no significant difference in decline between sexes, or for controlled speed versus non-speed tests. They did find, however, a slightly greater and earlier decline on performance subtests than on verbal tests. Eisdorfer (5) also discovered greater performance decline on 130 subjects over sixty years old. He divided his group by sex, race, socio-economic level, intellectual level, and health, but found that none of these variables could explain the differential decline. Ghiselli (7), unlike the investigators already mentioned, noted no downward trend in a group of 1400 subjects aged twenty to sixty-five. His testing conditions put no premium on speed and he used well-educated subjects—both crucial factors in *IQ* change with age according to his hypothesis. Over 1000 rural New England villagers, age ten to sixty, were studied by Jones and Conrad (11) using the Army Alpha Test. Their overall finding was that peak performance occurs between eighteen and twenty-one years with a gradual decline to fifty-five years of age. These investigators were unable to explain their findings on the basis of lack of motivation, lack of test practice, remoteness from school, speed control, or failing perceptual abilities. They did point out, as other investigators have (8, 9, 15, 21), that the decline varied among subtests, and that there were greater individual differences *within* adult age groups than *between* the ages.

In general then, there is disagreement among cross-sectional studies over whether performance on mental tests universally begins to decline after twenty years, in what populations it does

decline, and the factors associated with *IQ* changes during the last
half of life. We have found no data derived from cross-sectional
studies that help to explain *IQ* changes at different age levels in
adult populations.

CORRELATES OF CHANGE IN IQ —
LONGITUDINAL STUDIES

One of the first longitudinal studies in this area was Owens'
investigation (20) of the performance of 127 males on the Army
Alpha Test over a thirty year period. Owens found a general
increase in scores, although this increase was greatest for subjects
under fifty at the time of the second test. Owens related his
mental test results to answer on a "Personal Information Sheet"
and found that some educational and socio-economic factors differentiated changes in performance on specific subtests. Performance data on the Terman Group Test for 110 men and women
in the Oakland Growth Study was reported by Jones (10). Over
a sixteen year interval (17-33 years of age) 95 per cent of the
group showed a gain in total score, half of which was attributed
to improvement in vocabulary. Bayley and Oden (1) were unable
to account for similar changes occurring over a twelve year period
with Terman's gifted subjects; they suggested that differences in
motivation might play a role, but they presented no evidence for
this conjecture.

The Fels Research Institute's study of changes in *IQ* in children (23) tested serially from two and a half to twelve years of
age demonstrated a strong relationship between personality variables and changes in *IQ*. The authors postulated that changes
in performance on a Binet, or any mental test, would be related
to the ways and means an individual develops in an attempt to
achieve emotional comfort. In short, the nature of his psychological defenses and devices—whether his motivation was toward
independent functioning, problem-solving and competition, or
towards eliciting warmth and acceptance by peer and adult
groups—was the vital determinant of improvement or deterioration
in his performance. If the person sought social acceptance and
he was a "people's people," the motivation to acquire new intel-

lectual skills and to compete in an intellectual atmosphere was minimum. The individual did not take maximum advantage of opportunities in these areas. On the other hand, if the individual did not seek dependent gratification excessively, and developed mastery at problems, intellectual achievement, and successful competition as a source of reassurance, he acquired those skills that led to better performance on the Binet and other mental tests. Of the 140 children studied, all of whom had had Binets administered regularly, one-fourth increased a minimum of twelve and a maximum of 57.8 *IQ* points over a five and a half year period, and one-fourth decreased from 10.7 to 27.7 *IQ* points over the same period (age 5½ to 11). Ratings of behavior and personality variables on these children at age six and ten were used to test the hypotheses described above. The materials rated were records and observations obtained in the home, school, and nursery school over the first twelve years of life. The evidence supported the hypothesis. Ratings at age ten of independence, aggressiveness. self-initiation, problem-solving, competitiveness, and competitiveness in a scholastic situation, were clearly related to *IQ* increase. These results suggested the wisdom of assessing the validity of this general hypothesis on an older group.

ADULT IQ DATA

As a part of the total longitudinal effort at the Fels Research Institute, the parents of the children have also been studied. The group is primarily of French, English, German and Irish extraction. They are a middle class southern Ohio population who, in the main, have been residents of the state for at least two generations. The high educational achievement of the entire Fels group is illustrated by the fact that 61 percent of the men and 65 per cent of the women have one or more years of college.

Seventy-two women and fifty-nine men, who are parents of the children in our longitudinal study, were administered two Otis Mental Tests. The women's mean age at the first test was thirty-two (range of 20-46 years), and the mean age for the men at the first test was thirty-five (range 23-56 years). For both groups, the mean interval between the first and second Otis tests was seventeen years (10-23 year range). The mean *IQ* score for the women at the first test at age thirty-two was 105.8 with a standard deviation of 14.1, and at the second test, 105.1 with a standard deviation of 13.9. The *IQ* of the men at the first test (mean age 35) was 105.8 with a standard deviation of 17.7, almost exactly that of the woman, and at the second test it was 104.6 with a standard deviation of 16.4. The mean change in Otis *IQ* of the women was −.7 points and of the men, −1.2 points. Neither of these declines is statistically significant. There was, however, great variation among individuals. In both sexes some individuals improved their score at the second test, and some declined. Two women increased 11 points, and one lost 12 points. Among the men, the greatest increase was 11 points, and the greatest decrease was 16 points. While these changes are of a smaller magnitude than were found in the study of children's *IQ*s, they are sufficienty large to provoke a search for possible correlates or explanations of these changes. One hypothesis advanced was that some of the psychological defenses and devices associated with the rises and declines in the *IQ*s of children might be operative in the adult changes. We attempted, therefore, to appraise personality variables by means of ratings made from psychiatric interviews.

PSYCHIATRIC INTERVIEW RATINGS

The subjects available for the interview sessions were twenty-two of the seventy-two women who had mental tests administered at seventeen year intervals. For this group of twenty-two, the average interval between tests was eighteen years (mean age Test I, 33; Test II, 51). The distribution of scores for Test I had a mean of 103.4 and standard deviation of 15.4: the mean score on the second test was 102.5 with a standard deviation of 13.4, and the overall change was − .9 *IQ* points. These parameters are not appreciably different from the total group.

For the interview, a rating scale was devised to assess personality variables and social habits. Scatter diagrams were drawn plotting the ratings for each interview variable against the change in *IQ*. The statistical significance of each relationship was assessed by the Fisher Exact Probability Test (22). Table I below lists the thirty interview variables and the relation of each to *IQ* increases.

TABLE 1

RELATION BETWEEN PSYCHIATRIC INTERVIEW RATINGS AND IQ
INCREASE (DETERMINED BY THE FISHER EXACT PROBABILITY TEST)

Variable	Direction	Significance Level
Need for dependence on spouse	Neg.	.10[a]
Degree of gratification of that need		NS
Need for dependence on children		NS
Degree of gratification of that need		NS
Dependence on boss		NS
Dependence on church		NS
Dependence on peer groups and organizations	Neg.	.02[a]
Feelings of financial security		NS
Dependency conflict		NS
Inhibitions of striving for dependent gratification	Neg.	.04[b]
Hostility to life		NS
Hostility to employers	Pos.	.07[c]
Hostility to spouse		NS
Hostility to children	Neg.	.10[a]
Degree of expression of hostility		NS
Self image		NS
Degree to which mastery is basis of self satisfaction		NS
Intellectual mastery		NS
Problem or skill mastery	Pos.	.10[a]
Anxiety		NS
Depression		NS
Psychosomatic illness		NS
Hypochondria		NS
Passive-active-social (degree of social activity)	Neg.	.01[a]
Passive-active-to task obstacles		NS
Anxiety for the future		NS
Reaction to test procedure		NS
Impulsive behavior in life		NS
Degree of affect expressed		NS
Freedom of disclosing life history		NS

[a] $N = 22$
[b] $N = 9$
[c] $N = 16$

It is evident from a glance at the rating scale variables and the significance of their relationship to *IQ* increase or decrease that the theme of dependence-independence is of importance. Need for dependence on spouse is negatively related to *IQ* increase at a suggestive, but not statistically significant, level. Dependence on peer groups and organizations, social activity, and inhibitions of dependent need, all bear a high *negative* relationship to *IQ* increase, as was found in the previous study of children's *IQ* change. The variable of skill mastery has a suggestive, but not statistically significant positive relationship to *IQ* increase. The marginal level of significance might be ascribed to the fact that women in the fifty year age range have restricted opportunity to engage in problem-solving situations.

At this point the question must be asked as to whether rise or fall in *IQ* may not be dependent on initial level of *IQ* and represent a regression to the mean. There was no statistically significant relation between the level of *IQ* at the first or second Otis test and whether it rose or fell for the entire sample of seventy-two women. Neither is there any significant relation between initial or second *IQ* and dependency on spouse, peer groups and organizations, inhibition of dependent need, or degree of social activity.

During the time the interviews were conducted, other Fels investigators were conducting experiments with portions of our sample of seventy-two women. Two areas are included in this study because of relevant results from other, usually younger, samples suggesting the possibility that these areas might provide clues to the enigma of adult *IQ* change. The two problem areas are Dr. John Lacey's autonomic activity measures, and Dr. Jerome Kagan's work on conceptual styles. To date, these data are available on only a part of the group of women and not on the men.

AUTONOMIC ACTIVITY

Twenty-two of the mothers participated in a study in the Psychophysiology Department. The primary measure discussed here is the magnitude of the sinus arrhythmia (fluctuations in heart rate) during periods of rest. Experiments with these mothers give support to the Laceys' theory that the amount of fluctuation of heart rate at rest, "reliably characterize(s) an individual." The individual's pattern is reproducible under different forms of stress, in other words, "with varying physiological and psychological demands on the organism, and they are persistent over long periods of time." One can be characterized as an autonomic "stabile" (i.e., identified by minimal amplitude of oscillation in heart rate) in contrast to a cardiac "labile" who displays a maximum amplitude in cardiac oscillation (16).

Study of the behavioral significance of differences in cardiac arrhythmia have led to experiments on speed of reaction in simple motor tasks. The results of these studies suggest a relationship between reaction time as a function of the foreperiod and cardiac arrhythmia. The "foreperiod" in a reaction time task is the preparation period. The subject is alerted that the stimulus will soon appear, and the time that elapses between this warning and the signal is called the foreperiod. The individual's expectation of the length of this waiting period influences his speed of response. Thus, if the *preceding* foreperiod is short and his expectation for the current trial is for a short foreperiod, the reaction time of his response may be affected. The effect of this expectation on performance was found to differ for stabiles and labiles. The reaction times of stabiles were more affected by variations in current and preceding foreperiods than that of labiles, suggesting that stabiles are more passive and compliant to the environment. Labiles show a faster reaction time than stabiles under all conditions and greater ability to maintain a readiness to respond (15).

Moreover, among thirty Fels males, age nineteen-twenty-nine, Dr. Kagan found that cardiac labiles were rated significantly higher than stabiles on the following psychological variables: reluctance to be dependent on love objects; conflict over dependency; strivings for achievement; anxiety over erotic activity; compulsive behavior vacillation with decisions; and introspectiveness (13).

These provocative findings aroused our curiosity about the possible relationship among the magnitude of sinus arrhythmia at rest, the psychiatric interview ratings, and *IQ* change in our middle aged female group. The significance levels for these variables were determined with the Fisher Exact Probability Test as previously described and are listed in the following table.

TABLE 2

RELATION BETWEEN PSYCHOLOGICAL VARIABLES (INTERVIEW
RATINGS AND IQ INCREASE) AND CARDIAC LABILITY SCORES
(DETERMINED BY THE FISHER EXACT PROBABILITY TEST)

Variable	Direction	Significance Level
Need for dependence on spouse		NS
Degree of gratification of that need		NS
Need for dependence on children		NS
Degree of gratification of that need		NS
Dependence on boss		NS
Dependence on church		NS
Dependence on peer groups and organizations ..	Pos.	.08[a]
Feelings of financial security		NS
Dependency conflict		NS
Inhibitions of striving for dep. grat.		NS
Hostility to life		NS
Hostility to employers		NS
Hostility to spouse		NS
Hostility to children		NS
Degree of expression of hostility		NS
Self image		NS
Degree mastery is basis of self satisfaction		NS
Intellectual mastery		NS
Problem or skill mastery		NS
Anxiety		NS
Depression	Neg.	.05[a]
Psychosomatic illness		NS
Hypochondria	Neg.	.05[a]
Passive-active-social	Pos.	.02[a]
Passive-active-to task obstacles		NS
Anxiety for the future		NS
Reaction to test procedure	Pos.	.08[a]
Impulsive behavior in life		NS
Degree of affect expressed		NS
Freedom of disclosing life history	Neg.	.01[a]
IQ increase	Neg.	.02[b]

[a] N = 22
[b] N = 18

Few conclusive statements can be made from these results, but several points are worth noting. The socially passive individuals tended to be stabile, a fact which agrees with the suggestion from the reaction time experiments that stabiles are passive to the environment. In the case of *IQ* performance, the more labile women *decreased* in *IQ* over the years. This result is out of phase with Kagan's personality findings, from which one would expect the less dependent, more introspective labiles to increase in *IQ* score. Since Kagan's findings were on males and ours on females, the sex of the subject may be critical in this relationship. The most significant finding statistically was that labiles typically received a lower rating than stabiles on "freedom of disclosing life history" in the interview. Perhaps the stabiles respond more freely to the possibilities for dependence and sociability in the interview situation while labiles would be reluctant to participate on either basis. One can only conjecture from the available data.

PERCEPTUAL-COGNITIVE FUNCTIONING

Dr. Jerome Kagan of the Fels Psychology Department, administered two perceptual-conceptual tests to the mothers. One was a perceptual learning task in which twenty-six mothers participated. They were asked to learn to associate eight nonsense words with each of eight geometric designs. After learning to a criterion, each mother was presented with only a part of the original design. A figure, ground, form, or element was presented and she had to apply the correct syllable. The second test was the Gottschaldt Embedded Figures Test, in which the subjects were to find a hidden figure embedded in a complex design.

The rationale behind the administration of these tests follows. Witkin (27) has suggested that superior performance on the Embedded Figures Test was an index of field independence. Field independent subjects typically are rated as more independent socially, more self-confident and less likely to withdraw from difficult tasks, than field-*dependent* subjects. Such characteristics should be associated with *IQ* increases

Kagan has unpublished data to indicate that the degree to which the subject fractionates a visual stimulus during learning is positively associated with a less impulsive and more reflective approach to problems. One might conjecture that a reflective approach to problems would facilitate performance on a variety of mental tests, including the Otis. Thus, fractionation of the visual designs (as reflected in correct labeling of the solitary elements of the design on the transfer task) was expected to be related to *IQ* increase.

We administered these two perceptual tests—fractionation of a design during learning and the Embedded Figures Test—to a group of middle-aged women to see if field independence and/or fractionation were related to increase in *IQ*, high ratings of intellectual mastery, problem and skill mastery, and low dependency and sociability ratings, as one might expect from the findings with Fels children. The Fisher Exact Probability scores for these relationships are listed below.

TABLE 3

Fisher Exact Probability Scores for the Relation Between the Psychological Variables (Interview Ratings and IQ Increased), and Figure Recognition, and Ground Recognition, and Errors in the Embedded Figures Test

Interview Variables	Figure Recognition Dir. Sig. Level		Ground Recognition Dir. Sig. Level		EFT Errors Dir. Sig. Level	
Need for dependence on spouse	NS		NS		NS	
Degree of gratification of that need	NS		NS		NS	
Need for dependence on children	NS		NS		NS	
Degree of gratification of that need	NS		NS		NS	
Dependence on boss	NS		NS		NS	
Dependence on church	NS		NS		NS	
Dependence on peer groups and organizations	NS		Neg.	.02[a]	NS	
Feelings of financial security	NS		NS		NS	
Dependency conflict	NS		NS		NS	
Inhibitions of striving for dep. grat.	NS		NS		NS	

Interview Variables	Figure Recognition Dir. Sig. Level		Ground Recognition Dir. Sig. Level		EFT Errors Dir. Sig. Level	
Hostility to life	NS		NS		NS	
Hostility to employers	NS		NS		NS	
Hostility to spouse	NS		NS		NS	
Hostility to children	NS		NS		NS	
Degree of expression of hostility	NS		NS		NS	
Self image	NS		NS		NS	
Degree mastery is basis of self satisfaction	NS		NS		NS	
Intellectual mastery	NS		NS		NS	
Problem or skill mastery ...	NS		NS		NS	
Anxiety	NS		NS		NS	
Depression	NS		NS		NS	
Psychosomatic illness	NS		NS		NS	
Hypochondria	NS		NS		NS	
Passive-active-social	NS		Neg.	.06[a]	NS	
Passive-active-to task obstacles	NS		NS		NS	
Anxiety for the future	NS		NS		NS	
Reaction to test procedure..	NS		NS		NS	
Impulsive behavior in life ..	NS		NS		NS	
Degree of affect expressed ..	NS		NS		NS	
Freedom of disclosing life history	NS		NS		NS	
IQ increase	NS		NS		Pos.	.08[b]

[a] $N = 26$
[b] $N = 20$

As can be seen from the table, "dependence on peer groups and organizations," and "passive-active-social" ratings showed a significant negative relation to accurate labeling of the ground components of the geometric designs. Thus, low fractionation went with passivity. An individual who was dependent on peer groups and organizations and who was socially active was likely to perform poorly when asked to recognize the background of a complex design. While such results are far from conclusive, they do represent a trend in the expected direction. Occurrence of IQ increase was only moderately related to Embedded Figures Test performance and in a direction not predicted. Errors on the Embedded Figures Test were related to *increases* in *IQ*.

SUMMARY AND CONCLUSIONS

Otis Mental Ability Test scores of seventy-two women and fifty-nine men showed no significant change in level of *IQ* over a mean period of seventeen years. Within the group, many individuals did change, in some instances up and in others, down. Since childhood changes in *IQ* from age two and one half to twelve were related to certain characteristics of personality structure, a group of twenty-two Fels mothers were given psychiatric interviews and were subsequently rated on thirty personality and behavioral variables. Significance of the relationship of these variables to *IQ* change (and other characteristics) was tested by means of the Fisher Exact Probability Test. The results, like those in the study of Fels children's *IQ* changes, showed that the highly social and dependent personality is more likely to have a declining *IQ*. The relationship between certain aspects of autonomic behavior and cognitive style, on the one hand, and interview ratings and *IQ* change on the other, yielded some positive and suggestive results.

REFERENCES

1. Bayley, N., and Oden, M. H.: The maintenance of intellectual ability in gifted adults. *J. Geront., 10*:91-107, 1955.

2. Birren, J. E.: Psychological limitations that occur with age. *Publ. Hlth. Rep., Wash., 71*:1173-1178, 1956.

3. Cohen, J.: The factorial structure of the WAIS between early adulthood and old age. *J. Consult. Psychol., 21*:283-290, 1957.

4. Doppelt, J. E., and Wallace, W. L.: Standardization of the Wechsler Adult Intelligence Scale for older persons. *J. Abnorm. Soc. Psychol., 51*:312-330, 1955.

5. Eisdorfer, C., Busse, E. W., and Cohen, L. D.: The WAIS performance of an aged sample: the relationship between verbal and performance IQs. *J. Geront., 14*:197-201, 1959.

6. Fox, C., and Birren, J. E.: The differential decline of subtest scores of the Wechsler-Bellevue Intelligence Scale in 60-69 year old individuals. *J. Genet. Psychol., 77*:313-317, 1950.

7. Ghiselli, E. E.: The relationship between intelligence and age among superior adults. *J. Genet. Psychol., 90*:131-142, 1957.

8. Howell, R. J.: Changes in Wechsler subtest scores with age. *J. Consult. Psychol., 19:*47-50, 1955.

9. Howell, R. J.: Sex differences and educational influences on a mental deterioration scale. *J. Geront., 10:*190-193, 1955.

10. Jones, H. E.: Consistency and change in early maturity. *Vita Humana, 1:*43-51, 1958.

11. Jones, H. E., and Conrad, H. S.: The growth and decline of intelligence, etc. *Genet. Psychol. Monog., XIII:*223-298, 1933.

12. Kagan, J., Moss, H., and Sigel, I.: Conceptual style and the use of affect labels. *Merrill-Palmer Quarterly of Behavior and Development.* No. 4, *6,* 1960.

13. Kagan, J.: Unpublished paper.

14. Kamin, L. J.: Differential changes in mental abilities in old age. *J. Geront., 12:*66-70, 1957.

15. Lacey, J. I., and Lacey, B. C.: The relationship of resting autonomic activity to motor impulsivity. *Res. Publ. Assn. Res. Nerv. & Ment. Dis., 36:*144-209, 1958.

16. Lacey, J. I. and Lacey, B. C.: (In preparation)

17. Lorge, I.: The influence of the test upon the nature of mental decline as a function of age. *J. Ed. Psychol., 27:*100-110, 1936.

18. McHugh, R. B., and Owens, W. A.: Age changes in mental organization—a longitudinal study. *J. Geront., 9:*296-302, 1954.

19. Miles, C. C., and Miles, W. R.: The correlation of intelligence scores and chronological age from early to late maturity. *Amer. J. of Psychol., 44:*44-78, 1932.

20. Owens, W. A.: Age and mental abilities: a longitudinal study. *Genet. Psychol. Mong., 48:*3-52, 1953.

21. Schaie, K. W.: Rigidity-flexibility and intelligence: a cross-sectional study of the adult life span from 20 to 70 years. *Psychol. Monog., 72:*26, 1958.

22. Siegel, S.: *Nonparametric Statistics.* McGraw-Hill Book Co., Inc. 1956, 96-100.

23. Sontag, L. W., Baker, C. T., and Nelson, V. L.: Mental Growth and personality development: a longitudinal study. *Monograph of the Society for Research in Child Development, 23:* Serial No. 68, No. 2, 1958.

24. Sorenson, H.: Mental ability over a wide range of adult ages. *J. of Applied Psychol., 17:*729-744, 1933.

25. Stoddard, G. D.: *The Meaning of Intelligence.* The MacMillan Co., Part III, New York, 1945.

26. Wechsler, D.: The effect and the burden of age. Chapter in *Range of Human Capacities.* 2nd ed., Williams & Wilkins Company, Baltimore, 1952.

27. Witkin, H. A., Dyk, R. B., Faterson, H. F., Goodenough, D. R., and Karp, S. A.: *Psychological Differentiation.* John Wiley & Sons, Inc., 1962.

SECTION D
Personality and Social Process

Chapter 11

PERSONALITY MEASUREMENT IN THE OAKLAND GROWTH STUDY*

JOHN A. CLAUSEN

The Oakland Growth Study, or as it was originally called, the Adolescent Growth Study, began in 1931 with a population of fifth graders in five elementary schools in Oakland California. The initial sample consisted of slightly more than two hundred subjects who signified their intention of going to the junior high school selected as the center of observation for the study, and whose families agreed to cooperate in the research program. This group was studied intensively through the six years of junior and senior high school. Data were secured through a wide variety of techniques, including physiological and physical measurements, intelligence and achievement tests, ratings by adult project staff of the subjects' behavior in social situations, sociometric ratings by classmates, the subjects' self-reports on a wide variety of inventories of adjustment, interest and attitude, projective materials, teachers' ratings, and interviews with the mothers. More detailed descriptions of study design and data collection techniques are given in references 2, 6 and 7.

By the senior year of high school, the sample had decreased to approximately one hundred and fifty subjects, though not all of these were included in all parts of the data collection. The bulk of subjects lost to the study during the high school years moved out of the school district, though not necessarily out of the Bay

* Revised version of a paper presented at the meetings of the Gerontological Society, Miami, Florida, November 8, 1962.

Area. A recent assessment of the nature of sample attrition found no significant differences in social status, intelligence or adjustment (as of the early study years) among groups of subjects who dropped out of the sample during high school, those who remained through high school but could not be included in the adult follow-up and the current study population (4).

There was no systematic collection of data from the time the subjects left high school until they were in their early thirties, when two follow-up studies were undertaken. These reached from sixty to eighty of the most accessible subjects. Included were physiological studies, personality tests and interviews relating to occupational and marital adjustment. A more intensive follow-up study, reaching one hundred of the subjects, was carried out from 1957 to 1960 under a grant from the Ford Foundation. It is the data from this most recent follow-up, when the subjects averaged thirty-seven to thirty-eight years of age, with which the present paper is primarily concerned.

As in earlier phases of the study, the adult follow-up made use of a variety of types of data, including interviews, personality inventories, projective tests and physiological measures. Of primary interest in our attempts to characterize adult personality, however, is the series of intensive interviews which averaged more than twelve hours in length. The topics covered included recollections of adolescence, with particular reference to school, peer relations, family patterns and dating; occupational plans and current achievement; heterosexual relationships, marriage and child rearing; and a wide variety of attitudinal explorations designed to provide information about personal orientations—their flexibility and change—and patterns of relationship. This interview schedule was largely designed by the late Else Frenkel-Brunswik and her co-worker the late Suzanne Reichard, to permit assessment of personality dynamics using a set of ratings which was essentially an enlarged version of those used in the study of eighty-seven older workers as reported in *Aging and Personality* by Suzanne Reichard and her associates (9). Cluster analyses of these ratings have been carried out by Drs. John Hatfield and Albert Shapiro. They are now examining the relationships between selected aspects of adolescent development and dominant patterns of adult ego functioning.

Given the wealth of data available, several other conceptualizations of personality are equally feasible. After much discussion we have decided to use as our primary method for handling personality data the California Q-set developed by Dr. Jack Block (1), who is co-director of the project. This is a set of 100 descriptive items, constituting a standard language for characterizing persons. The items cover a wide range of observed behaviors and characteristic impressions which resemble and indeed include many of the kinds of statements used in everyday attempts to formulate what other persons are like. These items have the great advantage that they can be used by clinically experienced judges to make systematic, and hence comparable, characterizations based on a wide variety of sources of information about the subject—direct observation, interview, self-ratings (always, however, coupled with other data), projective techniques, etc. Therefore, they permit classifications to be made from partial or incomplete data, an important consideration when one is faced with the task of summarizing voluminous materials which have a number of gaps as a consequence of unavailability of subjects in certain phases of the data collection.

From judgments based on the adult interviews alone, an individual is described via the Q-set in terms of his most dominant or salient attributes. One can then seek clusters of dominant tendencies in behavior, and perhaps typologies of individuals who show roughly similar patterns. In addition to the adult Q-set, we have developed an overlapping, comparable set of items specifically designed to tap significant aspects of adolescent behavior and personality. This set is being applied independently by randomized groupings of three judges each to describe our subjects as they were in junior high school and by other trios of judges to describe them as they were in senior high school. Thus, we seek to assess the amount and nature of change from early to late adolescence and from late adolescence to age thirty-seven or thirty-eight for each of our subjects. Certain of the self-report inventories and ratings in adolescence and the psychological inventories and projective techniques used in the adult follow-up have, however, been withheld from the judges, so that we shall have other, independent bases for classification and analysis of trends.

Before turning to a general discussion of our strategy of analysis of adolescent-adult continuity and change, mention should be made of a third set of ratings of the adult interview data. These are less holistic in nature, consisting of ratings of the mechanisms of coping and defense. The defense mechanisms are the standard set of psychoanalytic derivation, as elaborated by Anna Freud. The coping mechanisms are seen as positive counterparts of the defense mechanisms, permitting flexible, adaptive responses in handling the same kinds of problematic situations as might be dealt with defensively. The coping conceptualizations of the mechanisms were developed or elaborated by Theodore Kroeber and Norma Haan, who have also spelled out the criteria for rating subjects with reference to both sets of mechanisms. Analyses thus far carried out with these mechanisms not only bear out the obvious expectation that intelligence should contribute substantially to high coping scores but also suggest that increase in tested intelligence, from adolescence to adulthood, in terms of ranking within the study population, is associated with high scores on certain of the coping mechanisms and low scores on defense mechanisms (5).

GENERAL PLANS FOR DATA ANALYSIS

The questions to which data analysis is being addressed derive from several different perspectives: developmental, psychodynamic, sociological. We are interested in delineating developmental sequences in salient aspects of personality conceived in terms of the individual's manifest motives, needs and sources of satisfaction, his modes of coping and defense, his effectiveness in various types of social roles and his reported feelings about self and others. To the extent that it is possible to use comparable classifications of adolescent and adult behaviors, and of inferred motives, an attempt will be made to examine both continuities and shifts in personality orientations.

One of the major advantages of the use of the Q technique is that an individual's characterization in adolescence can be correlated with his adult description. In addition to asking which characteristics tend in general to show continuity over time, one can ask which individuals change little and which change a good deal.

In instances in which substantial reorientations of personality have taken place, one may seek the social and experimental antecedents of such reorientation, as contrasted with antecedents in subjects showing greater stability. Examination of some of the case histories, over the entire period, by one not involved in the rating process, suggests that predictions based on adolescent personality dynamics and high school success were sometimes wide of the mark because of the development both of the individual's resources and of unexpected contingencies in the environment. Such contingencies led to the crystallization of new goals and self-images for some subjects and the dissolution of goals for others. This is not to say that discontinuity is more often found than continuity, but striking reorientations and less striking but significant shifts have occurred for a number of subjects.

In viewing the adolescent subject, one tends to see his development as the resultant of the interplay between gentic potentiality, general patternings of relationship and expectation surrounding him, and salient experiences of self and others, all within a social-cultural matrix that provides general definitions of individual experience. Stature, physical attractiveness, rate of maturing, intellectual potential, and temperament interact with family structure, parental personalities, and the subcultural and ecological correlates of position within the social structure. As individuals mature, the constraints of their original social matrix become less compelling. They not only respond to environmental pressures and potentialities; they select them. They commit themselves to lines of activity and to other persons, as well as to conceptions of themselves. As a consequence, one expects not only changing personal attributes and changing saliences of attributes and values but also a changed relationship between the way the person sees himself and the ways that he is seen by others.

Perhaps the most ambitious and most original aspect of data collection during the adolescence of our subjects was that involving direct observation in a wide variety of contexts—on the schoolground, in a clubhouse, on excursions arranged for the study group, at dances, during other phases of data collection (e.g., intelligence testing and physical examination) and in informal contact with study staff. Several different levels of rating were attempted, ranging from situationally manifest behaviors and attributes (e.g., self-expressiveness, emotional tensions, etc.) through general traits explicitly intended to describe overt phenotypic levels of behavior (e.g., generally self-confident vs. overtly insecure, introverted vs. extraverted, etc.) to "drive ratings," adapted from Murray's list of "needs," entailing inferences of motivations underlying behavior observed in a wide variety of situations.

Else Frenkel-Brunswik (2) examined in detail the interrelationships among the several sets of ratings of the adolescent subjects. She also explored the relationships between judges' ratings and the self-reports of the subjects, given in a response to a comprehensive inventory touching most heavily upon personal adjustment in family, school and peer group. From profiles of behavior ratings it was possible to distinguish four groups of subjects; those who were socially successful and who appeared to be emotionally well adjusted; those socially successful but emotionally maladjusted; those socially unsuccessful but emotionally adjusted; and a group of the unsuccessful and maladjusted. These sub-groups showed quite different profiles of drive ratings, with the socially successful but maladjusted appearing to be "driven,"—that is, having the highest ratings on need for social ties, recognition, control and aggression—and the socially unsuccessful but adjusted appearing to be relatively passive, with very low ratings on these same drives. In general, ratings on these drives were only slightly correlated with self-ratings on the adjustment inventory. On the other hand, drive ratings of abasement (tendency to self-blame or belittlement) and of succorance (desire for support from outside), which were less closely related to ratings of social success or adjustment, were significantly related to self-reports on the inventory of adjustment, especially for boys. Thus, boys rated by the judges as wanting support from others and as tending toward self-depreciation did indeed manifest these behavioral tendencies in responding to the inventory. On the whole, general traits rated by the judges were more closely related to self-reports than were drive ratings. Correlations were highest in those instances in which the traits rated entailed an element of self-disclosure or manifest emotional security.

Some of the adolescent subjects who were seen by the judges

as aggressive and maladjusted saw themselves in a much more favorable light—or at least reported that they did. For other subjects, the reverse was true. Our adult ratings are based on interviews rather than observations of behavior in varied situations. Nevertheless, in the interiew sessions (usually four) the interviewer had a fairly substantial sample of the subject's behavior which could be viewed in other terms than substantive self-report. To a degree it will again be possible to check judges' ratings against self-reports both in the interview and in response to personality inventories. In the former instance, the comparison will reveal primarily whether or not the interviewer tended to accept the subjects interpretations of himself. In the latter—judges ratings vs. inventory classifications—we shall have a parallel with the earlier comparisons made by Frenkel-Brunswik.

The requirements for success in occupational and family roles are markedly different from those prevailing in the adolescent society of the high school. One would anticipate that some of the subjects who had been unsure of themselves in adolescence, especially those who were socially and intellectually competent but not highly successful in high school society, would have achieved both social success and self-confidence in adulthood. One task in data analysis will be to examine the nature of the relative changes between judges' ratings and self-ratings. Another will entail an attempt to establish patterns of change for persons characterized by particular combinations or profiles of ratings and self-reports. Equally important will be the delineation of dominant patterns of adult functioning—especially as revealed by Q technique and ratings of ego mechanisms—and the investigation of their varied antecedents in adolescence. Thus both holistic and segmental classifications will be used in atempting to bridge the twenty years between adolescence and the follow-up study.

One of the great advantages of our longitudinal data is that we know something of the social matrix from which the adolescent came and we know the nature of the matrix in which the adult is functioning when on the threshold of middle age. We know something of the skills which were developed by our subjects early in life and the courses to which they have committed themselves in their adult careers. Others studies have suggested that the chang-

ing salience of skills in various phases of the life-cycle may have
differential effects upon occupational success and the evaluations
of others—and hence on self-evaluation. Thus, the worker whose
status rests upon physical strength and skills is likely to experience
a decline in status earlier than the worker whose status rests upon
intellectual skills, although the economic effects of declining physical strength and skill may be offset by the operation of seniority
principles in industry (11).

When our subjects were adolescents, it was clearly apparent
that some were far more gifted than others. Some had had clear
goals while others seemed to have no idea of where they were
going. Some were closely integrated into their families, some on
the verge of breaking away. The pictures they gave of themselves,
and the pictures that those who observed them, whether peer
or adult, formed of these subjects depended in part on the nature
of the gifts already displayed, the structure of the goals presented
and the state of their family and other group memberships.

As we see these subjects now as parents, many with children
older than they were at the time they entered the Adolescent
Growth Study, we find that there are substantial changes in the
structure of the goals they hold. A number had been successful
in occupations to which they were pointed at the time they left
high school. Others have only recently defined their occupational
niche with any clarity. For some the occupational trajectory shows
no sign of approaching a limit. For others, it is already apparent
that they are at or near their ceiling. The structuring of their
goals must of necessity be different for the two groups.

We anticipate that, in general, continuity in occupational and
personal commitments will be associated with greater stability of
attitudes and motivational dispositions as measured by the various
personality inventories and ratings. Analyses now in process relating to the ratings of ego mechanisms suggest that current social
status is more highly related to adult patterns of coping and
defense than is social status in childhood and adolescence, a finding
anticipated from cross-sectional research (10). Or, to rephrase the
relationship, persons who are upwardly mobile occupationally
appear to differ from those who originally came from and stayed
at the same status level. The upwardly mobile achieve many of

the personality correlates associated with life-long high status. In further analyses we have explanatory tasks relating both to adolescence and to adulthood. There is, for example, the task of seeking to delineate the characteristics evident in adolescence which may explain the upward mobility. Equally important is the task of assessing the consequences in the middle years of the orientation toward and fact of mobility. Has occupational commitment become a more overriding concern for these subjects? How have family and occupational careers meshed, and how have the meanings of phases of the family cycle been influenced by this meshing?

CONSIDERATIONS RELATING TO FUTURE RESEARCH

Any longitudinal study acquires a tremendous investment in its subjects. Each segment of study represents a potential pressure to seek still more data within the existing conceptual and data-gathering framework. Yet each longitudinal investigation must face the fact that the developmental process through which its subjects pass is only one of several types of change that must be dealt with. Conceptual tools and measurement techniques relating to personality are themselves constantly changing. Moreover, the aspects of personality that are most salient for role performance at one age level (or in one social group) may not be equally salient at another. The effects of early or late maturing upon the social skills and self-confidence of adolescents appear, for example, to be marked, but these effects may not persist significantly into the later years. Or perhaps there will be persistent effects only if early and late maturing tend to lead to different choices and commitments during the adolescent period. For example, to the extent that occupational choice and choice of marital partner are predictably influenced by physical and emotional development in adolescence, we may expect that groups differing in developmental processes in adolescence will continue to differ or even to diverge still further in adulthood.

As yet it must be confessed that the developmental perspective of the Oakland Growth Study has not been extended much beyond the middle years. We have not attempted to speculate on patterns of change in the later years as an outcome of processes of development to date. Yet if additional data are to be secured—as they probably will when our subjects approach fifty—there will almost inevitably be a shift in our perspectives. Other studies have suggested that with advancing age comes a shift from active to passive modes of mastery in dealing with the environment and with impulse life, increasing introversion, and either a decline or a redirection of emotional investment. Neugarten (8) has stressed that some of these tendencies begin to manifest themselves in the 40's, well before the "losses" of aging can be said to begin. To address such issues we shall have some relevant material from interviews and projective techniques, especially as these relate to problematic situations with which the person has had to cope or may have to cope in the future. The next step will require an attempt to bridge between such data available for our subjects in their late thirties and the data to be sought at some future date. Almost certainly our future work will entail the use of the more adequate techniques of studying personality processes in aging which are now being developed.

It has been said that the personality becomes more clearly revealed with advancing age. For some students of personality, this may be taken to mean that there is an underlying, coherent organization of tendencies of thought, behavior and feeling which becomes more clearly manifest in the later years. For others, the notion of a relatively fixed psyche seems improbable; what appears to be more clearly revealed is the individual's concerns and feelings—and most strikingly, of course, his idiosyncracies. Yet, somewhat paradoxically, comparisons of older with younger persons in large surveys of self-attitudes and concerns—as, for example, in the volume *Americans View Their Mental Health* (3)—reveal that the older respondents report fewer problems, fewer dissatisfactions with parenthood and job situations, less psychological immobilization. In such comparisons, however, one never knows what the objective circumstances have been or how they would have been reported by the subject ten years earlier—or later. It is the advantage of having such knowledge, accruing to the long-term longitudinal study, that would seem to be the primary justification for continuing to pursue an ever dwindling, ever less definably representative sample of respondents down the years.

REFERENCES

1. Block, Jack: *The Q-Sort Method in Personality Assessment and Psychiatric Research,* Springfield, Thomas, 1961.

2. Frenkel-Brunswik, Else: Motivation and Behavior, *Genetic Psychology Monographs, 26:*121-265, 1942.

3. Gurin, Gerald *et al.: Americans View Their Mental Health.* New York, Basic Books, 1960.

4. Haan, Norma: "Some Comparisons of Various Oakland Growth Study Subsamples on Selected Variables," Dittoed, Berkeley, California, Institute of Human Development, 1962.

5. Haan, Norma: A Proposed Model of Ego Functioning: Coping and Defense Mechanisms in Relationship to I.Q. Change, *Psychological Monographs 77:*Whole No. 571., 1963.

6. Jones, Harold E.: The California Adolescent Growth Study, *Journal of Educational Research, 31:*561-567, 1938.

7. Jones, Harold E. *et al.:* A Progress Report on Growth Studies at the University of California, *Vita Humana, 3:*17-31, 1959.

8. Neugarten, Bernice: "A developmental view of adult personality. Chapter 12, this volume.

9. Reichard, Suzanne *et al.: Aging and Personality,* New York, John Wiley and sons, 1962.

10. Srole, Leo *et al.: Mental Health in the Metropolls,* New York, McGraw-Hill, 1962.

11. Wilensky, Harold L.: Life Cycle, Work Situation and Participation in Formal Organizations, in *Aging and Leisure: Research Perspectives on the Meaningful Use of Time,* edited by Robert W. Kleemeier. New York, Oxford University Press, 1961.

Chapter 12

A DEVELOPMENTAL VIEW OF
ADULT PERSONALITY*

BERNICE L. NEUGARTEN

The focus of this paper is upon adult personality as it is seen from the perspective of the student of human development. Personality is conceptualized in dynamic terms, as a set of processes that have a course of growth and change from earliest childhood through old age. The structure of the adult personality is seen as continuous with, but not identical with, that of the child or the adolescent. In seeking ways to describe how the adult differs from the child, the investigator focuses attention upon the importance of the "self," and upon those elements in the personality that involve choice, self-direction, and the manipulation of outcomes. Personality is to be studied, in this sense, as a set of independent, not dependent variables in accounting for the varieties of adult behavior.

From this perspective, very little is yet known about adult personality. There are few theories that may be regarded as useful; and few empirical studies now available on which to build a developmental theory.

* Prepared with the assistance of Mr. Mark Skinner, Research Associate, Committee on Human Development. This paper is an adaptation of one entitled, "Personality Changes During the Adult Years," which appears in the proceedings of a symposium, *Psychological Backgrounds of Adult Education,* edited by Raymond G. Kuhlen, published by the Center for the Study of Liberal Education for Adults, Chicago, 1963. The paper has been adapted and reprinted with the permission of the Center.

After a few comments regarding problems of method and problems of theory, this paper will deal with two main topics: first, the issue of continuity of personality over long time intervals; and second, the nature of personality change in the adult years. In the first part, the focus is upon affective rather than upon cognitive processes; and upon the period from youth to old age rather than the longer period that encompasses childhood and adolescence as well. In the second part of the paper, there is a tentative formulation of the nature of adult personality development, in which the focus is narrowed even more to deal with change in certain intra-psychic processes.

Problems of Method

Knowledge of the personality changes that occur in adulthood is scanty for various reasons, first, because of problems related to method. The problems of sampling alone become increasingly acute as one moves through the age-range. The captive research groups available in nurseries, schools, and colleges must be foregone; adults have different, often decreasing, motivation for participating in research projects; and investigators are aware that, as the age of subjects increases, they must be increasingly wary about generalizing from what may be deviant to normal groups (such as generalizing from volunteers to non-volunteers, or from institutionalized to non-institutionalized aged).

There is difficulty also in that the rhythm of change is different in adulthood from that in childhood. A year, which is so long an interval in the early stages of life, is a very short interval in later life: long intervals must be used as units of time. Yet there is the difficulty that the longer the time-intervals, or the more the sub-samples are separated by chronological age in the attempt to highlight age differences, the more other characteristics will operate to confound the age variable itself. For instance, if the attempt is made to equate a group of twenty year olds with a group of forty year olds for educational level, the investigator is likely to introduce systematic bias with regard to socioeconomic level. This bias grows in geometric proportion as the age interval is enlarged between groups.

To make matters worse, the investigator cannot estimate the

effects of survival bias: that is, what types of individuals have died, and what types, survived. Yet it is known that the effects of this bias become greater and greater at advanced ages, so that the problem of equating samples of young and old persons on grounds that they will be equally representative becomes, in most studies, nearly impossible.

If, furthermore, the researcher is loath to draw his inferences with regard to developmental changes from studies based on cross-sectional data, then he faces the tremendous difficulties inherent in carrying out longitudinal research over the long time-intervals required to produce meaningful findings.

This is to say nothing of the difficulty involved in disentangling the effects of historical and secular changes in the society from the effects of increasing age: as, for example, when studies report an increase in conservative attitudes in successive age groups.[1] Do persons *become* more conservative with age? Or is it that older persons formed many of their social attitudes at a different time in history? It is a rare instance in which a study can be designed to control for this factor—a study in which observations are carried out, say, on a group of persons when they are twenty, and again when they are forty; in which observations are carried out also on a second group who are twenty at the same time that the first group reaches forty; and in which comparisons are then drawn between the Time 1-Time 2 difference and the Group 1-Group 2 difference.

Such problems of method, while they do not distinguish research in personality from research in many other areas, may nevertheless provide special hurdles to the student of personality processes. One problem does arise to plague the student of personality more often perhaps than in other areas: that is the problem of generalizing from behavior in the experimentally-controlled situation to behavior in the real-life situation. Without going into this issue at greater length, it can perhaps be argued that the problem becomes more acute with regard to adult behavior than with child behavior, for it is confounded by questions regarding suitable pre-

---

[1] The fact that cultural change contaminates both-sectional and longitudinal studies is discussed in a recent paper by Raymond G. Kuhlen (1963).

dictors in the lives of adults. What shall be the criteria in adulthood by which experimental findings should be evaluated?

Problems of Theory

Over and above problems of method, the student of adult personality suffers from the lack of theory to guide him in conceptualizing personality change, in making observations, and in determining the kinds of measures to devise.

The investigator in this field is faced with a strange anomaly. Psychologists are becoming increasingly impressed with developmental issues, as witnessed in the growing rapprochement going on, for instance, between learning theory and psychoanalytic theory; and in another instance, between developmental theory and research in cognitive processes. Furthermore, most psychologists are committed to the concepts of developmental change in children and in adolescents; the view that although behavior is always molded by social transactions, growth and change are also inherent in the organism; and the view that the changes observable through time are dictated by a variety of factors, not all of them external.

This point of view, although it has been more elegantly stated by others, needs no great elaboration when it refers to childhood and adolescence. Psychologists are accustomed to the thought that the child is not a *tabula rasa;* that there are inner processes and needs which change with time; and that the personality of the child cannot be accounted for solely on the basis of his social experiences.

For the most part, however, personality theorists have not carried the same view forward into adulthood. This in an over-simplification, of course; but by and large there is no developmental theory of adulthood. Psychoanalytic theory, tremendous as its influence has been, has given little attention to personality change after the crises of adolescence have been mastered. The personality is generally regarded as stabilized (if not fixed) by the time early adulthood is reached; and there are few developmental psychologists who have extended their theories upward in the attempt to account for perceivable changes in adult behavior.

Thus problems of theory as well as problems of method stand in the way of the student of adult personality.

CONTINUITY OF PERSONALITY THROUGH TIME

Stability of personality, or continuity of personality through time, is a major issue to students of human development. Most of the empiricial evidence with regard to stability has come thus far from studies of children and adolescents, and to that extent, is only partially useful with regard to adulthood. There are just now appearing, however, a few reports of longitudinal data in which Ss are now adults.

From Youth to Young Adulthood

At the Institute of Human Development, University of California, longitudinal studies have been in process for more than twenty-five years, and data are available concerning some 300 persons who are now in their thirties and forties. There are presently emerging from that body of data a number of empirical findings with regard to continuity of personality through the period of young adulthood.

In a study by Mussen (1961), for example, boys who were rated as more and less masculine were restudied when they were in their thirties. Those who had been low in masculinity in adolescence were found still to be low with regard to masculine interests and attitudes. The more masculine boys became the more masculine adults.

Tuddenham (1959), to take another example, interviewed seventy-two men and women in their early thirties who had been studied at length some nineteen years earlier. He rated these young adults on fifty-three personality variables, some of them variables of observed behavior, others, of inferred drives. Correlations between Time 1 and Time 2 were positive, but very low (average r was .27 for men, and .24 for women). Although Tuddenham concluded that "there is clearly a significant measure of temporal stability in personality across the developmental span from early adolescence to mature adulthood," he concluded also that the correlations were much too low to permit individual prediction.

To take another example from the California studies: Of 139 subjects who had been followed from birth through age eighteen by Macfarlane, and who were then seen again twelve years later as thirty year olds, early predictions appeared to be confirmed for certain personality make-ups, not for others. Although these particular data have not yet been processed quantitatively, it seems clear that the over-controlled, well-ordered, compulsive individuals tend to continue in that pattern, but a number who were hostile and dependent in childhood have grown up to become friendly and nurturant adults (Jones, 1960, p. 20).

Jones (1958), in a report of the work of the Institute, generalized from various studies of physical, physiological, intellectual, and personality development. Consonant with the findings emerging from other research centers, his conclusions were that the problem of age trend consistency is a more difficult one in the area of personality than in the other areas, among other reasons because the same research approaches cannot be used with adults as with children and adolescents. In spite of numerous instances of consistency between adolescent and adult measures, overall measures of adult adjustment showed little relation to strength of adolescent drives. Jones concluded: "The problem here may lie partly in the fact that over a long period behavioral consistency, when it occurs, may be countered by changes in the environment. The adaptive significance of a given behavior pattern can thus be interpreted only with reference to changing demands in the life situation" (1960, p. 20).

In line with the interpretation that there is relatively little continuity of personality observable from adolescence to adulthood is the study made by Rohrer and his associates (Rohrer and Edmonson, 1960). They traced a large majority of the Negro adolescents who had been described earlier by Davis and Dollard in the book *Children of Bondage* (1940); and they reported in considerable detail on twenty of those cases who were seen again after an interval of twenty years. Although the findings were not treated quantitatively, the net effect of these case materials is to highlight the great diversity of adult life patterns, only partly predictable from observations made during adolescence.

Different investigators, however, have differing interpretations with regard to continuity of personality. Symonds (1961), for instance, studied twenty-eight subjects who were aged twelve to eighteen at Time 1; and who were retested after an interval of thirteen years. He found what he regarded as high consistency in overt personality—such characteristics as aggressiveness in response to interviews and tests; a correlation of .54 between rankings at Time 1 and Time 2 for general adjustment; and even such marked persistence of phantasy themes as to enable the investigators to identify the narrator and to match stories told thirteen years apart. Symonds felt he had demonstrated "the remarkable persistence of personality over a thirteen year interval, and in particular, the fact that it is possible to estimate personality adjustment in later years from facts gathered about a person when he is adolescent."

Given such inconsistent points of view, it should be pointed out that the question of continuity has often been over-simplified by being stated only in terms of test-retest agreement on the same measures. The question is usually phrased: Is a specific response at Time 1 exhibited again at Time 2?

It is perhaps more meaningful to the student of human behavior to study antecedent-consequent relationships by asking the more complex questions concerning, not repetition, but derivation: *What* behaviors or what characteristics at Time 1 are predictive of *what* behaviors or what characteristics at Time 2?

Yet if we turn to studies of the latter type, the empirical findings are not necessarily more congruent.

In one such study, for instance, in which adjustment was being predicted, Anderson (1960) gathered data on all the children within a Minnesota county who were enrolled in school from grades four to twelve; then followed them up five to seven years later, by which time some were in their twenties. He reports that, as is true in other longitudinal studies of youngsters, cognitive abilities (intelligence, skill, knowledge) weighed more heavily than measures of personality in predicting adjustment at Time 2. (Independent of the problems of continuity and prediction, but also important to the present discussion, is Anderson's statement that cognitive measures were what he calls "age-bound"—that is, that scores increase as age increases; whereas personality measures were relatively "age-free.")

Kagan and Moss (1962) have just reported a major study based upon longitudinal data gathered at Fels Research Institute on a group of seventy-one men and women now in their twenties. Using interviews with parents, narrative reports, and behavior observations collected over the years, Ss were rated on a set of personality variables with regard to characteristic behavior at four periods in their childhood: infancy to age 3, 3 to 6, 6 to 10, and 10-14. A second investigator, with no knowledge of the earlier date, interviewed each young adult at length and made assessments of present personality. Taking the antecedent-consequent rather than the test-retest approach, and basing their interpretations upon correlations of the magnitude of .5 to .6, these investigators concluded: "... Many of the behaviors exhibited by the child aged six to ten, and a few during the age period three to six, were moderately good predictors of theoretically related behaviors during early adulthood. Passive withdrawal from stressful situations, dependency on family, ease-of-anger arousal, involvement in intellectual mastery, social interaction anxiety, sex-role identification, and pattern of sexual behavior in adulthood were each related to reasonably analogous behavioral dispositions during the early school years. . . . These results offer strong support for the generalization that aspects of adult personality begin to take form during early childhood" (pp. 266-268).

Yet in another broadly-designed study concerned with the prediction of performance in young adulthood, the conclusions were different. Hess and Davis (Hess, 1962) have followed up 350 young men and women whom they had studied eight years earlier when these Ss were seniors in high school. Assessments of these young adults have been made with regard to work-related achievement, social integration into the adult society, and psycho-social identity.

In general, these investigators were impressed with the difficulties in predicting performance in young adulthood from measures taken in adolescence. Although academic achievement in high school (school grades, but not IQ) was associated significantly with work-related achievement in young men, social experience and social skills in adolescence showed only low correlations with subsequent behavior in social, in work, or in identity areas.

Looking backward in time, furthermore, the measures of ego-identity established for these young adults were not consistently related to high school experience. In particular, measures of ego functions taken from projective tests of personality showed no significant correlations from Time 1 to Time 2.

These findings were true for the group as a whole, although more positive and consistent relationships between personality and achievement measures were found for the one-third of the group who fell at the extremes (those who were high achievers or low achievers at both Time 1 and Time 2).

Hess and Davis concluded not only that adult performance is apparently more closely related to events and experiences that occur after high school than to high school behavior (college attendance was the most significant factor); but that the high school years may constitute a kind of moratorium, and that it may be the transition from late adolescence into the twenties that is a more critical period of development than is adolescence.

It may be pertinent here to comment upon the problems that arise in generalizing from samples which differ in heterogeneity. The Hess-Davis study of young adults was based on a group of 350, all of whom graduated from high school—a relatively homogeneous group. Havighurst and his associates (1962), on the other hand, in still another recently reported study, tested all children in the sixth grade in a midwestern town (including children in public and parochial schools, the mentally retarded as well as the normal) and then examined them again nine years later, when they were age twenty. Substantial correlations with adjustment at age twenty were obtained for Time 1 measures of socioeconomic status, IQ, social leadership, and social adjustment by the California Psychological Inventory (rs were .48 to .58). Adjustment at age twenty was based upon ratings of educational progress, job success, marital success, and personal competence. These investigators conclude, somewhat contrary to Hess and Davis, that, given many exceptions, there is measurable continuity of personality. Children who are endowed with advantages make the most of these advantages during adolescence and become the most competent young adults.

These discrepant conclusions illustrate the difficulties involved in attempting to generalize about continuity of personality. There is variation from study to study, not only with regard to size and heterogeneity of sample, but also with regard to the interval between Time 1 and Time 2. Perhaps predictions can be made more accurately from late childhood to young adulthood than from adolescence to young adulthood. Perhaps adolescence is itself too unstable a period in development to provide a good base line. If so, this might account for at least some of the discrepancies just cited.

Another reason for the difficulties in evaluating the extent of consistency in personality through time is the fact that sometimes the focus has been upon the relatively overt, observable levels of behavior; at other times, upon the relatively covert, intrapsychic levels. To borrow terms from the biologist, the focus is at times upon phenotypic aspects of personality; at other times, upon genotypic. The same underlying trait can take a variety of overt forms; and sometimes it is this fact that plays havoc with the best-designed study. It is not always easy to move from phenotypic behavior at Time 1 to an accurate conceptualization of the genotypic trait that underlies it; and from that conceptualization to a different measure of phenotypic behavior appropriate to Time 2. It is this difficulty that may also account for some of the discrepancies just cited.

From Young- to Middle-adulthood

There are very few sets of findings available with regard to continuity of personality from young- to middle-adulthood—or, for that matter, from any preceding period of time to the period of middle age.

There is the notable exception of the Terman and Oden study (1959), in which Terman's group of gifted children have been followed now into their late forties. These were some 1,500 children who, in 1921, were in the top one per cent of the population in IQ. The data on personality have not been systematically treated with regard to continuity, nor have they been reported in terms of successive time intervals. However, the latest follow-up, after three and a half decades, has shown that, with few exceptions, the superior child has become the able adult, superior in nearly every aspect to the average person. From this point of view, and in these very gross terms, these findings support the generalization of continuity through time.

(An interesting point, although not directly related to the issue of continuity, is the investigators' conclusion that relates to the importance of personality factors in adult achievement. On the criteria of eminence, professional status, and recognized position in the community, the 150 most successful and the 150 least successful men were isolated from among this group of gifted subjects. The two subgroups differed most widely on four personality traits: persistence in the accomplishment of ends, integration toward goals, self-confidence, and freedom for inferiority feelings. In general, the investigators conclude, the greatest contrast between the two groups was in all-round emotional and social adjustment and in the drive to achieve. These findings suggest again the central importance, and perhaps the relative independence, of personality factors as research variables in human behavior.)

The second notable exception is the study of Kelly's (1955), in which 300 engaged couples were first studied in the 1930's and then re-tested in 1955 when they were in their forties. After correcting the correlations for attenuation, Kelly found that individual consistency was highest in the areas of values and vocational interests (r's were approximately .50); and was low but statistically significant with regard to self-ratings and other personality variables based upon responses to paper-and-pencil tests. (These latter co-efficients were of the order of .30.) Kelly leaves open the question of whether or not these findings should be interpreted as signifying high or low consistency. However, he does point out that there is obviously a great amount of individual variation, and he concludes: "Our findings indicate that significant changes in the human personality may continue to occur during the years of adulthood."

From Middle to Old Age

The degree to which we can speak of continuity when one moves from middle to old age is even more open to question. There are no longitudinal studies on personality yet available for individuals who have been studied in young adulthood or in middle adulthood and then again in old age.[2]

It has often been commented on by clinicians that the personality structure becomes more and more clearly revealed as individuals grow old. Dr. Martin Gumpert, a well-known geriatrician, once said: "With age, the outline of a psyche becomes more apparent." Yet there is little in the way of controlled investigations to demonstrate whether or not this observation is true. Findings about personality change in old age are thus far drawn from cross-sectional data; and strictly speaking, there is no systematic evidence regarding individual consistency over long periods of time when time relates to the latter half of the life span.

Before moving to findings from cross-sectional data, and granting that most of the longitudinal findings refer only to the first part of adulthood, there are nevertheless certain points that may bear restatement:

1. Test-retest on single variables or on sets of variables may not, indeed, provide the most meaningful approach to the problem of continuity. Any given trait, such as aggressiveness in males or expressivity in females, however the trait may be measured, may have quite different significance at Time 1 and Time 2 when seen within a wider pattern of variables. The individual may maintain his relative position on a given characteristic; but this fact may be less important than the way in which that characteristic is related to other characteristics at the two points in time. In this connection, for example, clinical observations have been frequently made that aggressivity may be adaptive in youth, but maladaptive in middle age; just as rigidity may be maladaptive in young adulthood, but adaptive in old age.

The more worthwhile question might be one to which certain of the longitudinal studies cited here have already been addressed: namely, What are the predictors at Time 1 for a particular trait or constellation of traits at Time 2? If, for instance, we wish to understand the antecedents of personal adjustment in middle age, to what variables should we attend when individuals are young

---

[2] Medorah Smith (1952) has reported observations made in childhood, and then again after an interval of fifty years; but only a half-dozen *S*s were involved, and the observations were largely uncontrolled.

adults? To carry this example further, there are a number of studies which indicate that intelligence or cognitive ability is perhaps the most powerful predictor of personal adjustment when Time 1 and Time 2 refer to childhood and adolescence, or to adolescence and young adulthood. The picture is not so clear, however, when we move beyond young adulthood. That is, it is not clear whether or not intelligence is a powerful predictor of personal adjustment at later ages.[3]

2. Whether the studies are test-retest or antecedent-consequent in design (in the sense described earlier), the general picture with regard to consistency of adult personality can be summarized by saying that measures taken at long time intervals tend to produce statistically reliable, but relatively low, correlations. (Coefficients are usually of the order of .30 to .40, only occasionally as high as .50). The indication is that while there is continuity of personality measurable by present techniques, the larger proportion of the variance in the measures used at Time 2 remains unaccounted for. Making allowance for the fallibility of measures with regard to reliability, the implication is that there is at least as much change as there is stability.

Empirical studies such as those cited here capture only part of the complexity of human behavior. While this is an obvious point, investigators sometimes overlook the obvious in pinning their sights upon the empirical, the controlled, and the experimental methods of observation. Most psychologists would readily agree that the individual, as he moves through the adult years, becomes transformed in his appearance, in his social life patterns, his interests, his personal and social relationships—in the outward or observable traits or characteristics. It is also highly probable that individuals change through the years of adulthood with regard to inner qualities of personality—for example, in ways of experiencing and expressing emotions, in motivations, in preoccupations—in the whole array of cognitive and affective processes that

---

[3] A study which comes to mind in this connection is one by Mulvey (1961), who studied the career patterns of several hundred middle-aged women, all of whom had graduated from high school, and who concluded that, of a variety of factors measured in youth, intelligence was the least important in influencing the kinds of career lines that ensued.

are involved in the day's traffic with the environment. The investigator has only to think of the waking, as well as the dreaming, thoughts that preoccupied him ten years ago, and the thoughts that preoccupy him now, to see that this is so. It is not the conviction that personality change occurs in adulthood, but the methods for measuring these changes, that psychologists are lacking.

Individual Differences

Intimately related to the question of continuity is the question of the extent to which individuals may be expected to vary, one from another, with increasing age. A developmental point of view leads to the search for patterns that are common to all members of a group, or for what are euphemistically referred to as "laws" of growth and change. On the other hand, longitudinal studies have also highlighted individual variation in growth patterns.

It is not clear to what extent the periods of adulthood and old age show the same general relationships between common patterns and idiosyncratic patterns as are shown in childhood—in other words, to what extent all people are alike and to what extent they are all different, once the period of growth is over. From the biologist's point of view, the forces of natural selection—if they may still be said to apply in our man-made environment—are no longer operative once the reproductive period of life is over. If a trait is neither biologically adaptive nor non-adaptive for the species, in the sense that it does not affect the rate of reproduction (a trait related to senescence, as compared with a trait related to growth), then it does not become eliminated from the population. It may be, therefore, that a greater variety of patterns develop in the last half of life than in the first half; and the more that man controls the effects of natural selection by creating a protective environment for less hardy biological specimens, the more variation we can expect in older organisms. Within the social and cultural realms, we can expect differences between individuals to be accentuated with time, as educational, vocational, and social events accumulate one after another to create more and more differentiated sets of experiences from one person to the next.

Whatever the net effects of these factors might be; and making allowance for the extent to which common social roles lead to increased similarities and therefore to greater homogeneity, whatever the effects upon personality; it is not unreasonable to expect that variation will increase as a group of persons moves from youth through adulthood. There is the factor of personal choice; and the factor of ever-increasing differentiation, once initial choices are made in one or another direction. There are also the ever-increasing effects of personal commitments and institutional structures that tend to produce increased individual differences between persons. Any high-school class may be said to be more alike at the time of graduation than at age twenty-five or forty or sixty in life patterns, interests, and abilities; so also it is likely, if appropriate measurements were obtainable, that the members would prove to be more similar in personality at the time of graduation than at later ages.

It is a fact, on the other hand, that empirical studies presently available produce an unclear picture with regard to increased differentiation with age. Some studies indicate greater individual differences with increasing age; some do not. There are major problems in interpreting these empirical findings, for the actual age groups being compared differ from study to study. In one case twenty year olds are being compared with forty year olds; in another, with sixty year olds. Above all, samples tend to be poorly controlled.

THE NATURE OF PERSONALITY CHANGE
IN ADULTHOOD

There are hundreds of investigations carried out with adult subjects which substantiate the phenomenon of personality change in adulthood; and which, if they were to be evaluated and ordered from a common perspective, could perhaps be reduced to a more or less coherent description of the nature of the changes from one age level to the next. Rather than any such summary, however, a more meaningful context for the formulation that follows can perhaps be provided by mentioning certain of the concepts upon which it relies, concepts drawn primarily from ego psychology. As represented in the work of Hartmann (1958), Hartmann, Kris, and Lowenstein (1946), Murray (1938), Rapaport (1959) and others, and especially in the work of Erikson (1959) and White (1960), these concepts constitute important modifications of psychoanalytic theory. Attention is focused upon the "executive" processes of personality, those that mediate between impulses and external demands, and those which "test" reality. The emphasis is upon processes of adaptation and choice; the growth of competence in dealing with the environment; and upon mental processes such as reasoning and cognition.

The concept of mutuality is stressed—that is, that human character is by nature social, and that there is a crucial and continual coordination between the individual and his human environment. "Thus, it is not assumed that societal norms are grafted upon the genetically *a*social individual by 'disciplines' and 'socialization,' but that the society into which the individual is born makes him its member by influencing the manner in which he solves the tasks posed by each phase of his epigenetic development" (Rapaport, 1959, p. 15).

Although there have been various stage theories set forth by psychoanalysts and by ego psychologists, Erikson (1959), unlike the others, has delineated stages of ego development specific to adulthood. (He has described eight stages in all. The first five, occurring in infancy, childhood, and adolescence, have to do with the formation of basic trust, autonomy, initiative, a sense of industry, and ego-identity or the sense of self). The first of the adult crises (the sixth of the eight stages) relates to the establishment of intimacy: the ability to merge one's self with the self of another; and to share intimately with another, as usually in the heterosexual relationship that becomes stabilized in marriage.

The next stage is called generativity: primarily the preoccupation with establishing and guiding the next generation; the sense of investment in the products of one's own creation (usually one's children, but also the products of one's work). Generativity involves also an identification with the future, and in this sense, a transcendance of the self and of the present.

The last stage is integrity: the view of one's life as meaningful and inevitable—"the acceptance of one's own and only life cycle, and of the people who have become significant to it, as something that had to be; and that, by necessity, permitted of no substitutions . . . ." The lack of ego integrity is signified by the feeling, conscious or unconscious, that death comes too soon because one needs a last desperate chance to make something different of one's life.

Another set of concepts that are of particular importance in differentiating adulthood from childhood are those that refer to the "self"; the importance of growing self-awareness and the impact of the self upon the environment.

Although a substantial portion of the theoretical literature deals with changes in self-image and with self-actualization (Maslow, 1943; Snygg and Combs, 1949; Rogers, 1951; Grinker, 1957; Buhler, 1962; Sherif, 1962; Shoben, 1962), certain of the concepts lead directly to the hypothesis that self-awareness increases throughout adulthood; that the self becomes increasingly more differentiated; and that the qualities related to the exercise of choice and to the manipulation of outcomes become increasingly salient in human behavior.[4]

Changes in Ego Processes

To summarize in advance of presenting the evidence, the view being set forth here is that there are sets of personality processes, primarily intrapsychic in nature, which show developmental changes throughout the life span. As the individual moves from childhood and adolescence into adulthood, ego processes become increasingly salient in personality dynamics. In the broadest terms, the development of the ego is, for the first two-thirds of the life span, outward toward the environment; for the last part of the life span, inward toward the self. In these impressionistic terms, it is as if the ego, in childhood, is focused upon the development of physical, mental, and emotional tools with which to deal with both the inner and the outer worlds, and with which to carry on its transactions with the environment. In young adulthood,

---

[4] Charlotte Buhler (1962) views the life span as primarily governed by two variables: a biologial variable she calls aging, characterized by growth and decline; and a psychological variable she calls development, which involves the whole individual in movement from the beginning of life to the end, movement defined in terms of goals set by the individual for attainment within his lifetime.

the thrust is toward the outer world, and toward mastery of the environment. In middle age, there comes a realignment and restructuring of ego processes; and, to the extent to which these processes become conscious, a re-examination of the self. In old age, there is a turning inward, a withdrawal of investment from the outer world, and a new preoccupation with the inner world. Finally, there is a stage in which the ego undergoes something of a last restructuring preparatory to death.

This is but a gross approximation of a developmental view of ego processes—a view which has, as yet, only limited evidence to support it. It is, nevertheless, against this framework that certain concepts and certain sets of empirical findings can be elaborated.

From Youth to Young Adulthood

The transition from adolescence into adulthood is, of course, a period marked by major transformation in the *social* personality, as the individual meets the major developmental tasks connected with vocational achievement, marital adjustment, home-making, and child-rearing. As already implied in the earlier discussion of continuity, however, findings are less clear with regard to changes in intrapsychic processes. It is an interesting fact that there have been relatively few studies in which age-groups in the twenties and thirties are compared on the same measures with groups just younger or just older. (Even in the longitudinal studies referred to earlier, the results are usually reported in terms of change in relative position of individuals within the group, and not in terms of those characteristics that may be regarded as most salient in young adulthood.) With the growth of interest in gerontology, there are large numbers of studies now appearing in which young adults are compared with old; but only a few of these studies have been couched in terms of ego processes.

Judging from descriptions of personality that emerge from a wide variety of studies, both experimental and observational, the generalization is probably warranted that development from adolescence to young adulthood is marked by an increase in expressivity, in expansiveness, and in extraversion. The high anxiety characteristic of adolescence seems to decrease. Feelings of autonomy, of

competence, and of stability increase, as social roles become stabilized. There is probably more equilibrium in mood, more integration of ego processes with impulse life, and relative stabilization
of ego identity. A few of the studies which lead to these generalizations are those by Nawas (1961), Brožek (1955), Schaefer (1962),
Willoughby (1937-38), Cattell (1957), Rongved (1961), and
White (1952).

This is the tenor, for instance, of Sanford's conclusions, based
upon studies of Vassar alumnae: "The evidence is that, in general,
gains in the direction of greater complexity of personality, made in
college, are maintained three to four years after graduation. But
change does not usually continue after college. Instead, what
seems to occur mainly is a kind of stabilization. When groups of
young alumnae were retested with the use of a variety of personality tests three or four years after graduation, the only really
significant differences lay in the greater stability, freedom from
anxiety, and general psychological well-being shown in the later
testing. . . . [We are] led to assume that there is a developmental
phase, marked primarily by increasing stabilization of personality,
that begins around the junior year in college and extends well into
the alumnae years" (Sanford, 1962, p. 808).

From Young to Middle Adulthood

To continue at this level of generalization, overt behavior and
social personality seem to become even more stabilized in the
period from young to middle adulthood. People move into a
plateau in the middle years with regard to role performance, as
family, work, and recreational patterns show less change than at
earlier or later periods in the life line. Self-reports, particularly
those of middle-class and professional groups, tend to emphasize
greater self-confidence, a sense of achievement and mastery, and
an awareness of maturity. There are, for example, the well-known
studies by Strong (1931, 1951) of changes of interests. In the first
study more change was found for professional men aged twenty to
fifty-nine in the decade from twenty-five to thirty-five than in the
two decades that followed. In the second, data based upon test-
retest of high school seniors and college students after an interval

of twenty-one years showed that those whose interests were similar to those of engineers, lawyers, or ministers on the first occasion were persons whose interests were similar to those same criterion groups on the second occasion. There is also the early study of Willoughby (1937-38), which indicates a drop in emotionality and mental stress by the forties; there is the work of Cattell (1957), which shows a consistent increase in the direction of greater adjustment between ages fifteen and fifty-five; and there is at least one study (Neugarten and Peterson, 1957) in which the forties were reported as the "prime" of life by middle-class respondents.

It is probable, furthermore, that, with regard to intrapsychic processes, the period from young adulthood to middle adulthood is marked by a decrease in emotional reactivity, a decrease in tension, greater introversion, and a certain degree of "constriction" (probably a reflection of the greater preoccupation with the self that begins in middle adulthood).

Beginning in the forties, however, there seem to be the first signs of the major redirection of ego cathexis from outer to inner concerns.

In an early investigation of adult personality made within the Committee on Human Development at the University of Chicago, for example, three groups of men were studied, of mean ages thirty, forty, and fifty, all of whom were employed in administrative positions in business (Schaw and Henry, 1956). In this study, responses to the Thematic Apperception Test were analyzed for dominant themes. The thirty year olds were found to hold a view of the outer world as achievement-demanding. These men seemed willing to follow assertively the cues provided by the outer world; and seemed confident that one achieved one's goals by devotion to those demands, and by relating directly and forcefully to an environment which is relatively uncomplicated. The forty year olds, however, saw the world in more complex and conflictual terms. There was a re-examination of inner drives and a questioning of achievement demands, those demands which seemed so right and reasonable to the younger men. There was also an increased self-awareness and a preoccupation with one's emotions.

The fifty year olds seemed also to experience outer world events as complex and conflictual; but they appeared to find resolutions by moving to abstract integrative systems as means of dealing with the environment, and by preoccupying themselves with thought rather than with action. The basic nature of the age change appeared to be a movement from an active, combative, outer-world orientation to the beginnings of an adaptive, conforming and more inner-world orientation.

(In the absence of other studies which bear directly upon this redirection of ego cathexis, there are those in which the findings are indirectly corroborative: the study by Willoughby (1937-38) which showed increased introversion in both sexes in their late forties; a study by Gray (1947) which showed decreased extraversion through the middle-adult years; and a study by Hays (1952) which showed a significant trend toward constriction and introversion in Rorschach test performances beginning in the fifties.)

From Middle to Old Age

There are several related studies of middle and old age, not all of them published, which have been carried out as part of the larger set of inquiries that have come to be known as the Kansas City Studies of Adult Life. They are all based upon large samples of normal people, and, with the exception of one group of very aged, upon samples drawn by probability techniques from the community at large. Although these are cross-sectional studies, they have been designed specifically to clarify differences between age groups with regard to ego processes.

In describing these investigations and in high-lighting the transitions from middle to old age, it will be noticed that the usual procedure is being reversed—the procedure in which changes in the first part of life are utilized in drawing implications for later stages. In this instance, by focusing upon the last half of the life span, certain implications have appeared with regard to the first half.

There have been, in the Kansas City studies, three different lines of investigation that bear upon personality. The first relates to the social personality, where attention has been focused upon gross patterns of social interaction and social competence, and upon behavior that is relatively overt and public. The second relates to personal adjustment and life satisfaction. The third is focused upon the more covert and less readily observed aspects of personality, the intrapsychic processes.

The inconsistent findings that have emerged in each of these three areas with regard to age differences are important in clarifying developmental changes in ego processes.

In the studies of social competence, there are neither significant nor consistent age changes in the years from forty to sixty-five, but marked shifts thereafter. Thus, Havighurst (1957) rated the performance of 240 men and women from varying social class levels in nine major roles (worker, parent, spouse, homemaker, user of leisure time, friend, citizen, club and association member, and church member) and found that the quality of role performance did not vary appreciably in the period from forty to sixty-five. Not until individuals reached the mid-sixties, on the average, did patterns of social interaction show marked changes. This is demonstrated also in studies in which various measures of social interaction were utilized (Cumming and Henry, 1961): the number of social roles, the number of hours of a typical day spent in interaction with others, and the total number of interactions with different kinds of people over an interval of one month. Here, with a sample of more than 200 persons aged fifty through eighty-five, the most marked changes appeared around age sixty-five.

Studies of adjustment and/or life satisfaction in Kansas City residents have shown no consistent relations with age. For instance, Peck and Berkowitz (1959) rated overall adjustment for a sample of 120 persons aged forty to sixty-four from all social class levels, and found no relationship to chronological age. Similarly, in a study by Neugarten, Havighurst, and Tobin (1961) based upon four rounds of interviews taken over a period of two years with more than 200 persons aged fifty to eighty-five, ratings made on different components of life satisfaction (the individual's zest for life; his mood tone; his sense of resolution or fortitude; the congruence between his desired and achieved life goals; and the degree to which the self is positively regarded) showed no correlations with age. It appears, then, that age is not a significant variable with respect to adjustment, not only in the twenty-five year age span prior to sixty-five, but probably in the decades of the seventies and eighties as well.[5]

By contrast, when the investigations were concerned with issues such as the perception of the self vis-a-vis the external environment, the handling of impulse life, or the nature of ego boundaries, the findings led to the conclusion that there are significant and consistent age differences from age forty onward. These differences become clear in moving to successively more covert measures of personality as, for example, from measures based upon interview data to measures based upon projective data analyzed blind for age of respondent.[6]

The first of these projective studies was one based on responses of 131 men and women aged forty to seventy to a specially-drawn TAT-type picture (Neugarten and Gutmann, 1958). Although this study was primarily an investigation of perceptions of age-sex roles, the data suggested consistent age differences in personality. Forty year olds seemed to see themselves as possessing energy congruent with the opportunities perceived in the outer world; the environment was seen as rewarding boldness and risk-taking; and the individual obtained from the outer world what he put into it. For older respondents, the world was seen as complex and dangerous, no longer to be reformed in line with one's own wishes; and the individual was seen as con-

---

[5] This finding relative to life satisfaction at the older ages must be interpreted with great caution, since the seventy and eighty year old subjects in these studies were individuals who suffered neither from major illness nor from economic deprivation, and thus constituted a relatively select group of survivors.

[6] There are special problems of research method involved in studies of adult, as compared to child, personality. Not only is the adult subject more practised than the child in controlling the information revealed in an interview or on a test; but the investigator himself has difficulty in avoiding a shifting frame of reference in making evaluation judgments of performance in forty-year-olds as compared, say, to seventy-year-olds. These problems are avoided to a considerable degree in studies based on projective test responses. Although the studies being reported here involve primarily the Thematic Apperception Test, inspection of other projective data on the same persons based on Sentence Completion and Draw-a-Person tests were corroborative of the overall findings with regard to age.

forming and accommodating to outer world demands. The protagonist was no longer a forceful manipulator of the object world, but a relatively passive object manipulated by the environment.

This study indicated also that with increasing age, ego functions are turned inward, as it were; and while rational thought processes are still important in the personality, thought becomes less relevant to action.

The same study suggested important differences between men and women as they age. For instance, men seem to become more receptive to their own affiliative, nurturant, and sensual promptings; while women seem to become more responsive toward, and less guilty about, their own aggressive, egocentric impulses.[7]

In another study (Gutmann, Henry, and Neugarten, 1959), the stories told by 144 men to four standard TAT cards were analyzed. The most frequent stories given by men in the forty to forty-nine age group were those in which virility and resistance to coercion were stressed, and in which there was energetic and motoric approach to the environment. Stories given by fifty year olds were frequently those in which passive and deferent, rather than rebellious or defiant, heroes were projected. In the stories given by sixty year olds, these conflicts seemed to have been resolved. The most frequent stories were now those in which heroes were conforming, abasive, meek, friendly, mild, and in which aggression was perceived only in the external world. The stories were also those in which parental figures or impersonal institutional demands were important in the story outcomes.

A somewhat different approach was used in another study in which the hypothesis was tested that with increased age there is a decrease in energy available to the

---

[7] Sex differences are consistent and often striking in studies of adult personality, just as they are in studies of child and adolescent personality. While the topic cannot be adequately treated within the limits of the present paper, there is considerable evidence that the sexes become increasingly divergent with age.

ego for responding to outer world events (Rosen and Neugarten, 1960). Four dimensions of ego function were measured from TAT data: the ability to integrate wide ranges of stimuli; the readiness to perceive or to deal with complicated, challenging, or conflictual situations; the tendency toward vigorous and assertive activity ascribed to story characters; and the tendency to perceive feelings and affects as they play a part in life situations. With a sample of 144 men and women aged forty to seventy-one divided into equal subgroups by age, sex, and social class, a three-way analysis of variance indicated that age was the significant factor in accounting for differences in the responses. Scores decreased regularly with age in the predicted direction.

Gutmann has proceeded to investigate further the indication that concerns with inner life increase as aging progresses. Again working inductively from projective data (but drawing also, at later stages in the analysis, from other sets of data on the same individuals, including ratings and interview responses), he has formulated five personality types in men aged forty to seventy-one, based upon these dimensions: 1) major concerns and preoccupations, especially in the area of impulse life; 2) the ego defenses or coping mechanisms elaborated in response to such preoccupations; and 3) the relative success or failure of these coping mechanisms. For women he also delineated five types, although the most salient psychological issues for women are not identical with those for men. For women, the dimensions underlying the typology include also the extent to which personal conflicts are externalized and projected onto the outside world; and the extent of intropunitiveness or extrapunitiveness. For both sexes, there was a consistent relationship between personality type and age, with a clear movement from active to passive to "magical" approaches to the environment. Although the increased concern with self is projected in different ways by men and women, both sexes move to more egocentric, self-preoccupied positions, and attend more to the control or to the satisfaction of personal needs (Gutmann, 1961).

In summary, these studies demonstrated significant age differences in regard to intrapsychic aspects of personality. These differences refer primarily to the *modes* of relating to the environment and of dealing with impulse life. There is a change from active to passive modes of mastery, and a movement of energy away from an outer-world to an inner-world orientation.

That these processes begin to be measurable by the time persons reach their forties is one point to be stressed, since in these years gross measures of social personality show no age changes.

The findings from these studies carried out at Chicago are generally congruent with the findings of other investigators, even though they have been formulated in somewhat different terms. Others have reported over and over again increased introversion in old age, decline in intellectual efficiency, reduction in activities and interests. There are other findings described in terms of increased rigidity of personality,[8] stereotypy, flattened affect, conservation of energy, avoidance of stimuli, and what some investigators choose to call "regression."

The direction of change from outer- to inner-world preoccupation is not identical with the change from expansion to restriction, as this process has often been described by others (Kuhlen, 1959, for instance). The latter may, indeed, be an accurate description of personality change in the adult years as, for instance, physical energy declines and as losses occur in many of those biological functions that are usually regarded as operating in the service of the ego—visual and aural acuity, memory, speed of reaction time, to mention only a few. The expansion-restriction interpretation is usually presented, however, in terms somewhat different from the ones used here—that is, as reactions to gains in early maturity, and as reactions to losses in old age. It is primarily with the concept of personality as a reactive set of processes that the present formulation differs.

The findings just described can, indeed, be interpreted differ-

---

[8] In an extensive review of the literature by Chown (1959), however, the concept of rigidity as a personality trait seems to have been put to rest. She has marshalled the evidence to show that there are many types and many components of rigidity; and that rigidity cannot be generalized from one situation to another.

ently: for instance, that as the individual ages he suffers sensory deprivation—or, more accurately, perhaps, both sensory and social deprivation; and that the response is "depressive" in reaction to the losses. Whether or not the change in personality has inherent as well as reactive qualities cannot yet be established, given the findings presently available. The major reason for interpreting certain of these changes as primarily inherent, or developmental, is that they seem to occur well before the "losses" of aging can be said to begin. In other words, the fact that these personality changes appear by the mid-forties in a group of well-functioning adults seems congruent with a developmental, rather than with a reactive, view of personality.

Engagement-disengagement

The studies just described have contributed to the theory of disengagement stated by Cumming and Henry (1961). These studies suggest a set of psychological processes which may be primarily intrinsic, and which contribute to a state of decreased interaction between the aging person and others in the social group to which he belongs. The psychological aspects of disengagement include a change in behavioral motivation, with possibly a lessened desire for approval, increased freedom of choice of life rewards, an increased tendency to select short-run gratifications, and finally, a withdrawal from intense emotional attachments to people and objects.[9]

On the hypothesis that psychological disengagement occurs in old age, the implication is that in youth and young adulthood, as the individual's network of social interaction becomes progressively more complex and more engrossing, there is an accompanying increase in psychological engagement with the world of persons and objects. In short, the implication is that the ego becomes increasingly preoccupied with the external world up through middle age; and that disengagement has its corollary, if not its forerunner,

---

[9] The theory of disengagement as set forth in the book *Growing Old* (Cumming and Henry, 1961) is being analyzed further in the light of new sets of data. Although all these data are not yet processed, it is likely that the theory will not only be elaborated, but also modified in major respects.

in the redirection of psychological cathexis from external to internal stimuli.

Perceptions of Time and of Death

It will be noted the middle years of life—probably the decade of the fifty's for most persons—represent an important turning-point in personality organization. Schilder (1940) undoubtedly had a similar point in mind when he spoke of the phase of "libidinous rearrangement" as the first phase in aging.

This change seems to occur somewhat later than Erikson's generativity crisis in ego development. Although Erikson has not attached specific chronological ages to his stages of adult personality, the concept of generativity is centered upon involvement with children and upon the sense that one has contributed to the future. Accordingly, the restructuring of the ego in terms of generativity is one that must occur, for most persons, before they reach the empty nest in the family cycle.

It appears also that Erikson's intimacy and generativity are both stages in which the ego is focused upon objects outside the self; and that they are both encompassed, accordingly, within that longer time period when the ego's primary preoccupation is with the outer world.

In any case, there is another process which promotes change in personality and which seems to occur in the middle years of life: the re-evaluation of time, and the formulation of new perceptions of time and of death. Others have described these processes (Cumming and Henry, 1961, for instance) in somewhat different words; but whatever are the most appropriate terms to describe it, there comes a time, usually in the middle years, when the individual realizes that time is not infinite, and that the self will die. Along with this realization may come, also, an end to measuring one's life-time from the date of one's birth, and measuring it, instead, from the distance from one's death. This is the period when it is typical to begin to take stock of one's life and to ponder what one may yet accomplish (or what one may yet obtain) in the time remaining. Time takes on a new saliency for a great many, if not all persons; to judge, at least, from anecdotal and self-report data. It is at this point in the life line that introspection increases and contemplation of one's inner thoughts becomes a characteristic form of mental life.

The implication is not that the introspection of middle age is the same as the reminiscence of old age; but it is its fore-runner. It is probably a preparatory step in the final restructuring of the ego that, in Erikson's terms, is the attainment of integrity, the symbolic putting of one's house in order before one dies.

The hypothesis that personality change occurs at the very end of life should not be relegated entirely to the realm of speculation. Recent work by Kleemeier (1961) on changes in IQ performance demonstrates a factor which influences the rate of observed decline and which, within the period of old age, is related to the imminence of death rather than to the age of the individual.

Similarly, there is the ongoing work by Lieberman (1962) on Bender-Gestalt and Figure-Drawing tests. In a small group of aged persons measured repeatedly at four-week intervals, there seems to come a point in time for each individual when his drawings of the human figure and his ability to reproduce the geometric figures of the Bender test undergo dramatic and irrversible change. The timing of these changes seems related to the time of death, and seems to occur in the absence of other observable social or biological changes that might be acting as precipitating events.

Whether or not these changes in performance are symptoms that herald imminent biological collapse, they are psychological in nature. Both these studies indicate personality change in the same general direction being described here—a shift in ego-organization and a shift in the direction of cathexis.

There is also the work of Butler (1963) who, drawing upon his clinical observations of aged persons, postulates the universal occurrence of what he calls the "life review." This is a process in which the aged individual, perceiving his approaching death, utilizes reminiscence to review his life. There is a progressive return to consciousness of past experience and unresolved conflicts, in which these experiences are surveyed and reintegrated. While the process can lead to destructive as well as to constructive outcomes, it represents personality change that is often profound. Within the present framework, Butler's observations are of special interest because he believes the life review occurs irrespective of environmental conditions.

If indeed the life review occurs in most persons, it is but another manifestation of the ego processes described here; and it implies that the ego undergoes a final restructuring in preparing for death —another evidence of personality change that is developmental.

In summary, the thesis of this paper may be restated as follows: As is true in childhood and adolescence, changes in personality occur throughout the long period of life we call adulthood. Although the evidence is inadequate, there are data to support the position that changes occur in intrapsychic processes as well as in more readily observable behavior; such changes are orderly and developmental in nature; there is a general direction of change from active to passive modes of relating to the environment; there is a general movement of energy from an outer-world to an inner-world orientation. The realignment and redirection of ego processes begins in middle, rather than in old age.

REFERENCES

1. Anderson, J. E.: Prediction of adjustment over time. In Iscoe, I., and Stevenson, H. A. (Eds.): *Personality Development in Children.* Austin, Univ. of Texas Press, 1960, pp. 28-72.

2. Brožek, J.: Personality changes with age. *J. Geront., 10:*194-206, 1955.

3. Buhler, Charlotte: Genetic aspects of the self. In Harms, E. (Ed.): Fundamentals of psychology: the psychology of the self. *Ann. New York Acad. Sci., 96:*730-764, 1962 and Social roles and the life cycle. Paper presented at the annual meeting of the Amer. Soc. Assn., Washington, D.C., 1962.

4. Butler, R. N.: The life review: an interpretation of reminiscence in the aged. *Psychiatry, 26:*65-76, 1963.

5. Cattell, R. B.: *Personality and Motivation Structure and Measurement.* New York, World, 1957.

6. Chown, Sheila M.: Rigidity — a flexible concept. *Psychol. Bull.,* 56:195-223, 1959.

7. Cumming, Elaine, and Henry, W. E.: *Growing Old.* New York, Basic Books, 1961.

8. Davis, A., and Dollard, J.: *Children of Bondage.* Washington, D.C., Amer. Council on Education, 1940.

9. Erikson, E. H.: Identity and the life cycle: selected papers. *Psychol. Issues,* 1959, Monograph No. 1.

10. Gray, H.: Psychological types and changes with age. *J. clin. Psychol.,* 3:273-277, 1947.

11. Grinker, R. R.: On identification. *Int. J. Psychoanal., 38*:1-12, 1957.

12. Gutman, D. L.: Personality in middle and later life: a Thematic Apperception Test study. Unpublished paper on file with the Committee on Human Development, University of Chicago, 1961.

13. Gutmann, D. L., Henry, W. E., and Neugarten, Bernice L.: Personality development in middle aged men. Paper read at Amer. Psychol. Assn., Cincinnati, September, 1959.

14. Hartmann, H.: *Ego Psychology and the Problem of Adaptation.* New York, Int. Universities Press, 1958.

15. Hartmann, H., Kris, E., and Lowenstein, R. M.: Comments on the formation of psychic structure. *Psychoanalytic Study of the Child, 2*: 11-38, 1946.

16. Havighurst, R. J.: Social competence of middle-aged people. *Genet. Psychol. Monogr., 56*:297-375, 1957.

17. Havighurst, R. J., Bowman, P. H., Liddle, G. P., Matthews, C. V., and Pierce, J. V.: *Growing Up in River City.* New York, Wiley, 1962.

18. Hays, W.: Age and sex differences on the Rorschach Experience Balance. *J. abnorm. soc. Psychol., 47*:390-393, 1952.

19. Hess, R. D.: High school antecedents of young adult performance. Paper read at Amer. Educ. Res. Assn., Atlantic City, February, 1962.

20. Jones, H. E.: Consistency and change in early maturity. *Vit. Hum., 1*: 43-51, 1958.

21. Jones, H. E., Macfarlane, Jean W., and Eichorn, Dorothy H.: Progress report on growth studies at the University of California. *Vit. Hum., 3*:17-31, 1960.

22. Kagan, J., and Moss, H. A.: *Birth to Maturity.* New York, Wiley, 1962.

23. Kelly, E. L.: Consistency of the adult personality. *Amer. Psychologist, 10*:659-681, 1955.

24. Kleemeier, R. W.: Intellectual changes in the senium, or death and the I.Q. Paper read at Amer. Psychol. Ass., St. Louis, September, 1961.

25. Kuhlen, R. G.: Age and intelligence: the significance of cultural change in longitudinal vs. cross-sectional findings. *Vit. Hum., 6*:113-124, 1963; and Aging and life-adjustment. In J. E. Birren (Ed.), *Handbook of Aging and the Individual.* Chicago, Univer. of Chicago Press, 1959, pp. 852-897.

26. Lieberman, M. A.: Personal communication. August, 1962.

27. Maslow, A. H.: A theory of human motivation. *Psychol. Rev., 50:*370-396, 1943.

28. Mulvey, Mary C.: Psychological and sociological factors in the prediction of career patterns of women. Unpublished doctoral dissertation, Harvard University, 1961.

29. Murray, H. A. and others: *Explorations of Personality.* New York, Oxford Univer. Press, 1938.

30. Mussen, P.: Some antecedents and consequents of masculine sex typing in adolescent boys. *Psychol. Monogr., 75:* No. 2 (Whole No. 506), 1961.

31. Nawas, M. M.: Longitudinal study of the changes in ego sufficiency and complexity from adolescence to young adulthood as reflected in the TAT. Unpublished doctoral dissertation, Univer. of Chicago, 1961.

32. Neugarten, Bernice L., and Gutmann, D. L.: Age-sex roles and personality in middle age: a thematic apperception study. *Psychol. Monogr., 72:* No. 17 (Whole No. 470), 1958.

33. Neugarten, Bernice L., Havighurst, R. J., and Tobin, S. S.: The measurement of life satisfaction. *J. Geront., 16:*134-143, 1961.

34. Neugarten, Bernice L., and Peterson, W. A.: Study of the American age-grade system. *Proc. Fourth Congr. Int. Ass. Geront., Merano, It., July 14-19, 1957,* Vol. 3, pp. 497-502.

35. Peck, R. F., and Berkowitz, H.: Personality and adjustment in middle age. Unpublished manuscript on file with the Committee on Human Development, Univer. of Chicago, 1959.

36. Rapaport, D.: Historical survey of psychoanalytic ego psychology. *Psychol. Issues,* Monograph No. 1, pp. 5-17, 1959.

37. Rogers, C. R.: *Client-centered Therapy.* Boston, Houghton-Mifflin, 1951.

38. Rohrer, J. H., and Edmonson, M. S. (Eds.): *The Eighth Generation.* New York, Harper, 1960.

39. Rongved, M: Sex and age differences in self perception. *Vit. Hum., 4:* 148-158, 1961.

40. Rosen, Jacqueline L., and Neugarten, Bernice L.: Ego functions in the middle and later years: a thematic apperception study of normal adults. *J. Geront., 15:*62-67, 1960.

41. Sanford, N. (Ed.): *The American College: A New Psychological and Social Interpretation of Higher Learning.* New York, Wiley, 1962.

42. Schaw, L. C., and Henry, W. E.: A method for the comparison of groups: a study in thematic apperception. *Genet. Psychol. Monogr., 54:*207-253, 1956.

43. Schaefer, Judith B.: Stability and change in thematic apperception test response from adolescence to adulthood. Unpublished doctoral dissertation, Univer. of Chicago, 1962.

44. Schilder, P.: Psychiatric aspects of old age and aging. *Amer. J. Orthopsychiat., 10:*62-69, 1940.

45. Sherif, M.: The self and reference groups: meeting ground of individual and group approaches. In E. Harms (Ed.), Fundamentals of psychology: the psychology of the self. *Ann. New York Acad. Sci., 96*: 797-813, 1962.

46. Shoben, E. J., Jr.: Behavioral aspects of the self. In E. Harms (Ed.), Fundamentals of psychology: the psychology of the self. *Ann. New York Acad. Sci., 96*:765-773, 1962.

47. Smith, Medorah: A comparison of certain personality traits as rated in the same individuals in childhood and 50 years later. *Child Develp., 23*:161-180, 1952.

48. Strong, E. K., Jr.: *Change of Interests with Age.* Stanford: Stanford Univer. Press, 1931; and Permanence of interest scores over 22 years. *J. appl. Psychol., 35*:89-91, 1951.

49. Symonds, P. M.: *From Adolescent to Adult.* New York, Columbia Univer. Press, 1961.

50. Terman, L. M., and Oden, M. H.: *The Gifted Group at Mid-life.* Stanford Univer. Press, 1959.

51. Tuddenham, R. D.: Constancy of personality ratings over two decades. *Genet. Psychol. Monogr., 60*:3-29, 1959.

52. White, R. W.: Competence and the psychosexual stages of development. In M. R. Jones (Ed.): *Nebraska Symposium on Motivation: 1960.* Lincoln, Univer. of Nebraska Press, 1960, pp. 97-143.

53. White, R. W.: *Lives in Progress.* New York, Dryden, 1952.

54. Willoughby, R. R.: The relationship to emotionality of age, sex, and conjugal condition. *Amer. J. Soc., 43:*920-931, 1937-38.

Chapter 13

DEVELOPMENTAL CHANGES IN MOTIVATION DURING THE ADULT YEARS*

Raymond G. Kuhlen

Whatever the specific role assigned to motivation by psychologists interested in learning and performance, there is little disagreement that it is an important variable, especially in more complex types of learning and "real life" situations. The psychological needs of individuals determine in part those aspects of the environment to which they attend and respond, the direction in which efforts are expended, and the amount of energy thrown into a task. But in addition, motivational concepts have proved extremely useful in understanding the behavior of individuals and groups at any one point in time, and define some of the more important variables determining the course of development as the years pass.

After consideration of some of the circumstances that result in developmental changes in motivation, the bulk of the present discussion will focus, first, upon growth-expansion motives, and second, upon anxiety and threat as a source of motivation. As one views the course of human life growth-expansion motives seem to dominate the first half of the adult years, with needs stemming from insecurity and threat becoming important in the later years.

---

* Adapted slightly from a paper entitled "Motivational Changes During The Adult Years" in R. G. Kuhlen (Ed.) *Psychological Backgrounds of Adult Education.* Chicago, Center for the Study of Liberal Education for Adults, 1963. Parts of the present chapter have also appeared in a chapter by R. G. Kuhlen in Philip Worchel and Donn Byrne (eds.) *Personality Change,* N. Y.: Wiley, 1964.

While this is obviously an oversimplification of the picture, and circumstances will vary greatly from individual to individual and from group to group, these contrasting trends appear to emerge from various studies of the adult life span.

FACTORS INFLUENCING DEVELOPMENTAL CHANGES IN ADULT MOTIVATION

At the outset, it may be worthwhile to examine some of the factors that are likely to result in important differences between people of various ages in their motivational patterns. Whether a need is aroused and influential or quiescent and latent in particular phases of adult life will likely be a function of a number of the variables to be discussed below.

Changes in Arousal Cues, Environmental Stimulation and Expectations

It is a matter of common observation, as well as a conclusion from psychological research, that even relatively satiated human desires can be aroused given the proper environmental stimulation, that motives may be weakened to the point of near disappearance if long periods of years are encountered with little opportunity for gratification of reinforcement, and that new motivational tendencies may appear if new types of stimulation or expectation (and reinforcement) are encountered. A society or culture decrees in many subtle ways, and in some not so subtle, that certain types of stimulation will be brought to bear on certain age groups and largely withheld from those of other ages. One of the problems that has plagued investigators of adult learning, for example, is the fact that once he has mastered his job, the typical adult is neither stimulated nor required to master new skills or understandings. The sameness of stimulation—whether on the job, in recreation, in marriage and sex—may be an important factor in the apparent decline of certain motivational tendencies, such as curiosity. An important, though unanswered, question concerns the nature of age trends under circumstances which permit or require that older individuals be subjected to new types of stimulation. Does a middle-aged person who changes jobs or spouses find career or sex drives rekindled, for example?

Moreover, since the motivational tendencies of people are very largely learned as a result of the reward and punishment systems to which they are exposed during the course of early development, it is reasonable to expect that motives may be *changed* during adulthood if the individual is exposed to a new set of punishment and reward patterns. Thus, as an individual moves into a new role, e.g., is perceived by others as being middle-aged or old, he may be subjected to a new pattern of expectations, a new set of approvals and disapprovals, with the result that in due course new motives may appear.

Satisfaction of Needs and Changing Motivation

It is helpful in understanding some of the motivational changes that occur during the adult years to assume that human beings have a number of "needs" which vary in importance. In a sense they are arranged in a hierarchy with the influence of higher level needs being to a considerable extent dependent upon the state of affairs with respect to lower level needs. Maslow (1943), among others, has argued that, generally speaking, more basic needs must be satisfied before higher level needs become operative. This particular conception of the relationship among psychological needs is useful in explaining some of the changes in motivation that come with adult years.

Among middle-class Americans, for example, career drives are likely to take precedence over many other psychological needs, and dominate the years of young adulthood, perhaps even to the point of resulting in minimal contact with family. If by forty or forty-five, the career-oriented individual has achieved economic security and success, the need to "get ahead" (the achievement need) may be much less in evidence, and the former career-oriented individual may turn more frequently to family or to community activities as sources of gratification. "Affiliation" or "service" needs then may be more important. A similar change in the importance of sex as a drive may occur with the passage of years, and in part for the same reasons. In addition to having a strong sex drive in sheer biological terms, the adolescent or young adult is likely to be frustrated in his free expression and satisfaction of this drive. With marriage and more ready satisfaction of sex needs other motivations may emerge as important. One may speculate that Maslow's conception may partially account for the fact that sex needs may take precedence over convention in adolescence whereas the reverse may be true of the parents of adolescents.

In sum, needs that are important in one phase of life may fade out and give way to others simply because they have become relatively satisfied. However, if circumstances should again arise which result in the frustration of a need previously satisfied that need may again become active. For example, autonomy needs may be strong in youth, but become submerged as the individual becomes independent and self-directing. But if a situation should later arise where his autonomy is threatened, by a domineering employer or even by the protective cloak of kindness with which we sometimes envelop old people, then the need to be self-directive and independent may reassert itself.

Age-Related Frustration of Needs

It was suggested above that lower level or more basic needs may become inoperative and thus give way to higher level needs *when they are satisfied*. It is also not unlikely that chronic frustration will tend similarly to make need inoperative. Lewin and his students pointed out some years ago that when children were unable to obtain an attractive goal object, such as toys within their vision but out of reach, they soon behaved as though the toys were no longer a part of their psychological field. Similarly, long and chronic frustration of some need may result in the individual turning to other sources of satisfaction. His behavior seems subsequently to reflect other motivations. Thus, while a person may experience a reduction in achievement need and career drive because he has been successful, by like token he may experience a similar decrease because he has been chronically unsuccessful.

Because frustration may play a pervasive role in motivational changes, as suggested in the preceding paragraphs as well as in the preceding pages, it may be worthwhile to specify some of the age-related factors that may prove frustrating and hence influence the motivational complex of the adult. Five sources of frustration merit comment.

First is the degree of status accorded people of different ages in the particular society in which they live out their lives. There seems to be general agreement that the American society tends to be geared to and to idealize youth, with the result that older individuals not only are frustrated somewhat with respect to status needs, but are very likely to encounter reduced opportunities for gratification of other rather important needs.

In the second place, people of different ages are likely to experience limitations and pressures of time and money. Man is a time-bound organism, in the sense that he has only twenty-four hours a day at his disposal.* This fact forces people, especially those in certain age ranges, to make choices, to push aside certain interests and activities which they previously enjoyed. Unpracticed and unreinforced, often for many years, certain motivational tendencies may essentially disappear. As in the case of time, unavailability of money can result in certain "needs" dropping out of the picture, because of lack of practice and lack of reinforcement, whereas increasing availability of funds may result in their reappearance and the development and cultivation of new needs.

Whereas time is relatively absolute and can be stretched only a little by efficiencies, money can be made to increase by appropriate expenditure of effort. Some data suggest that economic demands are greater in the thirty to forty decade (Johnson, 1951). At such a point in life, the economic drives can be highly motivating force. Economic pressures, coupled and merged with career advancement desires, probably accounts for a large share of the young adults enrolled in adult education programs. The force of the economic drive is apparent even in the history of geniuses whose productivity often bears a striking relationship to their need for money.

A third frustrating or limiting circumstance influencing motivation at different ages involves physical change and decline. The decline in physical energy, resiliency, strength and reaction time—the general slowing down of the organism—has a pervasive effect upon behavior, perhaps as evident as anywhere in the recreational pursuits which people of different ages engage in. While it is

---

* Man also has a relatively finite life span. Time perspectives, in this sense, will be mentioned later.

generally assumed that physiological drives are important motivators in infancy and early childhood, to be replaced gradually by
the socially derived motives which soon come to dominate the
behavioral scene, the question may well be raised as to whether
physiological pressures and tensions may not again become important motivators in the later years. One may argue that such would
be the case due to the fact that as frustrating agents they demand
attention. In some cases there does seem to be general concern
and preoccupation with physiological functioning, but how general this may be is uncertain. But if physiological pressures again
become important, they become so in a different psychological
context. In early infancy social needs have not yet developed. In
old age the difficulties of physiological function, of digestion and
elimination, for example, and greater susceptibility to fatigue and
illness may make satisfaction of derived needs more difficult or
impossible and require greater attention to diet and general regi-
men. A re-emergence of physiological pressures as a motivating
force may result.

Fourth, a middle-aged or older person may feel threatened and
insecure because of skill deficits generated by rapid technological
advance that has left him outdated. It should be noted that gains
on vocabulary and information subtests of general ability tests may
obscure this fact suggesting, as they do, increasing cognitive
resources as experience accumulates.

Fifth, and finally, is the greater threat and frustration that
people may encounter because of their inability to do anything
about some of the disturbing circumstances and sources of unhappiness which they experience. A person tends to get "locked in"
particular circumstances as he marries, has children, invests in
property, accumulates training and seniority, and may find himself unable to move out of a frustrating situation from which the
younger uncommitted individual could easily free himself. Threats,
such as of loss of job, are thus much more serious for the committed, and older, individual than for the younger.

Critical Periods and Motivational Changes

The foregoing discussion has suggested that certain motives
may be stronger at some periods of life than at others because of

the degree to which special stimulation, special frustration, or satisfaction is encountered at those ages. Are there to be found any particularly critical periods in the life span? Do, for example, changes such as those associated with the menopause result in a reorganization of the motivational structure of the individual? While the evidence seems to be essentially negative with respect to the menopause period, it does seem probable that various factors combine to concentrate satisfactions and threats at particular periods of life. Scott and others (1951) have advanced the hypothesis that "critical periods" may be found at various points throughout the life span, particularly at those points when important changes in the social relationships of individuals occur. If this hypothesis has merit, it may be expected that such events as marriage, becoming a parent or grandparent, or loss of spouse or job would influence in important ways the motivational pattern of an individual. Sometimes the effects may be dramatic, as in the instance of an elderly spinster who became quite a different person subsequent to the death of the domineering sister with whom she had lived her entire adult life.

Changing time perspectives represent another factor causing critical periods in the motivational history of the individual. The point in life, perhaps the late thirty's or early forty's, when one comes to the realization that time and life is not infinite probably has quite a significant effect upon one's orientation and motivation. The here and now becomes much more important; if goals are to be achieved, they must be achieved soon. One is almost forced to structure his psychological present and future on a "real" rather than an "unreal" level. Biology and culture combine to set particular sublimits within the total span of life. Thus, thirty seems to be a critical time for the single woman hoping for marriage; the forty's for the individual striving for success in career but not yet achieving it; the late forties for the woman who has married late and wants children; retirement age for the professor who wants to finish a book before leaving the university.

Depending upon the circumstances in individual cases, critical points introduced by changing time perspectives may very well result in reorientations of such magnitude that one can in a very real sense think of an important change, not simple in goal object but in motivation pattern, or one might anticipate heightened motivation as time begins to run out. For others there may be a building up of unhappiness and anxiety, which in themselves represent strong motivating forces. And at any and all of these points there may be periods of serious self-appraisal.

GROWTH-EXPANSION MOTIVES

In the introductory paragraphs to this paper it was pointed out that discussion would focuss upon (a) growth-expansion motives and (b) anxiety and threat as a source of motivation. We turn to the first of these now, to an array of needs which can be considered together since they tend to have in common the promotion of growth and expansion. These needs include those commonly assigned such labels as *achievement, power, creativity* and *self-actualization,* as well as broader orientation, suggested by such phrases as need to attain and maintain a significant role, need for expansion and ongoingness, generative needs. Buhler (1951, 1957) who has written extensively on changing needs as major explanatory variables in the life cycle, tends to subsume such motives as just listed under the general category of *expansion,* and to urge that there is a continuing need for expansion throughout the life span. Though this is likely true, as will be suggested below, it is also probably true that such needs dominate behavior more obviously in the years up to middle age.

Achievement and Social Needs

A number of studies have demonstrated the greater importance of achievements needs in early adult years, especially for men (Kuhlen and Johnson, 1952; McClelland, 1953), and a recent study by means of projective pictures of a nationwide sample of adults showed high points in young adulthood and middle age followed by a decrease in need achievement, but an increase in need power (Veroff, Atkinson, Feld, and Gurin, 1960).

In another study by Neugarten and Gutmann (1958), young men were described as actively striving toward goals, as self-propelled, achievement oriented. In contrast the older men were inactive, submissive, and introspective. Interestingly enough, while the female subjects did not give responses that could be categorized in the same way, they did portray the older female in the picture as characterized by a marked increase in dominance and assertion.

The data are not entirely consistent, however. Reissman (1953) for example, has reported that older high achievers were more willing than young high achievers to undergo the inconvenience of moving to a new city and to accept limitations upon freedom of religious and political expression for the sale of a better position.

Affiliation needs and social interests play a prominent role in life, and are here classified under growth and "expansion" needs since it is through expanding social relationships with individuals and groups that many people are able to achieve a sense of significance. Although it is difficult to infer whether there are marked changes in strength of affiliation and related social needs with age (the data of Veroff *et al.*, 1960, suggest a decline in the case of women), certainly there are important shifts in ways in which such needs are satisfied. There is, as is well known, an upsurge of social interest during the course of adolescence and into the early twenties. But from that point on there seems to be less interest in extensive social interaction with large numbers of individuals, and a shift to a greater liking for closer relationships with fewer people. Studies by Strong (1943) and by Bendig (1960) are consistent with this observation.

Changes in Goals

The postulation of a need or set of needs for continuing growth and expansion serves to relate in a meaningful way the goals and interests of people of different ages. As Buhler points out, family and work constitute major avenues of expansion, until these no longer offer possibility of continued satisfaction, whereupon interests shift to other kinds of activity. This shift from one orientation to another as a result of continued frustration of the possibility of "expanding" along the lines of marriage and family on the part of single women is illustrated in a study by the present writer (Kuhlen and Johnson, 1952). The basic data are presented in Figure 1. When asked what they most wanted to be doing ten years hence, the vast majority of young single women gave marriage and family as a goal. This response dropped off rapidly by thirty or thirty-five and was succeeded by desire to get a new or better job, a shift not apparent among married women. Other studies suggest that this process of forced reorientation in major goals is likely to be accompanied by considerable stress. The

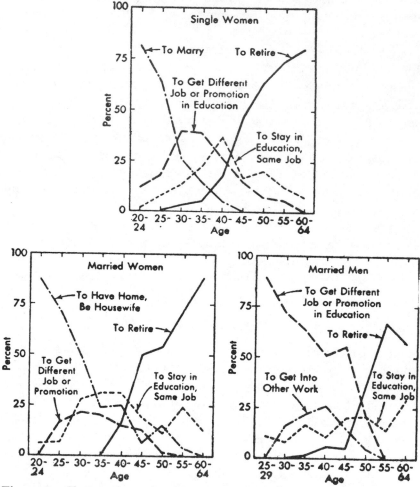

Figure 1. Changes in goals with increasing adult age as reflected in the responses of public school teachers to the question, "What would you most like to be doing ten years from now?" (From R. G. Kuhlen and G. H. Johnson, Change in goals with increasing adult age, *J. Consult. Psychol., 16*:1-4, 1952.

increasing participation of married women in organizational activities at around fifty years of age, as shown in another study done at Syracuse (Kuhlen 1951), may be interpreted as an effort to achieve a sense of significance in a new setting now that children have left home.

In total, analysis of changes in interests, activities, and orientations with increasing years reveal a shift from active direct gratifications of needs to gratifications obtained in more indirect and vicarious fashion. An illustration of this trend is found in a study by the present writer (Kuhlen, 1948) in which an age sequence emerged in reasons given for major happy episodes in life. Starting with the late teens or early twenties, the following sequence was evident: romance, marriage, birth of children, satisfaction with children's success. Presumably, through identification with one's own children, one achieves a sense of continuing expansion when one's own life becomes stagnant. It is of further interest, though not well documented in research, that people of older ages seem to evidence a greater interest in genealogy and in religion, particularly in a belief in immortality.* These orientations may well represent efforts, albeit unconscious, to maintain a sense of ongoingness even when it is recognized that one's own years are short.

Expansion, Constriction, and Degree of "Investment" in Life

Presumably, if Buhler is correct that needs for expansion are continuing, such shifts as just noted may reflect not so much a decrease in need strength (at least over a wide range of years) as a change in method of gratification necessitated by decreasing capacity or opportunity to obtain the gratifications as actively and directly as was possible at an earlier age. Figure 2 illustrates, nonetheless, that life tends to be characterized by a curve of expansion and constriction. Partly, constriction is forced upon the individual by extraneous circumstances. Retirement age is reached, spouse and friends dies, opportunities are withdrawn. But partly, too, the typical middle-aged or older person has less energy to invest, has less new experience to relish, and has less reason to exert himself. For such reasons, possibly, he "invests" less in life.

---

* See below, p. 000/ff, for a contrary view regarding interest in religion and further documentation of this point.

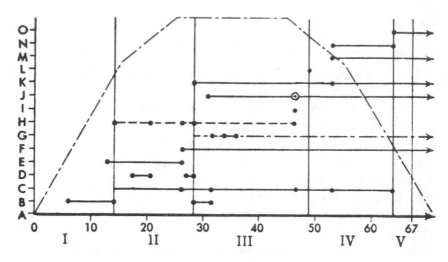

A. years
B. education
C. career
D. service in army
E. dating
F. marriage
G. children
H. change in domicile
I. extended trip

J. owns his own home
K. church and organizational membership
L. illness
M. children leave home and are on their own
N. operates own business
O. retirement

Figure 2. Schematic representation of Bill Robert's course of life. (From Buhler, Ch. Meaningful Living in the Mature Years, Chap. 12. pp. 345-387 in Kleemeier, R. W. (Ed.), *Aging and Leisure,* New York, Oxford University Press, 1961)

This decreased investment in living with increasing age has already been suggested by the less direct, more vicarious methods of achieving gratification characterizing the later years. In total, there sems to be a reduction in "drive level," a decrease in ego-involvement in life. The latter is reflected in analyses of Thematic Apperception Test stories obtained in the Kansas City study of middle and old age. Other people told less complex stories, introduced less conflict and peopled their stories with fewer inhabitants. Also a reduction in ego energy seems to occur, as reflected in a count of the number of assertive rather than passive activities described and in ratings of the emotional intensity of stories. The relevant data, reported in a paper by Rosen and Neugarten (1960), are summarized in Table 1. Gurin *et al.* (1960) reported older people to worry less than younger individuals, a finding which they also interpret as reflecting less investment in life.

TABLE 1

MEAN EGO-INVOLVEMENT AND EGO ENERGY SCORES OF MEN AND WOMEN COMBINED, DERIVED FROM TAT DATA. (ADAPTED FROM ROSEN AND NEUGARTEN, 1960)

		Ego-Involvement		Ego Energy	
Age	*Number Interviewed*	*Intro-duced Figures*	*Intro-duced Conflict*	*Assertive*	*Emo-tional Intensity*
40-49	48	2.23[a]	3.02[a]	13.19[a]	5.75
50-59	48	1.67[b]	2.38	12.27[b]	5.17[b]
64-71	48	.94[c]	2.35[c]	11.54[c]	4.08[c]

[a] Applying Tukey's test to the Studentized Range (Snedecor, 1956, pp. 251-252), the difference between means for the youngest and middle age groups is significant at or beyond the .05 level.

[b] The difference between means for the middle and oldest age groups is significant at or beyond the .05 level.

[c] The difference between means for the youngest and oldest age groups is significant at or beyond the .01 level.

Paralleling the shifts described in Figure 2 for an individual, is a general pattern of expansion and restriction in a whole array of life activities. This is evident in age curves relating to income, family size, participation in organizations (Kuhlen, 1951), and in the social life space as reflected in the relative number of psychological settings penetrated in the community (Barker, 1961). Similar to these patterns of expansion restriction, are the curves obtained by Schaie (1959) for scores on a social responsibility test. These scores increased until the mid-fifties and then decreased among a sample of 500 subjects ranging in age from twenty to seventy.

Disengagement

Presumably data such as the foregoing, but more especially data from the Kansas City study of middle and old age, led to the recent proposal of a theory of aging to which was given the label "disengagement," an interpretation first presented in 1960 by Cumming and her associates, and later given more formal form and elaboration in a book (Cumming and Henry, 1961). In a sense, this hypothesis asserts a reversal of a need for expansion, i.e., in later years the individual is motivated to disengagement. Though the point is not made as explicitly as might be wished, the implication is that the disengaged state of affairs is something *desired for its own sake* and not a second-best role adopted as a means of avoiding the threat developing in more significant participation or as a result of societal rejection from more significant roles.

This "theory" has not yet been subjected to extensive independent test, but some data are beginning to appear. Thus a recent study bears on the hypothesis implied by those proposing the disengagement theory that in old age psychological equilibrium accompanies passivity whereas at younger ages active participation is necessary for equilibrium. The data recently reported by Tobin and Neugarten (1961) do not support this view. They found that an index of life satisfaction was correlated *more* highly with participation in older years than in middle age. Although the supporters of the disengagement theory hypothesize that there would be no loss in morale with increased age or with retirement, available data suggest much loss does occur. Kutner and his associates (1956) have shown morale to decrease with age, and Phillips (1957) has reported more maladjustment among old people who have moved into less favored roles. Another study, by Filer and O'Connell (1962), is especially noteworthy in that it involved an *experimental* manipulation of environmental conditions. A special attempt was made to modify for an experimental group the environmental conditions. A special attempt was made to modify for an experimental group the environmental demands and expectancies in a veterans' domiciliary so as to provide a "useful-contribution" climate. Care was taken to avoid the appearance of a "special project" and the participants were probably not aware of the group they were in. Nor was the rater who evaluated their later adjustment. Significant gains in adjustment characterized the experimental group.

A recent report by Dean (1960), one of the collaborators in an early statement of the disengagement theory, has presented data on the decline of "instrumentality" in support of the theory. The present writer is inclined to place an opposite interpretation upon these findings, concluding that the data show oldsters to be quite unhappy about their lot because of their loss in instrumentality. The basic data in this study involved responses to the questions "What are the best things about being the age you are now?" and "What are the worst things about being the age you are now?" The responses were classified in several ways, but we focus our attention here on two categories: (1) "*Output:* responses emphasize active engagement in the social environment, with focus on achievement, responsibility, power and influence, utility, knowledge, experience." (2) "*Frustrated output:* The obverse of the above. Responses emphasize loss of ability to do, to achieve, to assume responsibility; loss of respect from others. This category includes responses about physical weakening, if this weakening is seen primarily as interfering with 'doing.'" It is significant that in response to the question concerning "best things" the "output" responses decline from 37 per cent in the fifties to 3 per cent in the eighties. This decline, in and of itself, does not indicate *purposeful* disengagement. Indeed, that people increasingly (with age) *resent* the loss of opportunity to achieve and assume responsibility is implied in the *increasing* frequency of responses to the "worst things" question, which fell in the "frustrated output" category. The percentages for four successive age groups (50's, 60's, 70's, 80's) were 22, 31, 53, and 48. In the two oldest age groups, 70-79, 80+, this response was the *most frequent* category, suggesting very real unhappiness at their inability to remain "engaged." *

One more example of inconsistency of data bearing on the disengagement hypothesis, that of religious interest, is appropriate inasmuch as there is no formalized pressure for a person to become "disengaged" from religious institutions as there is in the case of work. It will be recalled, also, that increased interest in religion in old age, particularly belief in immortality, was cited earlier as reflecting a need for continued "expansion." Cumming and

---

* One may also interpret an older study by Simmons (1946), Kutner, *et al.* *(1956) and Philip (1957)* as contradictory to the disengagement hypothesis.

Henry (1961, p. 91) are explicit on this point: "It is a common belief that religious piety and practice increase with age ... On the other hand, disengagement theory would predict a decrease in the interest in religion as normative control is lessened." Not only do the data reported by these authors seem to this writer inconsistent within themselves, and inconsistent with their own hypothesis, but other studies have indicated an increasing belief in immortality throughout the adult years (Barron, 1961) with unanimous or near unanimous belief in the very old age groups, e.g., over ninety (Cavan *et al.*, 1949). Although extensive participation in church programs drops off with age, attendance holds up remarkably well in view of the general decline with age in out-of-home activities. And almost all evidence that has come to the writer's attention bearing on "sedentary" participation—radio listening, reading,—shows an increasing interest in religion with age. Moreover, as Lehman (1953) has pointed out, more than any other organizations, religious organizations qualify as gerontocracies. It is not unlikely that the source of the differences of opinion regarding the importance of religion in old age lies in the fact that there are several possible indices of religiousness. It is probable that indices based on different definitions will show differing, in fact, contrasting trends with age.

Despite the contradictory lines of evidence summarized in the foregoing paragraphs, it is probable that the disengagement concept will have considerable heuristic value. Already it appears to have stimulated a variety of studies which have added to the store of empirical data on aging, and may well provide an appropriate explanation of aging trends in an, as yet undefined, segment of the population even though not applicable to the generality.

ANXIETY AND THREAT AS A SOURCE OF MOTIVATION

We turn now to another source of motivation, namely anxiety, which for reasons earlier noted, seems to increase and become more generalized as people move into the middle and later years of life. This anxiety may not only generate constructive efforts to reduce it, sometime through education or therapy, but is especially important as a generator of defensive and handicapping behavior patterns. As will be recalled, it was suggested in earlier pages of this chapter, as well as in the immediately preceeding paragraphs, that there is reason to believe that social and physical losses, coupled with increasing responsibilities and commitments, may well generate increasing anxiety with age. It is probable that the tendency to become anxious and susceptible to threat constitute an increasingly important motivating force in late middle-age and the older years of life. Indeed, a number of writers (e.g., Kaufman, 1940; Atkin, 1940) who have attempted theoretical explanations of the aging process, have seized upon anxiety generated by social and physical losses as the primary age-related independent variable. Various personality changes, such as conservatism, intolerance of ambiguity, and rigidity are construed as ego defenses, or maneuvers, utilized to control the anxiety so generated.

It should come as no surprise to the reader that this particular interpretation of aging is not well accepted by people in the middle-aged or older categories. Indeed, when the writer presented these views at an adult education conference some years ago, it was denounced as "a theory of decay." While, to be sure, there is much that is virtuous in an emphasis upon positive achievement and "expansion," a realistic approach requires that we take into account the "negative" side of the motivational picture as well. To this we turn next, and with sufficient reference to data to demonstrate the probability that such trends do indeed occur.

Anxiety is one among a number of symptoms of maladjustment. A recent factor analysis by Veroff, Feld, and Gurin (1962) of the symptoms of subjective "adjustment" and maladjustment has identified several dimensions that warrant our attention. Five factors were identified in the analysis of the data for males: (1) felt psychological disturbance, (2) unhappiness, (3) social inadequacy, (4) lack of identity, and (5) physical distress. All but the last of these factors were also apparent in the analysis for women. The data described below relate to age trends in a number of these variables.

Changes in Subjective "Happiness"

It is fairly axiomatic that a person is not well adjusted unless he is reasonably happy and contented. And about the only way one can discover whether this is so is to ask him. Subjective though the data are, they nonetheless have important implications for the issue at hand. Although the trends to be reported are for "happiness," it seems reasonable to assume that the trends for "unhappiness"—which are more directly suggestive of anxiety— would be essentially the mirror image of the curves for happiness, though a neutral group (neither happy nor unhappy) might vary in size from age to age and thus make the reflection less than exact.

One would anticipate that happiness would increase with age as important previously frustrated needs are satisfied. Thus, in young adulthood, in contrast to adolescence, sex needs and needs for autonomy are more likely to be satisfied, and important life developments in the area of family and work probably bring a sense of achievement and security, and presumably happiness. Later, as losses and limitations are encountered, these would presumably be given opportunities for direct need satisfaction, and happiness would be reduced. An unpublished study by Kuhlen (1948) shows this curvilinear relationship and studies by Morgan (1937), by Landis (1942), by Gurin and his associates (1960), and Caran and others (1949) show losses in middle and later years.

We have, then, in one important symptom of adjustment, an indication that as people get older, at least beyond middle-age, their reported happiness decreases on the average, and presumably the incidence of unhappiness increases.

Changes in "Self-Concept"

It is apparent that the well-adjusted individual will have positive self-regarding attitudes, whereas the individual who is maladjusted and insecure—and hence more susceptible to anxiety and threat—will tend to have a low regard of himself and be lacking in self-confidence. Again, one would anticipate that the character of the self-concept would vary curvilinearly with age, becoming more favorable during the periods of gains and increased status, and less favorable in the years beyond when losses are being experienced. Although there have been some interesting theoretical considerations of developmental changes in self-concept during the adult year (see particularly Erikson, 1959, and Buhler, 1962), there are relatively few developmental *data* available.

One of the few arrays of data with which this writer is acquainted that shows a curvilinear relationship of self-concept to age was assembled by Lehner and Gunderson (1953), utilizing a draw-a-person test. It was found that men tended to draw larger figures the older they got up to about age thirty and thereafter they draw smaller pictures, whereas women draw larger pictures up to age forty and then smaller pictures. Since it is often assumed that in such picture drawing the individual projects his self-image, it possibly may be inferred that these trends reflect trends in self-evaluation, and that the picture is drawn larger until the individual senses that he has passed the prime of life.

Some of the data bearing on the self-concept in later years are on the amusing side, though nonetheless revealing. For example, when taking intelligence tests in the course of an experiment, older college prefessors made twice as many self-belittling comments as did those younger (Sward, 1945). And older women,* particularly older single women, have a strong tendency to omit their ages from autobiographical sketches in such places as *Who's Who* and *American Men of Science* (Norman, 1949). Presumably this is done because such admission is painful to themselves, or viewed as self-damaging in the eyes of others. More systematic is the study by Mason (1954) who administered a number of measures of self-concept to several groups from different backgrounds. A group of institutionalized indigent old people had more negative self-concepts than did a group of independent, middle-class oldsters, and both, in turn, had more negative self-concepts than did a more youthful low economic group. However, individual differences among the old groups were greater then among the young, suggesting that reactions to the aging process vary substantially among individuals.

Still a further line of evidence is of interest here, particularly since it is often said that a person is as young—or as old—as he feels. Thus, how one classifies one's self age-wise may be construed as reflecting his self-concept. The surprising finding from several studies (Tuckman and Lorge, 1954; Phillips, 1957; Kutner *et al.*, 1956) is that many people of quite advanced years often describe

---

* Age, incidentally, was estimated by facts they gave regarding year of graduation from college.

themselves as "middle-aged"—half of over 300 individuals over seventy years of age in one of the studies and about a third of those over seventy-five in another. That one's subjective age has significant implications is suggested by the fact that, with actual age controlled, those oldsters who rated themselves as middle-aged in one study (Havighurst, 1953) were better adjusted on other measures, and that in another study (Kogan and Wallach, 1961) a relationship was found between subjective age and indices of caution, when chronological age was held constant. Curiously, however, this latter relationship was attributable almost entirely to a rather high relationship to subjective age and caution in that portion of the group that was low in measured anxiety. The investigators considered the lack of relationship between subjective age and "decision caution" in the high anxiety group to stem from the greater heterogeneity of this group, a circumstance they thought due to the different possible meanings of high anxiety for older people. For the low anxiety subjects, the theoretical interpretation stressed the importance of "image maintenance" in bringing about behavioral consistency.

This relationship between self-concept or self-image and "decision confidence" brings us to another major line of evidence relating to self-concept, namely, that bearing on the self-confidence of individuals of different ages. As suggested above, one would expect that individuals with positive self-concepts would be more self-confident, whereas those with negative self-concepts would be less self-confident. Following our expectation that self-concept would improve during those phases of the life span where there are pronounced gains and evidences of accomplishment, Brozek (1952) has shown that men around fifty were more self-confident on a questionnaire than those younger. Wallach and Kogan (1961) have compared younger adults (college age) and a group of older adults (between 47 and 85 years of age) on a number of measures of caution and self-confidence. They found a number of interesting relationships one of which involved the fact that the older group was more cautious than the younger group, and, in the case of men, less self-confident. The basic facts are presented in Table 2 where it is also shown that a reliable relationship between caution and age exists among the older group of women, but not among the men. These data suggest that aging experiences in the American culture affect the sexes differentially with respect to decline of confidence and caution, both with respect to timing and degree.

Another, possibly very significant, finding was the fact that the odd-even reliability of the test involving degree of caution (a dozen verbally described situations with respect to which the subjects were asked to reccommend action) was higher for the older group (*r*: males, .80; females, .80) than for the younger group (*r*: males, .53; females, .63). This finding may be interpreted as indicating a greater *generality* of caution, i.e., less dependence upon specific situational factors, among the old than among the young. This particular finding, if confirmed, has substantial theoretical significance. The fruitfulness of a theoretical interpretation of aging in terms of anxiety and threat depends in part upon the degree to which anxiety is shown to be generalized and not highly situational in origin.

Still another study (Kogan and Wallach, 1961) is of interest here, partly because of the fact that it utilized a different technique, but also because it compared the values placed upon dif-

TABLE 2

Age Differences in Self-Confidence and Caution
(Adapted from Wallach and Kogan, 1961)

	Young	*Old*	*p*	*r** *(Older Group)*
Confidence Index				
(Low scores indicate confidence)				
Men	2.83	3.19	<.01	...
Women	3.11	3.08	NS	...
p	<.01	NS		
Deterrence of Failure (Caution)				
(High scores indicate caution)				
Men	5.82	6.38	<.01	.05 (NS)
Women	5.88	6.36	<.02	.33 (p <.01)
p	NS	NS		

* Correlation is between age and "Deterrence of failure" score and age in the older group. "Older men" averaged 70.2 years (SD±7.3); women 69.5 years (SD±7.7). Number of subjects: 132 young women, 89 older women; 225 younger men, 65 older men. Young people were college students.

ferent phases of the life span by a younger and older group of subject. With respect to "self-concept," the concepts "myself" and "ideal person" were included among those studied by means of the semantic differential, with special reference to the evaluative factor score. Here again a decline in the favorability of the self-concept in old age appeared. The difference between the old and young was especially significant in the case of the "ideal person." This was interpreted by the authors as suggesting "that older individuals are either more willing to admit unfavorable elements into their image of the ideal or that the very connotation of the concept evokes a more negative reaction in an older person whose age status renders unrealistic any aspirations toward an unrealized ideal self. . . . However, such devaluation may have ego defensive properties for both old and young individuals."

Table 3 contains scores on the "evaluative factor" for those concepts relating to developmental stages in life. It will be noted that both young and old age groups of both sexes assign negative valuations to such concepts as elderly, old age, and death. However, the older individuals were reliably less negative toward old age and death than were the younger. Thus, while older people place a negative valuation upon their phase of life, they seem to achieve a certain adaptation to old age, and do not view it nearly as negatively as do young adults.

Changes in Incidence of Anxiety Symptoms

Evidence presented thus far in this section indicates rather clearly that as people get older, they are less happy, have more negative self-concepts, and have experienced a loss of self-confidence. One would expect increases in anxiety symptoms to parallel these changes. Trends should be examined under two conditions: first, under what might be considered "normal" circumstances of living, and second, under stressful or threatening conditions. Study in these two settings is desirable because, as is the the case of physiological functioning, the effects of aging are not likely to be so noticeable under normal conditions as under conditions of stress. Thus, we might anticipate that people would not show much in the way of trends in anxiety symptoms with age under

TABLE 3

AGE DIFFERENCES IN MEAN EVALUATIVE SCORES (SEMANTIC
DIFFERENTIAL) FOR SEVERAL LIFE STAGE CONCEPTS
(ADAPTED FROM KOGAN AND WALLACH, 1961)

| | *Concept* | | | | | |
	Baby	*Youth*	*Middle-Age*	*Elderly*	*Old-Age*	*Death*
Men						
Young ..	2.24	.99	.61	− .77	− .97	−3.02
Old	1.75	1.05	.29	− .69	− .11	−2.25
p	NS	NS	NS	NS	.02	NS
Women						
Young ..	2.32	1.17	.22	−1.02	−1.79	−4.28
Old	2.09	1.35	.20	−1.14	− .30	−2.33
p	NS	NS	NS	NS	.001	.001

normal conditions of living, but would under conditions of environmental or organic stress.

The bulk of the data obtained under ordinary conditions of living, seem to be consistent with this expectation. Despite the common expectation that "nervousness" would increase with age or be particularly noticeable at certain points, such as menopause, no particular age trends appear (Hamilton, 1942). Nor was an increase with age in the frequency of nervous symptoms evident among a large number of individuals taking health examinations in another study (Britten, 1931). No age trends or a trend toward decreased anxiety might well be expected, in view of the fact that people tend to seek out those circumstances in life which are positively rewarding and non-threatening. To the degree that one is successful in this, as he is likely to be as time (age) passes, and so long as this state of affairs is maintained, no increase with age in anxiety would be anticipated. This seems to be the finding of a number of *early* studies.

However, certain facts emanating from a recent national mental health survey appear to be contrary to the earlier findings and warrant particular attention because of the size and representativeness of the sample. The interview schedule utilized in this survey contained questions dealing with some twenty symptoms of psychological distress. A factor analysis suggested four factors which were labeled "psychological anxiety," "physical health," "immobilization," and "physical anxiety," Table 4 car-

TABLE 4

PERCENTAGE OF SUBJECTS OF VARIOUS AGES WHO RECEIVED HIGH SCORES (6, 7 OR 8) ON "PSYCHOLOGICAL ANXIETY," "IMMOBILIZATION," AND "PHYSICAL ANXIETY" (ADAPTED FROM GURIN, VEROFF, AND FELD, 1960)

	Age					
	21-24	25-34	35-44	45-54	55-64	65-plus
Psychological Anxiety						
Men	5	6	8	11	14	17
Women	10	14	17	20	29	34
Immobilization						
Men	22	10	10	3	1	2
Women	14	15	12	6	5	4
Physical Anxiety						
Men	3	4	4	8	13	17
Women	8	9	10	14	17	28
No. of Subjects						
Men	65	252	241	209	146	161
Women	98	344	307	250	183	191

ries the percentage of subjects in various age groups who evidenced high scores in three of these factors. It will be noted that there is a substantially greater incidence of anxiety symptoms among older people than among younger except in the instance of the factor dealing with immobilization.

These investigators offer the following interpretation of the greater incidence among young adults of anxiety symptoms classified under the tentative label of immobilization:

> Immobilization, ennui, and lack of energy are all psychological states that suggest lack of integration, rather than insurmountable, immediate psychological difficulty. In a life situation, where one is caught among different pressures for integration of the self—pressures that may operate at cross-purposes (such as the "achievement versus house-

wife" conflict for some women) or pressures that are so varied that they are not all attainable at the same time—one may frequently experience a lack of integration. Such pressures are more likely to occur early in life and then gradually diminish as patterns of integration are chosen. Until such integration occurs, however, one might expect that a common reaction to these cross-pressures which are too divergent or too numerous to handle would be withdrawal, with its concomitant restlessness and disruption. Since this problem is more often encountered by the young adults, perhaps this is one reason that young people are prone to symptoms of the immobilization type (Gurin, Veroff, and Feld, 1960, pages 191-192).*

Adequate explanations of the contrast between this recent study and earlier findings are not readily apparent. Differences in methodology or in sample may be responsible, or it may be that current times are confused and stressful compared to the social-political context of earlier research. As will be developed next, older individuals seem particularly susceptible to stress, and thus it is possible that under current "normal" conditions they may reflect more anxiety.

For more definitive evidence regarding reactions of people of different ages to stressful situations, one may cite reports of observations in "naturalistic settings" and studies which were specifically designed to check this phenomenon. Welford (1951), among others, offers as one explanation of the reluctance of older individuals to cooperate in experiments is their unwillingness to expose themselves to the threat of the new situation. Another study of younger adult years, done by the present writer (Kuhlen, 1951) during World War II, revealed a greater relationship between age and anxiety symptoms among enlisted naval personnel who were presumably in a more stressful situation than were others.

Two other studies, utilizing different procedures, suggest an increase in anxiety with age. In these studies, reaction time to

---

* This interpretation of the nature of the psychological task facing young adults is not unlike that suggested by Erikson (1959).

stimulus words was utilized as a measure of threat or stress. While data bearing on words representing different areas of life will be considered below, relevant to the current discussion is the reaction time to words such as *worry, afraid, unhappy, restless, anxious.* Such words may be considered generalized anxiety "stimuli" in contrast to a word like "church" which represent the religious area of life. Powell and Ferraro (1960) in one study and Olsen and Elder (1958) in another found reaction time to these words to increase with adult age. Since these generalized anxiety words were interspersed with words from potentially stressful areas of living, it is not clear whether the results should be construed as bearing on changes under "normal" circumstances of living or under "stressful" circumstances.

Although the data are by no means as extensive as one might wish, either with respect to the range of symptoms sampled or the range of ages, the evidence does suggest that increasing age brings increasing susceptibility to stress and threat. Presumably this threat is engendered by cultural and physical losses that are experienced with increasing age and by various and sundry commitments which are more binding as age increases and which make threats more serious. Certainly more careful studies should be undertaken of this variable, not only for the purpose of marking out the age relationships under different conditions, but also with respect to determining the degree to which increasing age brings with it a generalized type of anxiety which might be reflected in an array of behaviors, in contrast to anxiety which is fairly specific to certain situational changes that occur with age. In view of the theoretical importance of anxiety as a variable influencing personality and performance changes with age such studies assume great importance.

Specific Sources of Anxiety as Related to Age

The foregoing discussion has given some indication of age changes in the gross amount of anxiety present at different ages as this is reflected in the incidence of general anxiety symptoms. Data indicating particular sources of worry and anxiety are likely to be especially useful to those concerned with human betterment.

That there can be striking age differences in the source of

anxiety and tension during the young adult years and middle age is shown in the data presented in Figure 3. In this study, instead of using a verbal questionnaire, subjects were presented with

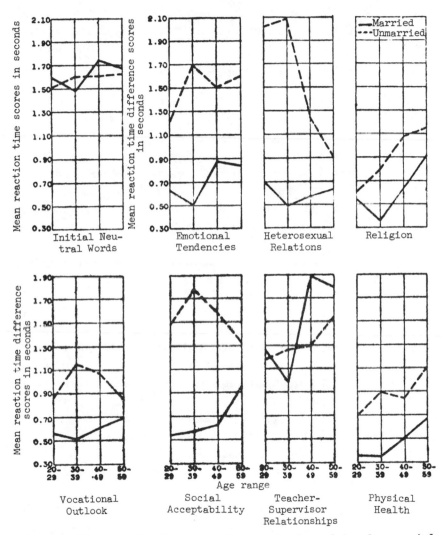

Figure 3. Mean reaction time scores in seconds of married and unmarried teachers at various age ranges to initial neutral words, and mean reaction time difference scores in seconds of married and unmarried teachers at various age ranges to "critical" words taken from various psychological adjustment areas. (From Powell and Ferraro, 1960)

words, taken one at a time, which were chosen to represent different areas of living. Since it is well known that people tend to block up, and thus to react more slowly to stimuli which are disturbing to them, comparison of their reactions to these critical words with their reactions to a list of neutral words can be taken as some indication of the degree to which particular area of life sampled by the critical words represents a source of anxiety or tension.

The subjects in this study were all white female public school elementary teachers, half of whom were married and half of whom were single, twenty-five of each group in each of the age categories shown in the chart. It is to be noted that there are important differences between those who are married and single, i.e., between those who occupy different roles in life and hence are exposed to different threats and have different opportunities for need satisfaction. Particularly striking is the anxiety evoked by heterosexual words among single women in the younger adult years and the rapid drop-off as age increases to sixty. Married women, who have greater opportunity for satisfaction of sex needs, show relatively little anxiety and relatively slight change with age. Single women, for whom career begins to become a primary source of satisfaction by around thirty, show a peak of concern with this area in the thirties, whereas married women show little age trend. Similar striking differences are found between the married and unmarried groups with respect to social acceptability, but in the instance of religion, physical health, and teacher-supervisor relationship the trends are similar, increasing with age in each instance. It is of some significance, that in each of the seven areas, with the exception of teacher-supervisor relationships, single women show more anxiety and concern than do married women. Whether this is due to selection, the more maladjusted being those who do not marry, or due to a generalized anxiety resulting from a "minority group" status is not clear.

Other data (Dykman, Heiman, and Kerr, 1952) confirm the fact that different ages in young adulthood and middle age are characterized by different problems, and suggest that changes in problems continue into old age. Morgan (1937) and Havighurst and Albrecht (1953), among others, have presented data describing specific worries of very old people.

INDIVIDUAL DIFFERENCES

It has been argued in this paper that the changing motivational picture of the adult years can be painted in two broad strokes, one emphasizing growth-expansion motives which are translated into a succession of goals, the other emphasizing anxiety, generated by physical and social losses, which constitutes the motivational source for various handicapping, but nonetheless protective, defense maneuvers. Although both motivational patterns are important throughout life, it has been suggested that the first more clearly dominates the young adult years, the latter the later years of life. Whatever merit such a conceptualization may have as far as the generality is concerned, it is obvious that there will be important differences among individuals as to how and the degree to which these tendencies are translated into specific goals or specific maneuvers, and the ages at which one tends to outweigh the other. As illustrative of differences among individuals, it will be instructive to examine certain contrasts between meaningful subgroups of the population where data are available.

Differences in the Onset of the Threat of Age

It may be hypothesized that a critical point, motivationally, in the life history of the individual is that point at which he senses that the process of expansion is concluding and begins to become sensitive to certain irreversible losses. Such a point would presumably be somewhat delayed in an oriental culture where age is venerated as compared to a typical western culture where an unfriendly attitude toward old age is probably more characteristic. Generally speaking, in those subcultures (or in those individuals) where age brings continuing success and status, there presumably would be less threat associated with the process than in a subculture (or in an individual) where losses are experienced relatively early.

While data are not available for all subcultures, the point can be made by selected sample data. Incidence of suicide varies greatly between the sexes and between Negroes and white groups. Whereas the rate constantly climbs for white males with age, for females it is a relatively level smoothly rounded curve, with an actual decline in the advanced years. These differences may be interpreted as reflecting the more stressful environment in which males live, and the fact that with increasing age it is more difficult for them to maintain their role. Geared as men are to the work life, career frustrations and inability to find useful employment presumably would be a serious blow to self-concept and the generator of unhappiness and anxiety.

Two lines of evidence are presented with respect to social economic and social class differences. The first involves social class differences in the way people perceive the prime of life and aging. In Table 5 which summarizes answers given by men and women with respect to certain matters, the most striking difference relates to answers to the question of when is a man "mature," "at the prime of life," "most confident." The lower-lower class individuals gave twenty-five years of age and those in successively higher social classes regularly raised the age until those in the upper middle class gave a mean age of forty. Similarly upper middle class individuals defined "middle age" and "old" as notably older than did those in lower-lower class groups. When women were

TABLE 5

Differences Among Social Class Groups in Their Perception of Aging (From p. 4a of *Aging and the Aged*, The University of Chicago Reports, Vol. 12, No. 2, November 1961)

	Upper Middle	Lower Middle	Upper Lower	Lower Lower
Men Look at Aging				
When is a man . . . ?				
"Mature," "at the prime of life,"				
"most confident."	40	35	30	25
"Middle-aged"	47	45	40	40
"Old"	70	70	60	60
Women Look at Aging				
When is a woman . . . ?				
"Good looking"	35	30	27	25
"Most confident"	38	35	30	35
"In her prime"	40	40	38	35
"Old"	70	70	67	65

PROPORTION EMPLOYED, ACCORDING TO AGE, FOR FOUR
OCCUPATIONAL CLASSES, UNITED STATES, 1940

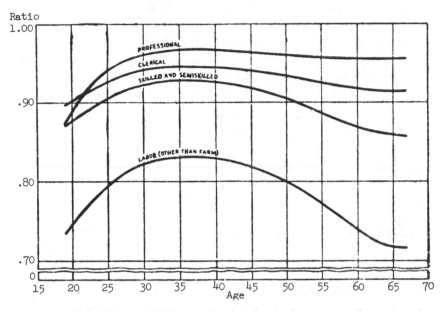

Figure 4. The differential threat of aging for various economic groups as
reflected in age trends in the percentage employed in different categories
at different ages. Data are for 1940, a time when cultural discrimination
would likely be better reflected than in times of peak employment. (From
L. I. Dublin and A. J. Lotka, *The Money Value of a Man*, revised ed., New
York, Ronald Press, 1946)

asked what age a woman was most "good looking," "most confident,", "in her prime," or "old," again the lower-lower class
groups gave younger ages than did those in the upper middle
classes.

But perhaps more critical than such perceptions is the age at
which economic threat is experienced by members of different
occupational categories. We go back to 1940, depression years,
for a good example of this phenomenon, since it would be under
conditions of economic stress that such threats would be most
clearly revealed. The data in Figure 5 show clearly that it is the
laboring group who experiences earliest and in most pronounced
fashion the threat of loss of employment. In the upper professional

group, very little change occurred with age. These people, even under stressful economic conditions, seemed not particularly threatened by loss of employment regardless of age.

Other significant subgroups of the population can very readily be identified. Buhler (1933) for example, has contrasted a "psychological curve" of life with the "biological" curve of life, and has pointed out that those individuals who are most dependant upon physical status—e.g., strength or attractiveness—have psychological curves closely approximating the biological curve of life, whereas those engaged in mental pursuits have a psychological curve lagging the physical curve. One would expect, for example, a narcissistic person, a chorus girl, or a prize fighter to feel the threat of age much earlier than a non-narcissistic person, a university professor, or a physician.

Differences in Degree of Future Orientation and Meaning of Life

A number of writers have commented on the fact that certain lives seem to have "unity," that certain individuals seem well integrated and "inner-directed." In contrast, other individuals seem responsive to the many different situations in which they find themselves. Some people seem "future-oriented" and work toward deferred gratifications; others live essentially for the present. Such differences are likely to be especially, but not exclusively, evident in the different meanings that work and career have for different individuals.

Differences of this nature assume importance in evaluating the generality of "expansion" needs in human lives, and in assessing the overall character of motivational changes during the adult years. Filer and O'Connel (1962), for example, have noted that despite a mean gain among a group of oldsters under conditions of a useful contributing climate (a finding which, as noted earlier, was interpreted as failing to substantiate the "disengagement" hypothesis), some individuals made no gain and some lost. Quite properly these authors have noted that any theory of aging must encompass such contrasting trends among individuals. What seems "disengagement" may not really be this if the individual were not "engaged" psychologically to begin with. And, for others, "disengagement" may actually mean "re-engagement," in the sense of retiring "to" rather than "from." Investigations into the personal meanings with which different people invest their goals and their varied behaviors, and the relationship of the specifics of their lives, singly and in patterns to their more fundamental motivations are very much needed.

Of those psychologists interested in aging, Charlotte Buhler has probably been most interested in fathoming the meaning and unity of the course of human life, and of describing this meaning in terms of changing motivations, sequences of goals and self-conceptions. In her most recent papers (1957, 1962), she has given especial emphasis to the meaningfulness of life, self-realization, and fulfillment. For many people, she argues, life is a meaningful project involving self-determination toward goals, with various episodes of self-assessment along the way, and ending in fulfillment or failure. Something of the range of individual differences is suggested by her categorization of those individuals interviewed (Buhler, 1961). Four groups were identified:

1. Those who felt they had done their lives' work and wanted to rest and relax and were content to do so.
2. Those who felt that their active life was never finished and who continued striving to the end.
3. Those who, though not satisfied with their lives and accomplishments, but lacking strength, ability or will-power to go on struggling, find an unhappy sort of resignation.
4. Those who led thoughtless and meaningless lives, and who are now not only frustrated but bothered by guilt and regret.

In her overall evaluation, Buhler concluded that more critical in old age maladjustment than functional decline and insecurity is the individual's self-assessment as to whether he did or did not reach fulfillment. This she felt was true of the person who had hoped for accomplishments, but often, as well, for the person who did not think of their lives as a whole at the outset but who later became aware of a pattern.

Although Buhler's generalizations reflect clinical impressions and are not so well-supported by empirical data as many psychologists might wish, her points seem well taken and square sufficiently with subjective observations and experiences to suggest an important area of research as well as hypotheses to give that research direction. The suggested focus is upon basic motivational tendencies, sequences of goals, meaningfulness and fulfillment— with attention to differences among individuals and the kinds of antecedent and concurrent conditions that have brought them about.

SUMMARY

It has been suggested in this paper that hypothesizing two broad motivational patterns—one of growth and expansion, the other of anxiety and threat—will serve to integrate a wide variety of data reflecting developmental changes during the adult life span. The major points made in the development of this notion are as follows:

1. It was suggested first that a number of factors interact to cause age changes in adult motivation. These include age-related differences in cultural stimulation and expectation, the degree to which satisfaction or chronic frustration of certain major motives over time paves the way for the emergence of other motives, and the degree to which people experience social and physical losses in highly valued areas. Becoming "locked" into a situation as is likely to occur as age increases) tends to make frustrations keener, and changing time perspectives seem to create critical points in the motivational history of individuals.

2. The postulation of a need for "growth-expansion" serves to integrate in a meaningful way the commonly observed goals and interests of people. One notes shifts in goals and interests from career and family, to community interests, to identification with children's success, to religious and philosophical interests. In general, although "growth-expansion" motives seem important throughout life, their satisfaction is by less direct and more vicarious means in older years. As age increases, there appears to be less personal investment (ego-involvement, energy) in life and in the satisfaction of needs.

3. The recently advanced "theory of disengagement," which suggests that people *seek* a disengaged state as something valued in its own right, seems not particularly supported by the data,

though this view is having a stimulating effect upon research.

4. The evidence seems particularly clear that anxiety and susceptibility to threat increase with the passage of time, and that this circumstance tends to be the motivational source for many of the behavioral (personality) changes that occur with age. This particular trend has important implications for adult educational methodology.

5. Individual differences are, of course, great, and important differences have been demonstrated with respect to sex and social-economic class. Among the important differences are the ages at which irreversible losses become evident, the degree to which one's life is seen as a meaningful pattern, and the ways in which various subgroups of the population translate their "needs" into specific goals or adapt particular patterns of defense against losses.

REFERENCES

1. Aging and the Aged, *The University of Chicago Reports,* Vol. *12,* No. 2, Nov. 1961.

2. Atkin, S.: Discussion of the paper by M. R. Kaufman, Old age and aging: the psychoanalytic point of view. *Amer. J. Orthopsychiat.. 10*:79-83, 1940.

3. Barker, R. G., and Barker, L. S.: The psychological ecology of old people in Midwest, Kansas, and Yoredale, Yorkshire. *J. Gerontol., 1961, 16*:144-149, 1961.

4. Barron, M.: *The Aging American.* New York, Crowell, 1961.

5. Bendig, A. W.: Age differences in the interscale factor structure of the Guilford-Zimmerman Temperament Survey. *J. Consult. Psychol., 24*:134-138, 1960.

6. Britten, R. H.: Sex differences in physical impairment in adult life. *Amer. J. Hyg., 13*:741-770, 1931.

7. Brozek, J.: Personality of young and middle-aged normal men: item analysis of a psychosomatic inventory. *J. Gerontol., 7*:410-418, 1952.

8. Buhler, Charlotte: Genetic aspects of the self. *Ann. New York Acad. Sci., 96*:730-764, 1962.

9. Buhler, Charlotte: *Der Menschliche Lebenslauf Als Psychologisches Problem.* Leipzig, Verlag von S. Hirzel, 1933.

10. Buhler, Charlotte: Maturation and motivation. *Personality, 1*:184-211, 1951.

11. Buhler, Charlotte: Meaningful leisure in the mature years, Chap. 12, pp. 345-387. In R. W. Kleemeier (ed.), *Aging and Leisure,* New York, Oxford University Press, 1961.

12. Buhler, Charlotte: Old age and fulfillment of life with consideration of the use of time in old age. *Vita hum., Basel,* 4:129-133, 1961.

13. Buhler, Charlotte: Zur Psychologie des menschlichen Lebenslaufes. *Psychol. Rdsch.,* 1957, 8, 1-15.

14. Cavan, R. S., Burgess, E. W., Havighurst, R. J., and Goldhamer, H.: *Personal Adjustment in Old Age.* Chicago, Science Research Associates, 1949.

15. Cumming, Elaine, and Henry, W. E.: *Growing Old,* New York, Basic Books, 1961.

16. Dean, Lois R.: Aging and the decline of instrumentality. *J. Gerontol.,* 15:440-446, 1960.

17. Dykman, R. A., Heimann, E. K., and Kerr, W. A.: Lifetime worry patterns of three diverse adult cultural groups. *J. Soc. Psychol.,* 35: 91-100, 1952.

18. Erikson, E. H.: *Identity and the Life Cycle.* New York, International Universities Press, 1959.

19. Filer, R. N., and O'Connell, D. D.: A useful contribution climate for the aging. *J. Gerontol.,* 17:51-57, 1962.

20. Gurin, G., Veroff, J., and Feld, Sheila: *Americans View Their Mental Health: A Nationwide Interview Survey.* New York, Basic Books, Inc., 1960.

21. Hamilton, G. V.: Changes in personality and psychosexual phenomena with age. In E. V. Cowdry (ed.), *Problems of Aging,* Chapt. XXX, pp. 810-831. 2nd ed. Baltimore, Williams & Wilkins Co., 1942.

22. Havighurst, R. J., and Albrecht, R.: *Older People.* New York, Longmans, Green, 1953.

23. Johnson, G. H.: Differences in the job satisfaction of urban teachers as related to age and other factors. Unpublished PhD. dissertation, Syracuse University, 1951.

24. Kaufman, M. R.: Old age and aging: the psychoanalytic point of view. *Amer. J. Orthopsychiat.,* 10:73-79, 1940.

25. Kerr, W. A., Newman, H. L., and Sadewic, A. R.: Lifetime worry patterns of American psychologists. *J. Consult. Psychol.,* 13:377-380, 1949.

26. Kleemeier, R. W.: *Aging and Leisure.* New York, Oxford University Press, 1961.

27. Kogan, N., and Wallach, M. A.: Age changes in values and attitudes. *J. Gerontol.,* 16:272-280, 1961.

28. Kuhlen, R. G.: Age trends in adjustment during the adult years as reflected in happiness ratings. Paper read at a meeting of the American Psychological Association, Boston, 1948.

29. Kuhlen, R. G.: Expansion and constriction of activities during the adult years as reflected in organizational, civic and political participa-

tion. Paper read at Second International Gerontological Congress, St. Louis, 1951.

30. Kuhlen, R. G.: Nervous symptoms among military personnel as related to age, combat experience and marital status. *J. Consult. Psychol., 15*:320-324, 1951.

31. Kuhlen, R. G., and Johnson, G. H.: Changes in goals with increasing adult age. *J. Consult. Psychol., 16*:1-4, 1952.

32. Kutner, B., Fanshel, D., Togo, Alice M., and Langer, T. S.: *Five Hundred Over Sixty: A Community Survey on Aging.* New York, Russell Sage Foundation, 1956.

33. Landis, J. T.: What is the happiest period of life? *Sch. Soc., 55*:643-45, 1942.

34. Lehman, H. C.: *Age and Achievement.* Princeton, Princeton University Press, 1953.

35. Lehner, G. F. J., and Gunderson, E. K.: Height relationships on the Draw-a-Person Test. *J. Pers., 21*:392-399, 1953.

36. Lewin, K.: Field theory and experiment in social psychology. *Amer. J. of Sociol. 44*:868-896, 1939.

37. Maslow, A. H.: A theory of human motivation. *Psychol. Rev., 50*:370-396, 1943.

38. Mason, Evelyn P.: Some correlates of self-judgments of the aged. *J. Gerontol. 9*:324-337, 1954.

39. McClelland, D. C.: *The Achievement Motive.* New York, Appleton-Century-Crofts, 1953.

40. Morgan, Christine F.: The attitudes and adjustments of recipients of old age assistance in upstate and metropolitan New York. *Arch. Psychol.,* No. 214, 1937.

41. Murray, H. A.: *Explorations in Personality.* New York, Oxford University Press, 1938.

42. Neugarten, B. L., and Gutmann, D. L.: Age-sex roles and personality in middle age: a thematic apperception study. *Psychol. Monogr., 72* (17, Whole No. 470), 1958.

43. Norman, R. D.: Concealment of age among psychologists: evidence for a popular stereotype. *J. Psychol., 30*:127-135, 1949.

44. Olsen, I. A., and Elder, J. H.: A word-association test of emotional disturbance in older women. *J. Gerontol., 13*:305-308, 1958.

45. Phillips, B. S.: A role theory approach to adjustment in old age. *Amer. Sociol. Rev., 22*:212-217, 1957.

46. Powell, M., and Ferraro, C. D. Sources of tension in married and single women teachers of different ages. *J. Educ. Psychol., 51*:92-101, 1960.

47. Reissman, L.: Levels of aspiration and social class. *Amer. Sociol. Rev., 18*:233-242, 1953.

48. Rosen, J. L., and Neugarten, B. L.: Ego functions in the middle and later years: thematic apperception study of normal adults. *J. Gerontol., 15*:62-67, 1960.

49. Schaie, K. W.: The effect of age on a scale of social responsibility. *J. Soc. Psychol., 5*:221-224, 1959.

50. Scott, J. P., Fredericson, E., and Fuller, J. L.: Experimental exploration of the critical period hypothesis. *Personality, 1*:162-183, 1951.

51. Simmons, L. W.: Attitudes toward aging and the aged: primitive societies. *J. Gerontol., 1*:72-95, 1946.

52. Strong, E. K., Jr.: *Vocational Interests of Men and Women,* Stanford, California, Stanford University Press, 1943.

53. Sward, K.: Age and mental ability in superior men. *Amer. J. Psychol., 58*:443-470, 1945.

54. Tobin, S. S., and Neugarten, Bernice L.: Life satisfaction and social interaction in the aging. *J. Gerontol., 16*:344-346, 1961.

55. Tuckman, J., and Lorge, I.: The best years in life: a study in ranking. *J. Psychol., 34*:137-149, 1952.

56. Veroff, J., Atkinson, J. W., Feld, Sheila, and Gurin, G.: The use of thematic apperception to assess motivation in a nationwide interview study. *Psychol. Monogr., 74* (12, Whole No. 499), 1960.

57. Veroff, J., Feld, Sheila, and Gurin, G.: Dimensions of subjective adjustment. *J. Abnorm. and Soc. Psychol., 64*:192-205, 1962.

58. Wallach, M. A., and Kogan, N.: Aspects of judgment and decision making: Interrelationships and changes with age. *Behav. Sci., 6*: 23-36, 1961.

59. Welford, A. G.: *Skill and Age.* London, Oxford University Press, 1951.

Chapter 14

DEVELOPMENTAL CONSIDERATIONS AND THE OLDER CLIENT

MARGARET BLENKNER

> *But what of the whole, and particularly what of the whole as it moves through segments of time? This is essentially the domain of developmental theory . . .*
> JOHN ANDERSON
> *Old Age is a phase of human life. It is part of the whole . . .* CHARLOTTE BUHLER
> *Death, when it approaches, ought not to take one by surprise. It should be part of the full expectancy of life . . .* MURIEL SPARK

The concept of development is fundamentally a biological notion. It has to do with the process by which a living system moves and changes through time in a species-specific manner. The process is *sequential, cumulative,* and *irreversible.* It is not, however, a simple unfolding of pre-existent organic mechanisms but a complex interaction of genetics and milieu, constitution and life experience. Together they shape the individual organism which throughout its life span is always in the process of becoming with what it becomes, in the end, limited by its nature. What the limits of that nature are, is in a sense, the subject of the behavioral sciences.

Development proceeds in *stages* which overlap; the transition from one stage to the next is more gradual than the *events* that signal the stage. (Schneirla, 1957). Thus, adolescence is a stage: menstruation the event that signals it in the human female. In a

247

different context, "disengagement" can be thought of as a developmental stage and retirement the signalling event. In either case,
something new is emerging which is unlike that which has gone
before although not independent of it. Change—to be labelled
developmental—must be cumulative but it must also "eventuate
in modes of organization not previously manifested in the history
of the developing system"... (Nagel, 1957). Developmental change
is irreversible. "A child who has once learned to talk can never be
returned to the state of one who has never talked" (Anderson,
1957) and—one might add—a man, once become adult, can never
again be child, though in senile decay he lie once more a-babbling.[1]
In a truly developmental view of the human life span, the characteristic properties emerging in successive stages cannot be wholly
described in terms of earlier behavior or earlier influences but must
be viewed in their own developmental context: the stage that is
becoming.

Despite this attribute of "becomingness," developmental theory
does not rest on a teleological view of nature (Nagel, 1957). It does
not assume the operation of purpose or final cause; it merely
specifies that a sequence of changes, to be considered developmental, must contribute to the generation of properties or qualities
which though new in the individual are characteristic of the
species. It is this latter quality of development, however, that introduces a logical paradox into its application to the latter half of the
life-span.   For if one substitutes "natural selection" for "final
cause" how can one view aging as anything but a series of random,
unprogrammed events? (Comfort, 1956). Yet, at the same time,
"to say that longevity is genetically determined is almost a truism"
(Birren, 1959). It is not proposed here to solve this problem except
to point out that the survival of a species may well be dependent
in some measure on knowledge and actions of members well past
the young-bearing stage or, as in the case of social insects, who
have no reproductive function.[2] Herd or pack animals, of which

---

[1] "... for after I saw him fumble with the sheets, and play with flowers,
and smile upon his finger's ends I knew there was but one way; for his
nose was sharp as a pen, and a'babbled of green fields." Death of Falstaff.
Henry V, Act II, Scene iii.

man is one, may be more dependent for species-survival on the emergence of qualities of sagacity, cooperation, and coexistence or—in the language I am about to move to—ego-transcendence than the popularized tooth-and-nail corruption of Darwinian fitness would have us believe.[3] Such animals have a proto-culture. There is some transmission of experience from one generation to the next so that a vigorous, surviving oldster, freed from the distractions of mating or bearing young, may well play a role in the survival of its race. Even in man, his ability to develop culture rests on a biological base and serves a biological need.[4]

Although teleology—that, to the scientist, "troublesome issue of purpose" (Harris, 1957)—is not inherent in the developmental view, there is a teleological or "teleonomic"[5] flavor in its application to man introduced by what appears to be an attribute unique to the species; "the attribute of futurity which humans have so distinctly... and [which] seems to be deeply involved in man's adaptive capacity" (Birren, 1959).

It is this sense of future—and here I come down to the subject matter about which I was asked to speak—that is, to me at least, so missing in the literature of social work practice and research

---

[2] "Selection of postreproductive characters or characters of non-reproductive individuals can be selected and can effect the evolution of the race because the unit of selection is not wholly confined to the individual organism but may be and often is the more inclusive population system" (Emerson, 1960. p. 327).

[3] "We have good evidence that two types of sociel or sub-social interactions exist among animals: the self-centered egoistic drives, which lead to personal advancement and self-preservation; and the group-centered, more or less altruistic drives, which lead to the preservation of the group ..." (Allee, 1958, p. 212).

[4] "I have felt that culture freed us from our biological base and separated us from our animal cousins, but it becomes clearer now that this ability is in a broader sense a biological mechanism serving a biological need" (Tax, 1960. p. 247).

[5] "... organic systems incorporate time dimensions ... end-directions are apparent in ontogenetic and phylogenetic time. Pittendrigh (1958) refers to such end-directedness as teleonomy without implying Aristotelian teleology as an efficient causal principle ... Population systems have such teleonomic properties as well as individual organisms, and the basic evolutionary processes are similar" (Emerson, 1960. p. 341).

in relation to the aging client although it permeates social work with children, adolescents, and the young adult. What is missing, I believe, is a frame of reference which induces a forward-impelled conception of the latter half of life; a frame in which developmental tasks are seen to be fully as important to the individual, and possibly to the race, as are the developmental tasks of infancy and childhood.[6] It is this lack which accounts for a certain sterility, a there's-nothing-different-about-the-aging attitude or the concrete-services orientation in even the best of social work literature on the subject. It may also, in large part, account for the reluctance of many of the best practitioners to enter the field— it, plus misapprehensions of the normal end-state of life, brought on by the overstress on pathology which pervades the social work curriculum (Butler, 1959) and which f u r t h e r re-inforces the worker's unconscious rejection of his own death. "Every social worker who proposes to work with the aging should force himself to meditate upon his own death."[7]

Social work teaching regarding individual growth and development is dominated by Freud's exposition of psychosexual development—the oral, anal, phallic and genital stages or levels. Butler (1959), after a review of course outlines submitted by the schools for the Social Work Curriculum Study, concludes Freud's theory (with one school excepted) was used with such emphasis as to suggest that it constitutes a theoretical base required for developing an understanding of human personality on which to base social work practice" (p. 15). Freud, however, did not extend his formulations of development much beyond childhood and his concept of Thanatos, the death instinct, offers little to build on. Quoting further, Butler also reports:

In those schools whose courses extended to the *adult period*,

---

[6] "As a social worker one inevitably is drawn to some organization or constellation of ideas related to general social work orientation ... Especially significant is the concept of the life cycle and life span. Related are the concepts of human development and growth, expansion, self-realization, as well as that of mastery" (Wasser, 1961. p. 15).

[7] E. Wasser in conversation with the author, October, 1962. As is often the case, the novelist may give us more genuine understanding of something we ourselves have not experienced than can any scientist. I know of no better work for this purpose than Muriel Spark's *Memento Mori* (1960).

coverage of that period was less systematic than for earlier phases of the life cycle. . . Reference to the menopausal period was made in a few schools. Concerning *the aged*, ideas and concepts appeared with little attempt at orderly arrangement. The distintegration of ego functioning as well as disturbances in physical functioning were noted. In one or two instances reference was made to death (p. 15).

It should be noted that current studies all point toward the health, not the pathology, of the aged. None uphold the prevailing stereotype.[8] (Blenkner, 1961; Cumming and Henry, 1961; Gurin, 1960; Reichard, 1962; Shanas, 1962).

In thinking of the aged, it is perhaps too easy to slip into thinking of them as all being in extreme condition. Actually only 2 per cent of the group sixty-five and over are bed-ridden, less than 10 per cent are in institutions. Relatively few ever become senile. . . Many old people reach the end of life without ever having been physically or mentally infirm (Reichard, 1962, p. 5.).

According to Shanas (1962), "The possibility of extended illness is the greatest single threat to the peace of mind of the elderly". Shanas also states:

Most people in the older age group have worked out some way of life, and even those with very small incomes make the best of their negligible resources; but the threat of illness remains. (p. 178).

Social work eagerly picked up the newer ego psychology as it developed out of class Freudianism but it has largely followed the direction set by Anna Freud:[9] the mechanisms of defense and their elaboration, not the direction set by Hartman: the processes of adaptation and mastery; the autonomous, conflict-free, intrinsically

[8] Research of the late Irving Lorge (1960) on such stereotypes indicates that social workers, physicians and nurses are more subject to stereotyped attitudes toward aged persons than are social scientists.

[9] In *Ego Psychology and Dynamic Casework* (Parad, 1958) there is not one reference in the index to "mastery." There are 15 to "defense."

pleasurable functions of the ego (Monroe, 1955).[10] Anna Freud needs no defense, if I may be permitted a pun, but some of her followers do, especially those who would see every behavior, every maneuver, even basic character structure as a system of defense. This absurd reductionism in which "ego devices which approach the normal or even the ideal are still 'defenses' " is not accidental. "The term arises from pathology, from the fact that psychoanalysis has developed a general theory of human psychology based upon principles discovered largely through investigation of the distortions of mental illness" (Monroe, 1955, p. 54).

One can speculate on the selective screening that may operate to introduce into the ranks of social workers a high proportion of persons who find it congenial to view life as something to be defended against rather than something to be mastered but that would lead us far afield. Nevertheless, the overwhelming emphasis on defense may have a good deal to do with the fact that most social workers shun work with the aging. Defense mechanisms may not be of too great help in thinking creatively about the aged, but they are certainly pertinent to understanding the average social worker's dealing with them.[11]

A look at what Hartman calls the ego-apparatuses (See Monroe, 1955)—the sensorium, memory, motility and the like— seem to me to point away from "defense" and toward "mastery" in treatment of the aging adult. These are the things that fail even in the best of us as we age. In their failure we are deprived

---

[10] Goldfarb (1955, 1956) following Meyer, Rado, and Kardiner, has presented his theoretical formulation of an ego-based psychotherapy for the older person with severely disordered behavior which makes particular use of the motivational dynamics of mastery and pleasure. Turner (1961) has incorporated some of this fomulation in her view of casework with the aged client. Both have, to date, written largely of the psychopathology of aging. One hopes they will at some point give us the benefit of their thinking regarding the larger group of normal, relatively healthy oldsters who also, at points of crises, can benefit from psychiatrically-oriented help.

[11] I am not arguing that understanding of the mechanisms of defense has no place in work with aging, but that it is not enough. An understanding of *character* (not character disorder, note) is fundamental to work with the aged. The dynamics of the neuroses when applied to an old person whose life and character are organized around mastery and control may cause a worker to err seriously in her diagnosis and treatment.

of familiar pleasures of mastery. Can casework not take a lead from a statement made by Harlow (1961) to group workers: "Old age is a possibility and a probability, the need remains to use what there is with a sense of mastery."

Of the various ego psychologists with whom social workers are familiar, Erikson (1950, 1959) offers the best starting-off point for considering the second half of life. Erikson's conception of the life cycle is a truly developmental one and he has been called the first of the psychoanalytic theorists to carry us beyond the stage of genital maturity (Rapaport, 1959). Erikson (1959), himself, speaks of the "epigentic principle, whereby:

Each item of the healthy personality . . . is systematically related to all others, and they all depend on the proper development in the proper sequence of each item and each exists in some form before "its" decisive and critical time normally arrives (p. 53).

Erikson conceived of eight distinct stages in the human life cycle. He posed his stages in terms of crises or tasks, successful solution of which lead to health; failure to pathology. The sequence he held to be universal, the typical solution dependent on the particular society of which the person is a member. His pairs of outcome are familiar to most of you. They carry us from infancy into old age. As phrased in his 1959 version, they are: Basic Trust *vs.* Basic Mistrust; Autonomy *vs.* Shame and Doubt; Initiative *vs.* Guilt; Industry *vs.* Inferiority; Identity *vs.* Identity Diffusion; Intimacy *vs.* Self-absorption; Generativity *vs.* Stagnation and, finally, Integrity *vs.* Despair. Mere repetition of these name tags cannot possibly convey the richness of Erikson's conception but I would point out to you the extent to which the art and literature of the last two decades reflects his "failures" in adolescence and adulthood. The question of *identity*, the *self-absorption*, the *stagnation*, above all, the *despair* reflected in the Theatre of the Absurd is but one example. (One cannot help but wonder what this most recent lost generation will be like in their seventies. I do not think they will be like the generation now at that age: today's old men and women were neither beat nor lost in their youth they may have suffered from inhibition but they did not ask who am I?)

Erikson's description of the healthy resolution of the last great developmental crisis, "the fruit of the seven stages," is a magnificent concept:

> I know no better word for it than integrity. . . . It is the acceptance of one's own and only life cycle and of the people who have become significant to it as something that had to be and that, by necessity, permitted of no substitutions.[12] It thus means a different love of one's parents, free of the wish that they should have been different, and acceptance of the fact that one's life is one's own responsibility. It is a sense of comradeship with men and women of distant times and of different pursuits, who have created orders and objects and sayings conveying human dignity and love. Although aware of the relativity of all the various life styles which have given meaning to human striving, the possessor of integrity is ready to defend the dignity of his own life against all physical and economic threats. For he knows that an individual life is the accidental coincidence of but one life cycle with but one segment of history; and that for him all human integrity stands and falls with the one style of integrity of which he partakes (p. 98, 1959).

Among those few behavioral scientists who have tried to formulate the last half of life in developmental terms, Peck and Buhler have perhaps the most to offer for social work consideration. Peck (1956) acknowledging fully his debt to Erikson, attempts to divide Erikson's final crisis (Integrity *vs.* Despair) into stages, for after all, Erickson's last crisis extends over forty years in the average life-span; more time than is covered by all his preceding seven.[13]

---

[12] Reichard *et al.* (1962) state their "data suggest that growing old, may, in itself, make it easier for some people to accept themselves and their past — and so achieve integrity."

[13] "Erikson has written a book about childhood, and he cannot be blamed for not writing one about old age, but it is a loss to us that he did not extend his analysis to include the responses of the retrenching organism" (Cumming and Henry, 1961, p. 7).

Peck first divides the last half of life into two broad chronlogical periods—Middle-age, the forties and fifties and Old-age, from sixty on. Within each of these periods he sees several stages or tasks. For middle age these are:

1. Valuing Wisdom *vs.* Valuing Physical Powers

   (Essentially an inversion of a previous value hierarchy so that wisdom becomes the standard for self-evaluation and the chief resource for solving life's problems.)

2. Socializing *vs.* Sexualizing

   (Brought on maturationally by the climacteric, this too introduces a shift in self-evaluation as well as a shift in one's valuation of others; people take on a new kind of value that stems from other drives than sex. Failure to make the shift is evidence that the person is still trying to work out unfulfilled need from an earlier age. (This writer is of the opinion that in understanding the dynamics of the psychiatrically disturbed oldster, the question is not so much "what symbolizes sex" as "what does sex symbolize.")

3. Cathectic Flexibility *vs.* Cathectic Impoverishment

   (This refers to a capacity to shift emotional investments from one person to another and from one activity to another and as such seems more of a trait than a stage, or if it is to be considered as a stage, it is perhaps, more appropriate in the context of the sixties and seventies than that of middle age. For the sixties and especially the seventies, a "generalized set toward making new cathexes" becomes of prime importance.)

4. Mental Flexibility *vs.* Mental Rigidity

   (This too seems more a trait than a stage. Peck admits it cuts across all life but holds it becomes a critical issue in middle-age. It is closely related to Frenkel-Brunswick's (1949), "tolerance of ambiguity" and Henry's (1956), "affective complexity.")

Peck's middle age stages are not as successful as his old age ones, to be described later. This, I believe is because he violates the developmental principle of sequence and maturation. Only his first two stages are tied to biological changes which are universal; the problems they pose do not quite fit the concept of the timing of the developmental task, "the teachable moment," which in Havighurst's (1952) apt phrases comes "When the body is ripe, and society requires, and the self is ready." I am not sure, either that the first two cannot be subsumed in some fashion under one theme. Data from several studies (e.g., Cumming and Henry [1961]) and developmental theory itself suggest a long, somewhat stable period or plateau at maturity.[14] Thus there may be but one major crisis in middle age. On the other hand, *old* age like childhood, may have a number of stages in relatively quick succession.

Buhler (1959), expressing her dissatisfaction with both classic Freudianism and ego psychology (including Erikson's model) as well as theories based on homeostatic equilibrium—because neither gives a sufficiently *primary* place to creativity or mastery—adopts a bio-physical model of the "open system" as her starting point. In this conception of the living open system, both *maintenance* and *change* are equally important; for while the system maintains itself in a steady state through continuous exchange with its environment, it also displays "spontaneous transition to a state of higher heterogeneity and complexity," or in Buhler's words, "The organism changes while maintaining itself and maintains itself while changing." (This, incidentally, ties in with the developmental concept of irreversability; no matter how much the older organism may seem to take on some of the aspects of infancy, aging is not a process of turning, at maturity, toward a simpler, more homogeneous state.) Buhler distinguishes two forms of maintenance: that which is directed to satisfying need and that which is directed to maintaining internal order; as well as two types of change—adaptation and creativity. From these she drives her four basic tendencies of life, the tendencies toward:

1. Need-satisfaction (maintenance)
2. Adaptive self-limitation (change)
3. Creative expansion (change)
4. Upholding internal order (maintenance)

---

[14] See also B. S. Bloom's Chapter 8, of this volume.

"In every human being all these four tendencies have to be in operation at all times, with one or the other prevailing depending on individuality and age. Developmentally their prevalence forms a maturational sequence" (Buhler, 1961 p. 365). Biological growth and decline, sociocultural influences, and motivation, together with maturation, are seen in Buhler's system as "co-determinants of human development."

In the normally developing human organism, the young child's prevalent tendency is to satisfy his needs, the older child is primarily involved in adaptive self-limitation; the adolescent and younger adult is engaged largely in creative expansion; the middle-aged adult in establishing internal order. Successful passage through each of these stages requires integrating as well as balancing the conflicting and competitive trends from the earlier stages with those in the new stage. In moving from middle age to old age, however, integration becomes particularly crucial. In middle age "an inner scrutiny develops, a self-assessment, a questioning of whatever order seemed to exist before." This *self-assessment of the climacteric* is seen by Buhler as of a different order than any earlier self-assessments. "It is a much more serious, much more consequential procedure, because it takes place with awareness of this being a critical period, a last moment for making changes, for improving on the results, for bringing in some of the harvest that everybody is hoping for" (1961, p. 368). (It is also, one might add, a time when most of us begin to realize our own parents are aging. How well they are doing so undoubtedly effects to what extent we, ourselves, react with panic or despair to our own first true self-consciousness of aging. How this effects our reactions to our parents' needs is also insufficiently recognized. Too often, for example, the son's or daughter's anxiety at placing a parent in a nursing home is seen only as guilt. It has other overtones. The parent is the child's future.) How well one comes out of Buhler's period of self-assessment will determine to a large extent how one faces old age.

Returning now to Peck, his formulation of the stages of old age is in many ways superb. The sequence is clear and necessary. The crises have the quality of universality. Old age, beginning somewhere in the sixties for most, poses the following developmental tasks or crises:

1. Ego-Differentiation *vs.* Work Role Preoccupation

   ("Am I a worthwhile person only insofar as I can do a full time job . . . or because of the kind of person I am?") Peck here is talking not just of shifts in social role and status but of attributes of personality and intra- as well as inter-personal relationships. Although precipitated by vocational retirement, it is, in my opinion, more biologically based than Peck gives it credit. Some may be forced into a "precocious" development by involuntary retirement but we really do not know whether, if society's values were different, if achieved standards of living could be maintained even though retired, how many people might choose to retire voluntarily at an even earlier stage than they do now. Evidence from several studies point in this direction (Gordon, 1961).

2. Body Transcendence *vs.* Body Preoccupation

   (This requires a re-definition of "happiness" and "comfort" if one is to handle the decline in physical powers, the lowered resistance to illness, and lessened recuperative powers or the increase in physical discomfort, which later life brings on. The "failures" at this stage of development will, I think, be recognized by every social worker and every physician. Many fail who, in outward reality, are not put to a very severe test but there are others whose gallantry under what seems unbearable trauma leaves one in humble wonderment at the triumph of the human spirit.)

3. Ego Transcendence *vs.* Ego Preoccupation

   (The task here is that of positive adaptation to the certain prospect of personal death—"the night of the ego." Success may be measured "both in terms of the individuals inner state of contentment or stress, and . . . his constructive or stress-inducing impact on those around him."[15] Peck's con-

---

[15] This is an important concept. Goldfarb, for example, often speaks of the "disturbed *and disturbing*" oldster.

ception of this last stage invokes an element of "adaptive, goal-seeking change which extends into the latest years of life . . . a vital gratifying absorption in the future, possibly the most complete kind of ego-realization.")

Thus, Peck, noting that "the concept of development often connotes an end-point—a teleological goal," summarizes his conception of that goal as follows

If the end-point be conceived not as some physiologically defined goal, but as an end-of-life state of mind whose vision shapes and colors all the actions of the older person, then might not the human end-point be this: to achieve the ability to live so fully, so generously, so unselfishly that the prospect of personal death looks and feels less important than the secure knowledge that one has built for a broader future, for one's children and one's society, than one ego could ever encompass" (1956, p. 43).

Buhler's concept of the last task is in many ways similar to Erikson's and Pecks. Although she does not phrase it in quite this way nor place it directly in the context of her discussion of the maturational sequence of her four basic tendencies, her concept of the proper concern of the old—the seventies on—seems to be that of finding an inner fulfillment, an inner meaning and integrity as one moves inevitably toward approaching death. This fulfillment, this meaning and integrity is a final reward of "that essentially human grandeur of attempting to build a lasting structure, a monument of life that survives ourself" (1961, p. 369).

All three of these thanatopses, these musing on the end-state— "delicate death"[16]—reviewed here present the end of life as a goal of human development. Aging is seen primarily as a natural process of change, not as a pathological system nor entirely as a response to one's environment (Breen, 1960). All three recognize that few persons attain the ideal state, just as few young adults reach com-

---

[16] Come lovely and soothing death,
 Undulate round the world, serenely arriving, arriving,
 In the day, in the night, to all, to each,
 Sooner or later delicate death. (Whitman, "When Lilacs Last in the Dooryard Bloomed." Stanza 14.)

plete "genital maturity." But all three hold that an approximation is possible for many and the evidence from studies of the very old supports them (Cumming and Parlegreco, 1961; Reichard, 1962). That the very old are also a special breed is likely.[17]

Although one of the more important recent theoretical formulations about the aging process is that of Elaine Cummings,[18] I have not chosen to dwell on it here, for though Cumming places old age in a developmental context she is primarily concerned with how the aging individual relates to his environment rather than to himself.[19] In her own words, she is, "not directly interested in the structure of personality or in the structure of society but, rather, in the interface between them" (Cumming and Henry, 1961, p. 10). I would however commend her recent book to you for its useful insights, its good sense and wry humor and especially, its trenchant criticism of what Cumming terms "the implicit theory of aging." I would also suggest careful study of her thoughts and her data on differences in the aging process that society imposes upon men and women. "The nature of the modern industrial world, which does not make use of the accumulated wisdom of men,

---

[17] There is some evidence that living to be over eighty . . . is associated with being a member of a biological, and possibly psychological elite. Furthermore, very old people often have surprisingly high level of social competence and seem able to maintain high spirits . . . there may be a group of people who, more than being merely survivors, have a special biological invulnerability to such things as hardened arteries and failing senses" (Cumming and Parlegreco, 1961, pp. 201-202).

"It must be recognized that persons who survive into old age may be psychologically stronger than those who do not. The established link between emotional stress and disease suggest that psychological factors may speed up the rate of physical decline and even play a part in precipitating fatal illness" (Reichard, 1962, p. 169).

[18] Cumming, herself, gives a succint statement of "disengagement theory" as follows:

This theory starts from the common-sense observation that here in America the old person is less involved in the life around him than he was when he was younger, and it proceeds without making assumptions about the desirability of this fact. Aging in the modal person is thought of in this theory as a mutual withdrawal or disengagement which takes place between the aging person and others in the social systems to which he belongs. He may withdraw more markedly from some classes of people and remain relatively close to others. This withdrawal may be accompanied from the outset by increased pre-

creates an important assymetry in old age. . . . There is no wise old man to match the widow Mary Worth. [It is an] assymetry which makes ours, in old age, a women's world" (p. 160). In Cumming's opinion, "If *health care and economic independence are guaranteed*" the only "true problem group" in American society are "those few retired men who cannot reintegrate with a membership [after retirement] and cannot shift their skills" (p. 153).

Talcott Parsons (1962) is groping—as only he can grope—for a role for the older man in American society.[20] He states hopefully but with full recognition that it may smack of "naive harmonism," that his "broadest suggestion is that a society which has been increasing in its 'production' of older people has at the same time been creating an increasing demand for their contributions." One such major contribution he suggests "has to do with trusteeship, not so much over social as over cultural values . . . in their link with moral standards. More generally it is guardianship of cultural traditions, not necessarily in the sense of traditionalism but rather of concern for the longest-run consideration of the society and its culture." This sounds familiar and is, I think, what anthropologists

occupation with himself. When the aging process is complete, the equilibrium which existed in middle life between the individual and his society has given way to a new equilibrium characterized by a greater distance and an altered type of relationship. In a previous report, we have presented data which suggest that one of the early stages of disengagement occurs when the aging individual withdraws investment from the environment. We have thought of the inner process being an ego change in which object cathexis is reduced; this results in an appearance of self-centeredness and an orientation to others which betrays less sense of mutual obligation. This is accompanied by a somewhat freer and more expressive manner. The fully disengaged person can be thought of as having transferred much of his cathexis to his own inner life; his memories, his fantasies, and his image of himself as someone who *was* something, and *did* accomplish things (Cumming and McCaffrey, 1961, p. 58).

[19] Cumming does speak of transitions, plateaus and crises and her theory would, I believe, lend itself to developmental structuring. It might well prove useful and clarifying to do so.

[20] Parsons has decanted the wine of Freud into his own bottles to formulate a theory of personality development but since it is Freudian wine he too has not yet got beyond "genital maturity" (Parsons, 1955). One of my colleagues at B.R.I., Martin Bloom, is currently attempting to extend the Parsonian formulation to the end of life (Bloom, 1962).

agree has been the function of old men in pre-literate societies. Erikson's, Peck's and Buhler's formulations suggest a further function for those who succeed in the last developmental task: to teach the rest of us how to die and thereby give us a philosophy by which to live.

In conclusion, I have some questions to ask of my fellow social workers. Before asking them, I want to make it perfectly clear that I am in no way implying criticism of those sturdy souls who find social work with the aging a rich and rewarding experience. They have either known intuitively or learned for themselves, much of what I have put down here. They have taught me. In turn, I hope some of what I have said may be of use to them.

To the caseworkers I would say—do not these conceptions of development in the last half of life give you a frame of reference for both diagnosis and treatment that holds more promise than a "needle-struck" concentration on "defense mechanisms"?[21] If one accepts the developmental frame of reference, what is more important to diagnose or evaluate in an older person; his particular resolution of the Oedipus complex or his philosophy of life? Which is more likely to offer you a dynamic you can use in treatment? In working with the older adult do you orient yourself to the task he has before him—*his developmental task*—just as in working with an adolescent, no matter what the immediate problem, you orient yourself to his overall task of leaving childhood and becoming adult? If casework is a problem-solving process do you know what your older client's real problem is? Are you fully aware of the counter-transference problem within you; that the older client may not be your parent but yourself?

Among the service methods of social work—casework, group work, and community organization—my identity is that of caseworker. In taking my casework colleagues to task, I take myself to task. Hence I am more free and more knowledgeable in my criticism of casework than I am in relation to my other colleagues, but

---

[21] Lest it be thought I exaggerate, I refer you to the proceedings of a seminar on casework held at Arden House in 1960 and particularly to the summary of workshop discussions under the heading Diagnostic Processes — *Ego Functioning,* p. 52 *(Casework With the Aging.* New York, Family Service Association of America, 1961).

of group work too, I would ask some questions: Are you perhaps selling your birthright, which was development, for a mess of undigested role theory? Is your phrase, "substitute roles," also a needle-stuck refrain? Is it substitute roles or *new roles* the old person needs for a *new task?* Do you too, look too much to your constituent's past and not enough to his future? What do you give that the old can carry with them to use when they can no longer come to your center? Do you teach philosophy or provide an opportunity for those who have it, to share it? Lastly, and with mischief aforethought, why are you so resistant to the term "disengagement?"

As for community organization, it is the method farthest from my ken. I am not familiar enough with its current literature to ask impertinent questions. I do know though that it also has a magic phrase—"power structure." I will however leave whatever implications this paper may have for that subject, or any other he cares to talk about, in the capable hand of our commentator, Bob Morris.

In closing, I would like to thank the organizers of this symposium for inviting my participation. I doubt very much that I have done what they expected of me. I have, instead, done what I wanted to do and thereby got a lot out of *my* "system." The feedback, I suspect, may be considerable!

My last remarks are addressed to the young now in schools of social work. They are not my words, they are Walt Whitman's as an old man:

> Youth, large, lusty, loving—Youth,
> full of grace, force, fascination,
> Do you know that Old Age may come
> After you with equal grace, force,
> fascination? (Youth, Day, Old Age and Night—1881).

REFERENCES

1. Allee, W. C.: *The Social Life of Animals.* Rev. Edition. Boston, Beacon Press, 1958.

2. Anderson, J. E.: Dynamics of development: Systems in process. *In* D. B. Harris (Ed.): *The Concept of Development,* Minneapolis, University of Minnesota Press, pp. 25-46, 1957.

3. Birren, J. E.: Principles of Research on Aging. *In* J. E. Birren (Ed.): *Handbook of Aging and the Individual: Psychological and Biological Aspects,* Chicago, University of Chicago Press, pp. 3-42, 1959.

4. Blenkner, M.: Study project in services to the aging. *In Institute of Welfare Research, Annual Report — 1960-1961,* New York, Community Service Society (Mimeographed), pp. 1-5.

5. Bloom, M.: Memorandum on life-span analysis. Cleveland, Benjamin Rose Institute (unpublished document), 1962.

6. Breen, L. Z.: The aging individual. *In* C. Tibbitts (Ed.): *Handbook of Social Gerontology: Societal Aspects of Aging,* Chicago, University of Chicago Press, pp. 145-162, 1960.

7. Buhler, C.: Theoretical observations about life's basic tendencies. *Journal of Psychotherapy, 13*:561-81, 1959.

8. ....: Meaningful living in the mature years. *In* R. W. Kleemeier (Ed.): *Aging and Leisure: A Research Perspective Into the Meaningful Use of Time,* New York, Oxford University Press, pp. 345-87, 1961.

9. Butler, R. M.: An orientation to knowledge of human growth and behavior in social work education. *Vol. VI Project Report of the Curriculum Study,* New York, Council on Social Work Education, 1959.

10. Comfort, A.: *The Biology of Senescence.* London, Routledge and Kegan Paul, 1956.

11. Cumming, E., and Henry, W. E.: *Growing Old: The Process of Disengagement,* New York, Basic Books, Inc., 1961.

12. Cumming, E., and McCaffrey, I.: Some conditions associated with morale among the aging. *In* P. Hoch and J. Zubin (Eds.): *Psychopathology of Aging,* New York, Grune and Stratton, pp. 57-68, 1961.

13. Cumming, E., and Parlegreco, M. L.: The very old. *In* E. Cumming and W. E. Henry, *Growing Old: The Process of Disengagement,* New York, Basic Books, Inc., pp. 201-09, 1961.

14. Emerson, A. E.: The evolution of adaptation in population systems. *In* S. Tax (Ed.): *The Evolution of Life: Its Origin History and Future,* Volume I in *Evolution after Darwin:* The University of Chicago centinnial, Chicago, University of Chicago Press, pp. 307-348, 1960.

15. Erikson, E. H.: *Childhood and Society,* New York, W. W. Norton & Co., 1950.

16. ....: Identity and the Life Cycle. *Psychological Issues, I*:1 (New York, International Universities Press) 1959.

17. Frenkel-Brunswick, E.: Intolerance of ambiguity as an emotional and perceptual variable. *Journal of Personality, 18*:108-143, 1949.

18. Goldfarb, A.: Psychotherapy of aged persons. IV. One aspect of the psychodynamics of the therapeutic situation with aged patients. *Psychoanalytic Review, 42(2)*:180-187, 1955.

19. ....: Psychotherapy of the aged: the use and value of an adaptational frame of reference. *Psychoanalytic Review, 43(1)*: 68-81, 1956.

20. Gordon, M. S.: Work and patterns of retirement. *In* R. W. Kleemeier (Ed.): *Aging and Leisure: A Research Perspective into the Meaningful Use of Time,* New York, Oxford University Press, pp. 5-53, 1961.

21. Gurin, G., Veroff, J., and Feld, S.: *Americans View Their Mental Health: A Nationwide Interview Survey,* New York, Basic Books, Inc., 1960.

22. Harlow, M.: Program content or group experience in a psychiatric hospital, Topeka, The Menninger Foundation (Mimeographed), 1961.

23. Harris, D. B.: Problems in formulating a scientific concept of development. *In* D. B. Harris (Ed.): *The Concept of Development,* Minneapolis, University of Minnesota Press, pp. 3-14, 1957.

24. Havighurst, R. J.: *Developmental Tasks and Education.* New York, Longmans, Green & Co., 2nd Edition, 1952.

25. Henry, W. E.: Affective complexity and role perceptions: Some suggestions for a conceptual framework for a study of adult personality. *In* J. E. Anderson (Ed.): *Psychological Aspects of Aging,* Washington, D.C., American Psychological Association, Inc., pp. 30-41, 1956.

26. Lorge, I.: Professional Practices with the Aging: A Challenge to Practitioners. Address to the National Health Council Forum, Miami, (Duplicated), March 15, 1960.

27. Monroe, R. L.: *Schools of Psychoanalytic Thought: An Exposition, Critique, and Attempt at Integration.* New York, The Dryden Press, 1955.

28. Nagel, E.: Determinism and development. *In* D. B. Harris (Ed.): *The Concept of Development,* Minneapolis, University of Minnesota Press, pp. 15-24, 1955.

29. Parad, H. J. (Ed.): *Ego Psychology and Dynamic Casework.* New York, Family Service Association of America, 1958.

30. Parsons, T.: Family structure and the socialization of the child. *In* T. Parsons and R. Bales: *Family, Socialization and Interaction Process,* Glencoe, Ill., The Free Press, pp. 35-131, 1955.

31. ....: The aging in American society. *Law and Contemporary Problems, 27(1)*:22-35, 1955.

32. Peck, R.: Psychological developments in the second half of life. *In* J. E. Anderson (Ed.): *Psychological Aspects of Aging,* Washington, D.C., American Psychological Association, Inc., pp. 42-53, 1956.

33. Pittendrigh, C. S.: Adaptation, natural selection and behavior. *In* A. Roe and G. G. Simpson (Eds.): *Behavior and Evolution,* New Haven, Yale University Press, pp 390-416, 1958.

34. Rapaport, D.: Historical introduction. *In E. Erikson: Identity and the Life Cycle, Psychological Issues, I(1)*:5-17, New York, International Universities Press, 1959.

35. Reichard, S., Livson, F., and Peterson, P. G.: *Aging and Personality: A Study of Eighty-Seven Older Men.* New York, John Wiley and Sons, 1962.

36. Schneirla, T. C.: The concept of development in comparative psychology. *In* D. B. Harris (Ed.): *The Concept of Development,* Minneapolis, University of Minnesota Press, pp. 78-108, 1957.

37. Shanas, E.: *The Health of Older People: A Social Survey.* Cambridge, Harvard University Press, 1962.

38. Spark, M.: *Memento Mori.* New York, Meridian Books, Inc., 1960.

39. Tax, S.: The celebration: a personal view. *In* S. Tax (Ed.): Issues in Evolution, Volume 3 in *Evolution after Darwin:* The University of Chicago Centinnial, Chicago, University of Chicago Press, pp. 271-82, 1960.

40. Turner, H. Use of the relationship in casework treatment of aged clients. *Social Casework, 42*:245-252, 1961.

41. Wasser, E.: Some considerations pertinent to personality theory of the aging. New York, Institute of Welfare Research, Community Service Society (unpublished document), 1961.

Chapter 15

THE INTERRELATIONSHIPS OF SOCIAL WELFARE THEORY, PRACTICE AND RESEARCH

ROBERT MORRIS

The difficulty this subject presents for social welfare and social workers is long-standing and imbedded in our history, training, and function. The lag between theory and practice has plagued many professions, but none more persistently than social work. Our task in society has been defined, for many years, as the coping with problems cast up by an industrialized, urbanized society; it has not been primarily our task to search for casual explanations of these problems, nor to frame basic policies which could modify our social and economic functioning sufficiently to attack them at their roots. True, we have maintained some commitment to prevention of social distress and to social action, but in fact our education, our alignment of technical resources, our sponsors and our ways of thinking have added up to a helping task—helping individuals to meet their private environments, and helping our communities live with the human wastage of an industrial society with built-in technology for rapid change.

This situation has not always existed, and it seems to be changing now. Prior to World War I, an effort was made to wed, in the National Conference of Charities and Corrections, the approaches of the analyst, theoretician and practitioner—the social scientist and the social worker. By 1920, Mary Richmond was able to assert that "social casework had contrived to slip from under the domination of the economists . . . generalizations about relief, family life, widowhood, desertion, immigrants and the rest served a useful purpose in that pioneer period but . . . casework achieved an even more important step forward."[1] This important step was the designing of a method for studying individual behavior on a case-by-case basis. Even in her eyes, however, the step was not an abandonment of research and theory, but the first step in creating a *new* theory by going back to the study of the individual units of human existance.

Between 1920 and 1945 we were, as a profession and with a few exceptions, little concerned with large theories of our own, content to work within the framework of dynamic psychology which explained individual behavior. Since then, a few social agencies and a few social workers have re-opened the path of social research which may lead to new and useful theories.

Having said this, I can still sense a subtle drawing back from the term "theory." It has many impediments. Social agencies have only recently agreed that interviewing can be carried on in a thera-peutic situation to serve two ends simultaneously—the therapeutic and the investigative. More often, they have been suspicious that research investigation would rupture the treatment relationship. The languages of the therapist and the researcher have often been incomprehensible to each other and neither has tried very hard to learn the useage of the other.

There has also been an underlying distrust of pure theory in our pragmatic workaday world. We have been mistrustful of general explanations and predictions, for we have known the complexity of man in society. Committed as we are to the uniqueness of the individual and his capacity to respond to his environment in his unique way, we still mistrust generalizations which classify groups of individuals for this limits the possibility of distinctiveness. All this has begun to change in recent years and for good reasons. Above all, our society has until recently tended to equate theory and fuzzy-minded impracticality, treating a theory as something which floats on cloud nine far above the earth, or which represents wishful dreaming not reality. We have been impelled to think more and more about prevention as well as treatment and care. The explo-sion of aged survivors in our society resulted from certain public

---

[1] Richmond, Mary: *The Long View*. New York, The Russell Sage Founda-tion, New York, 1930, p. 484.

health, medical and technological acts but we were wholly unprepared for the consequences. Not being prepared, we launched scores of programs, tried innumerable paths of trial and error, increased the numbers of agencies beyond counting.

This frank trial and error approach soon ran into difficulties—we had not enough money, and more importantly, not enough staff to perform all these exciting but unproven and untested duties at once. We have had to think deeply about the best means for applying our limited resources of dollar and personnel (limited in relation to the magnitude of the problem) effectively at the most vital leverage points. Such a more focused and selective approach has been demanded not only by our own professional pride; it is required if our competence to accept responsibility for such large problems is to be established and accepted.

I believe a case can be made that the building up of a body of theory by social work to explain more incisively the problems with which we deal is essential if we are to discharge the responsibilities thrust upon us. Before developing this theme, a slight detour may be in order to outline what I believe to be the relationship between a social welfare problem, research, theory and professional practice. In capsule form, these terms can be distinguished thusly: practice constitutes the things we do to deal with our professional responsibilities, (it can be built upon accumulated experience, trial and error selection or shared wisdom). Research is the systematic ordering of data about a problem (social work research has, by and large, concentrated on single sets of facts, such as those which measure the dimensions of social needs). Social theory seeks to do two things (a) to explain the abstract relationships between two or more sets of facts (e.g., what is the relationship between chronological, neurological deterioration and social withdrawal or isolation); and (b) to fix the basis for predicting events which can be expected to occur in the future (e.g., will interposed social activity reduce the rate of mental deterioration in persons over 65 years of age under specified conditions)?

Our history had led us to treat each problem on a case basis, to seek for the multiple factors which are intertwined in the behavior of each individual in response to his environment. We have helped individual older persons seek financial security, to find housing, to secure medical care, to resolve the personal issues of loneliness and estrangement from family, to face finally, the ultimate decline in human existence. Then our daily responsibilities led some of us to more systematic study of these one-by-one experiences and we entered into social research along several paths: one added up the measure of economic insecurity and led to the Social Security system; another threw light on functional ability and the distinctive health needs of the aged in and out of institutions, so we evolved home medical care programs, rehabilitation, and nursing care in homes for the aged; and a third path revealed the intricate patterns of family relationships which led to counseling and other supportive services for the three generation family.

None of this can be called theory building for the research did not yet seek to explain but rather sought to define the extent and charcter of our problems. We moved then to more subtle forms of research, now concerned with evaluating the caliber and effectiveness of our practices. This evaluative research has not been theoretical either, except as to research method, for it sought to define and judge the practices we have built by trial and error, in order to permit a more careful selection of effective over ineffective practices.

We have come far with this evolution, but have not yet a body of social welfare theory. Miss Blenkner's eloquent and concise paper is testimony to this truism, for the provocative theories she outlines have, by and large, been evolved by social scientists, not social workers. We have a great deal of experience about the development of human life and aging, but none of this has been ordered in theoretical form to enable us to say with certainty what the sequence of aging is, or to distinguish key changing elements in the path from birth to old age.

We need to ask ourselves candidly and honestly—can social work develop theory at all, in the sense I have defined it? True we have concepts we call social work theory but note that few, if any, of them are either our own, or explain cause and effect relationships between several sets of facts so that prediction is possible. The hallmark of our profession is the uniqueness of individual growth, not the prediction about the probable scope of limits of that growth for any class of individuals.

I believe that social work is ready to test its capacity to develop its own theory for use in its own practice, to supplement the theories borrowed from other disciplines. To suggest the possibility, I should like to draw upon two examples from research in community planning now being conducted at Brandeis University— examples which are incomplete first steps but which may illustrate how social welfare theory may differ from social welfare research, and how each may be valuable for an extension of our practice.

One of the repeated elements in social work planning is the concept of leadership as a key element in bringing about social change. We have done some research which defines the characteristics of persons in ascribed leadership positions. Other research has established that social work planning attracts middle-range influential persons but seldom attracts the most powerful persons in our communities. Meantime, our observations report that few welfare planning councils have yet given a high priority to aging with the result that many community leaders interested in the subject have been attracted to other organizations, setting up parallel planning bodies. Our usual response to these facts is to assert that strong leadership for aging must be brought into the welfare councils and that this, in turn, will lead to effective support for aging programs, provided the leadership acts with vigor and skill (terms not yet defined). Note that this approach ascribes planning weakness to a leadership lack in planning agencies, but does not seek to explain why this lack has so long persisted.

This research project attacked the problem from the viewpoint of theory building.[1] A review of published data and professional practice led to a decision to use one key factor with which to unravel the problem: What are the mechanisms for leadership in-put in voluntary welfare councils and in groups with special interests in aging? The investigation was limited to urban areas with voluntary welfare councils. Study of data established who were the leaders and decision-makers in general welfare planning

---

[1] Based on a forthcoming publication on "Leadership In-Put in Welfare Planning Councils and Aging" by Sanford Kravitz for the study of Community Organization for the Elderly, conducted by The Florence Heller Graduate School, Brandeis University; financed by The Ford Foundation; Principal Investigator, Robert Morris.

and for the aged. These data led to a theory, part of which is presented in oversimplified form:

1. Voluntary welfare councils draw their key leadership from two main sources: the social elite with established wealth and tradition; and the executive class of business or organization men. The key holders of economic power are seldom involved directly.

2. A subsidiary flow of leadership comes from certain minority groups *which maintain well-established social welfare agencies* similar to those previously incorporated in the welfare council.

3. There are a few token representatives of other groups, who exert no decisive voice in policy.

4. The "ticket of entry" from any of these groups to leadership has two parts: (a) policy influence or control in an "acceptable" social agency (defined variously in various cities); and (b) a willingness to abide by a few ground rules, the most important of which is acceptance of a balanced set of many programs as more important than the success or failure of any one program. Such leaders are first and foremost oriented to integration and balance of conflicting interests.

5. Key leaders in aging differ, by and large, as follows: (a) they are often drawn from political minority or labor groups without social agency experience or interests; (b) they are inclined to turn to governmental action for problem solution; (c) they are convinced that new programming for the aging is more important today than the pre-existing balance of other welfare activity. They are therefore *action*-oriented to the success of their particular interests; they are "cause oriented."

6. Social or economic "influentials" who became active in these aging groups are convinced of the primacy of this cause over others.

7. Therefore, the selection of persons by welfare councils to plan for aging excludes, by the dynamics of the leadership in-put system, those most interested in the subject.

8. Therefore, too, planning for aging is not likely to receive top priority in welfare councils.

9. Finally, it is unlikely that all welfare planning for the aged will be centralized within welfare councils for at least several years to come.

It is not necessary that this theory be proven right in every instance, and each of us will think of exceptions. What we need to ask is: Does this explain our acts well enough and often enough to make it possible to predict that planning will follow this course most of the time? This statement is not offered with the belief that it *is a proven* theory, but it is a theory, evolved from research and observation in several cities. It is advanced as a stimulator for our thinking. We are now ready to take the next step, to test this theory. If it is accurate we would expect to predict these outcomes: that aging would not receive a high priority in welfare council planning; that independent planning groups for the aging will develop apart from welfare councils; that there will be minimal overlap between *key* decision makers in councils and in aging groups for some time to come. The theory would then help us understand certain obstacles we face and pave the way for creative solutions which now elude us because we lack proper understanding of all the facts before us.

This theory, untested as it is, does not purport to answer all the problems of planning for the aged; it leaves untouched such questions as the proper patterning of programs, what structure will make greatest progress in getting action, and whether one or the other combination of leaders gets best results. What it does is *explain* certain facts with which we have all struggled: The proliferation of planning groups for the aged and the slowness with which welfare councils have moved into this field.

A second illustration[1] may make an indirect contribution to the current controversy over the Cumming theory of disengagement. Social workers are faced with this set of observations or collected data: (a) most persons in their early sixties are in a state of "retirement" from either paid employment or family obligations; (b) many retired persons seem to be socially lost, unhappy and disengaged from social affairs; (c) many other older people are either ill and handicapped or quite content with a socially passive life;

---

[1] Based on a study of the Manpower Potential Among Retired Persons by Camille Lambert, Jr. and Mrs. Mildred Guberman, conducted at The Florence Heller Graduate School, Brandeis University, and supported by a grant from the Community Health Services Program, U.S. Public Health Service and the Medical Foundation of Boston. (Robert Morris, Principal Investigator).

(d) our industrial world is fast making a permanent proportion of labor redundant, with automation and long-term unemployment coupled together; (e) the health and welfare services are constantly frustrated by a continuous shortage of manpower and limited citizen interest; (f) most social agencies have one or two older persons active in their work, as staff trustees or volunteers, but they are seldom considered "old" and the numbers do not grow.

With these facts, we confront a serious issue in aging: What is the role of the older citizen in our community life? We have various views about possible roles, most of which depend upon moral or ethical positions about the value of the human personality. Would a social work theory, not a social work conviction, help us deal with this issue? At the moment we have one borrowed concept of disengagement which, in its oversimplified form, could encourage us to help older persons make a graceful transition to this declining period of life, but it is in conflict with the ethical position just expressed. At Brandeis, we are advancing a crude theory and are beginning to test it. In capsule form it would read: Retirement is a function of rigidity in social organization, not personal adaptation. Retired persons can and will respond to opportunities for a high level of community service, thus shifting their energies into second careers of community service rather than retiring from early careers through a series of disengaging steps. This is spelled out in more detail thus: the survival of *large* numbers of older persons into their sixties and seventies and eighties is a new phenomenon in human society, one for which the history of social organization gives no precedent and for which our social institutions are poorly equipped. We not only have many aged persons surviving and healthy (reasonably so at least) but our economy no longer requires the full labor of all living persons, thanks to our technology, so most older persons have leisure. A predictable proportion of these will be interested in and capable of performing civic tasks. The characteristics of such persons can be defined as a basis for selection.

To make this theory work, it is necessary to change agency practices by re-structuring present professional tasks so that some manageable units can be delegated to older workers (as volunteers or employees) with minimal supervision by scarce professional staff; and then to arouse the interest of retired persons for these tasks. By this means a place for *all* interested older persons can be found in the modern world.

In a crude form, this has the elements of a theory suitable for practice. It can be tested by demonstration and research. Here I caution against undue optimism. Several hopeful efforts premised on *parts* of this theory have floundered either because social agencies were inflexible or older persons were not interested. Our own testing is proceeding by a careful examination of individual interests and capabilities of a random sample of retired persons while simultaneously we probe the conditions under which agency tasks can be restructured.

Although the testing is in its early stages we already have some findings which tend to support parts of the theory, but to discredit some of our agency practices. Thus we find that about a third of our study population of 300 have both interests and ample physical capacity for community service while another third have interest but uncertain physical capacity. The characteristics of each group can be charted. Interest in more activity and physical vigor bears no relationship to age for equal proportions of those between sixty-five and seventy-five, and over seventy-five seem to have both requirements. Predictable, too, is the fact that most agencies are reluctant to alter their current practices in order to deal with our initial problem, although we have located a few willing to experiment.

To our surprise, the active and interested one third are already leading quite busy lives and seem to say "we are too busy as it is, but if you have got something very interesting, which makes use of our maximum talents, we will consider it in place of some of the made work activity we now get into."

This example is not very sophisticated nor complicated, but I hope it suggests how a number of loosely related facts and observations can be brought together by a binding theory, with implications for our daily practice, to re-order our tasks to capitalize upon available excess manpower in new ways. It explains tentatively why the aged so often have a difficult time making a constructive place for themselves; and it explains why our ad hoc efforts to arouse interest among the aged has often failed. Finally, it suggests a way in which social work can contribute to the solution of a major social problem.

To be wholly effective for predicting the future, this theory would have to be improved by adding the explicit conditions under which social agencies will re-draft their work to use retired persons, and the more exact classification of older persons who can and want to serve their communities.

There are many among us, ready to develop such testable theories, drawn from research and practice—theories which will progressively alter our practice and provide a growing base for future research. Only in some such fashion will we build the improved society which has been our goal.

INDEX

N

GROWING OLD

An Arno Press Collection

Birren, James E., et al., editors. **Human Aging**. 1963

Birren, James E., editor. **Relations of Development and Aging**. 1964

Breckinridge, Elizabeth L. **Effective Use of Older Workers**. 1953

Brennan, Michael J., Philip Taft, and Mark Schupack. **The Economics of Age**. 1967

Cabot, Natalie H. **You Can't Count On Dying**. 1961

Clark, F. Le Gros. **Growing Old in a Mechanized World**. 1960

Clark, Margaret and Barbara G. Anderson. **Culture and Aging**. 1967

Crook, G[uy] H[amilton] and Martin Heinstein. **The Older Worker in Industry**. 1958

Derber, Milton, editor. **Aged and Society**. 1950

Donahue, Wilma, et al., editors. **Free Time**. 1958

Donahue, Wilma and Clark Tibbitts, editors. **New Frontiers of Aging**. 1957

Havighurst, Robert J. and Ruth Albrecht. **Older People**. 1953

International Association of Gerontology. **Old Age in the Modern World**. 1955

Kaplan, Oscar J., editor. **Mental Disorders in Later Life**. 1956

Kutner, Bernard, et al. **Five Hundred Over Sixty**. 1956

Lowenthal, Marjorie F. **Lives in Distress**. 1964

Munnichs, J.M.A. **Old Age and Finitude**. 1966

Nassau, Mabel L. **Old Age Poverty in Greenwich Village**. 1915

National Association of Social Workers. **Social Group Work with Older People**. 1963

Neugarten, Bernice L., et al. **Personality in Middle and Late Life**. 1964

Orton, Job. **Discourses to the Aged**. 1801

Pinner, Frank A., Paul Jacobs, and Philip Selznick. **Old Age and Political Behavior**. 1959

Reichard, Suzanne, Florine Livson and Paul G. Peterson. **Aging and Personality**. 1962

Rowntree, B. Seebohm. **Old People**. 1947

Rubinow, I[saac] M[ax]., editor. **Care of the Aged**. 1931

Shanas, Ethel. **The Health of Older People**. 1962

Shanas, Ethel, et al. **Old People in Three Industrial Societies**. 1968

Sheldon, J[oseph] H. **The Social Medicine of Old Age**. 1948

Shock, N[athan] W., editor. **Perspectives in Experimental Gerontology**. 1966

Tibbitts, Clark, editor. **Social Contribution by the Aging**. 1952

Tibbitts, Clark and Wilma Donahue, editors. **Social and Psychological Aspects of Aging**. 1962

U.S. Dept. of Health, Education, and Welfare. **Working With Older People**. 1970

Vischer, A[dolf] L[ucas]. **Old Age**. 1947

Welford, A[lan] T[raviss], and James E. Birren, editors. **Decision Making and Age**. 1969

Williams, Richard H., Clark Tibbitts, and Wilma Donahue, editors. **Processes of Aging**. 1963